Teaching, Training, and Administration in Graduate Psychology Programs

Teaching, Training, and Administration in Graduate Psychology Programs

A Psychoanalytic Perspective

David L. Downing, Marc Lubin, and Jed Yalof

ROWMAN & LITTLEFIELD
Lanham • Boulder • New York • London

Published by Rowman & Littlefield
A wholly owned subsidiary of The Rowman & Littlefield Publishing Group, Inc.
4501 Forbes Boulevard, Suite 200, Lanham, Maryland 20706
www.rowman.com

Unit A, Whitacre Mews, 26-34 Stannary Street, London SE11 4AB

British Library Cataloguing in Publication Information Available

Library of Congress Cataloging-in-Publication Data

978-1-4422-4496-2 (cloth)
978-1-4422-4498-6 (paper)
978-1-4422-4497-9 (electronic)

™ The paper used in this publication meets the minimum requirements of American National Standard for Information Sciences—Permanence of Paper for Printed Library Materials, ANSI/NISO Z39.48-1992.

Printed in the United States of America

To my family: sons, daughters-in-law, grandchildren, and brother. And to my parents, for their encouragement of all things educational, with love

David L. Downing, PsyD, ABPP

To Marco and Jake, our new grandsons, for their bright futures

Marc Lubin, PhD

To Barb, with love

Jed Yalof, PsyD, ABPP

Contents

Acknowledgments ix

1 Introduction 1

PART I: ADMINISTRATION 7

2 On Thinking Organizationally, Systemically, and Psychoanalytically: Part I—Foundations 9

3 On Thinking Organizationally, Systemically, and Psychoanalytically: Part II—Applications 25

PART II: TRAINING 43

4 Normotic Elements in Professional Discourse and Practice: Implications for Professional Identity Development 45

5 The *Psychoanalyst's* Capacity to Be Alone: A Brief Comment on Some Challenges in Preserving Psychoanalytical Diversity While Diversifying Psychoanalysis in the Academy—The "Position" of the Psychoanalyst in Organizational Space and Culture 69

6 Locating the Subject Matter in the Matter of the Subject: On the Education of Mental Health Professionals in a Cookbook Culture 87

PART III: TEACHING 109

7 How Psychoanalytic Perspectives and Processes Can Inform the Curriculum and the Teaching of Self-Observational Skills 111

8 Additional Perspectives on Instructional Models of Teaching Self-Observation 133

9 Teaching and Learning from Microanalysis of Exemplar Transcripts: Detailed Approaches to the Clinical Data 143

10 Concluding Remarks 179

References 181

Index 193

About the Authors 207

Acknowledgments

I wish to take this opportunity to acknowledge my two coauthors of this book, Dr. Marc Lubin and Jed Yalof, for their friendship and professional collaboration across many projects over the years, culminating in the composition of this book. Their presence and helpfulness as fellow teachers, practitioners, and administrators has been of enormous inspiration and support on many levels—but especially so with respect for creating and maintaining a space in academia for psychoanalytical pedagogy and praxis. Great appreciation is also extended for the guidance and professionalism of all at Rowman & Littlefield and their belief in this endeavor.

David L. Downing, PsyD, ABPP

I would like to thank both my colleagues for their supportive and engaged involvement in this project, and most especially Jed Yalof for his spirit and determination to move these series of individual papers into an edited book. His persistence has been a guiding force in this project.

Marc I. Lubin, PhD

I would like to acknowledge my co-contributors, Dr. David Downing and Dr. Marc Lubin, for encouraging the development of my ideas as they relate to administration and leadership in doctoral programs, and for their intellectual support and friendship. I would also like to acknowledge Molly White and Megan Manzano at Rowman & Littlefield publishing for helping us bring the book to fruition.

Jed Yalof, PsyD

Chapter 1

Introduction

Teaching, Training, and Administration in Graduate Psychology Programs: A Psychoanalytic Perspective offers a unique contribution to the literature by addressing psychoanalytic perspectives on teaching, training, and program administration. The integration of psychoanalytic theory with doctoral education in clinical psychology lurks in the shadows of the curriculum, clinging to its corner space and losing favor to the pursuit of the "numbers game," that is, a hot and heavy pursuit of demonstrably quantifiable outcomes, which, in its most extreme form, Amado (2013, p. 111) has termed "quantophrenic delirium." Scholars searching for an alternative voice might turn to the work of Britzman (1998, 2006, 2009), whose writings offer a dedicated, creative, and most thoughtful application of the psychoanalytic method to education. Yet securing a faculty quorum of sorts to embrace psychoanalytic psychology has been an uphill battle, as summarized recently by Yalof (2015). Indeed, there has been limited attention to the application of psychoanalytic ideas to teaching, training, and administration at the graduate level. Other recent contributions that touch the areas of teaching, training, and administration have lamented the problems with traditional psychoanalytic institutions in terms of their curriculum and teaching paradigms, or provided insight into organizational dynamics by applying psychoanalytic theory, but no book has been published in almost twenty years (Yalof, 1996) synthesizing the challenges that confront faculty members who use psychoanalytic theory to inform their teaching, training, and administration responsibilities in graduate psychology programs.

In writing this book we set as our main goal the synthesis of psychoanalytic ideas that transverse the core areas of the graduate psychology curriculum for faculty members and administrators: teaching, training, and administration. Each of us has had extensive teaching, training, and administrative responsibilities in leading accredited clinical psychology doctoral programs. Rarely has a day passed without a program conflict of sorts, be it student–faculty, faculty–administration, faculty–faculty, student–student, staff–student, or staff–faculty, that does not cross our desk or e-mail and, to varying degrees, involve and require our attention. Each of us is also a psychoanalytic clinician, practicing psychoanalysis and/or psychoanalytic psychotherapy, which colors both our worldview and the questions we ask when confronted with a challenge in the educational setting. Why, for example, did a policy issue emerge for which we have only vague procedures? How do we talk to a faculty member or student about a tense matter without evoking strong reactions, and how do we react internally and externally if the response is not what we had hoped for? Why does certain lecture material seem easy to explain, whereas other content seems grated with inhibition or uncertainty? How do we develop alliances with administrators without risking being perceived as disloyal by faculty? How do we oversee faculty as program leaders, even though we have faculty status? How do we advocate for budget requests in a sensible, justified, and planned manner without coming across as aggressive, and how do we maintain relationships with leaders of other university programs that do not regress into competitive exchanges? The nature and extent of conflict vary, but our approach is always psychoanalytic. These are the types of questions we address throughout the book.

The impetus for the book grew out of a series of symposia offered at the American Psychological Association's Division 39 (Psychoanalysis) Annual Spring Meeting. Each symposium, chaired by Dr. David Downing, included presentations on teaching (Dr. Marc Lubin), training (Dr. David Downing), and administration-program management (Dr. Jed Yalof). Symposia titles were (a) *When Holding and Containment Falter: High Conflict Moments in Teaching, Training, and Administering Graduate Psychology Programs* (2014); (b) *A Different Focus: Creative Applications of Psychoanalysis to the Work of the Psychoanalytically-Oriented Instructor Administrator, and Clinical Training Director* (2012); (c) *Making Sure We Matter: The Generative Functions of Psychoanalytical Education in Academia* (2011); (d) *From the Classroom and Academia to the Psychotherapist Office, and Back Again: Intensifying Self-Observing and Containing Skills in the Student, Supervisor/Consultant and Administrator* (2010); (e) *Against All Odds: Teaching Psychoanalytical Concepts and Process in an Era of Professional and Educational Resistance* (2009); and (f) (chaired by Dr. Martha Hadley) *Teaching Psychoanalysis to Clinical Doctoral Students in the Age of Managed Care and Short-Term Treatment* (2006).

This book is an attempt to distill these presentations (Yalof/Organization-Administration, Downing/Training, Lubin/Teaching) into a cohesive presentation that does justice to the depth of teaching, training, and administration.

As such, we divide the book into these three sections. The sections necessarily have some overlap; for example, teaching embeds training; that is, a teacher who brings psychoanalytic training to the teaching of graduate students necessarily conveys an attitude about treatment, training, and the importance of Schafer's (1983) "analytic attitude" to all aspects of clinical work. Training embeds the philosophy of the university and of the regulatory aspects of the profession, the psychoanalytic culture, and the organizational matrix within which training operates. Efforts to understand organizations psychoanalytically also must account for these same variables: university philosophy and values, professional guild requirements, and the manner in which the student-teacher-administrator experiences the culture of the organization. We provide a review of the psychoanalytic literature behind each central idea, case examples, and applications to graduate programs, and offer a distinctive presence in this area of applied psychoanalytic scholarship. The outline of the book is as follows.

PART I: ADMINISTRATION

Part I, under the primary direction of Dr. Jed Yalof, looks at organizational dynamics that affect program leadership and administration. Chapter 1 discusses how psychoanalytic theory informs academic programs from an organizational perspective, with a focus on the responsibilities of, and pressures experienced by, the program leader (e.g., Creswell, Wheeler, Seagren, Egly, & Beyer, 1990; Grotstein, 1981; Kernberg, 1980). There is a review of (a) psychoanalytic group psychology (Bion, 1961; Freud, 1921/1981), (b) the challenges associated with producing quantifiable outcomes (Amado, 2013), and (c) a range of other topics associated with psychoanalytical organizational psychology (e.g., Hirschhorn, 1988; Klein, Gabelnick, & Herr, 1998). Chapter 2 builds on chapter 1 by applying concepts to two published cases (Herrick, Kvale, & Goodykoontz, 1991; Trombly, Comer, & Villamil, 2002) and discussing them in relation to the psychodynamics of educational administration.

PART II: TRAINING

Part II, under the primary direction of Dr. David Downing, takes a different slant, highlighting how psychoanalytic theory helps us make sense of the pressure to conform to regulations that govern accreditation. These pressures force trainers to find a workable compromise between passive conformity and forging a curriculum that does not shy away from a psychoanalytic identity.

Chapter 4 points out how Bollas's (1987) concept of "normotic illness" and the pressure to conform impacts the academy and its training of doctoral students. Chapter 5 offers a discussion of the challenges that psychoanalytically informed faculty members might experience in academic settings. Winnicott's (1958) description of the capacity to be "alone" is relevant here. Chapter 6 endeavors to describe the effort to create and maintain a space for an intrapsychic focus, and subscribe to a psychoanalytical ethos (e.g., Freud, 1912a/1981, 1912b/1981, 1914a/1981, 1914b/1981, 1915/1981, 1921/1981, 1923/1981; Kohut, 1971; Winnicott, 1965) in a climate where concretized, quantified, and evidence-based education is the expectancy and presumptive gold standard.

PART III: TEACHING

Part III, under the primary direction of Dr. Marc Lubin, using the first-person "I" in order to best capture the experience, near-relationship between therapist–client, analyst–client, supervisor–supervisee, and teacher–student, addresses psychoanalytic teaching strategies for teaching psychoanalytic practice. Chapter 7 addresses the importance of teaching self-observation skills to both graduate and postgraduate students. Such skills are fundamental for eventual self-supervision when students are in settings prohibiting recordings, have minimal supervisory structures, and are in postgraduate private practice. This chapter contains a survey of teaching goals and targets, including the model of the nonjudgmental self-attitudes present in the mindfulness processes. The need for specific note-taking settings is also discussed. Apart from recalling the significant moments within a just-completed session, note taking was seen as activating a process leading to a deepened view of notes as a form of self-observation was included as a significant goal of the session notes. This approach also includes the creation of internal "space," as part of the curriculum is emphasized. An exam directed at training and assessing student self-reflective skills was discussed as a part of the instructional methodology. Chapter 8 continues a discussion of a range of instructional models. Major phase and tracking models are also discussed, including a micro-analytic approach to transcript reviews. The value of such an approach is also noted in terms of transcript tracking and phase perspectives emphasizing sequential process in review of transcripts. Chapter 9 presents a discussion of how specific applications of approaches to self-observation connect to the same process of accessing countertransference. To do so, a micro-analytic focus to the transcripts of two expert therapists (i.e., psychotherapist, psychoanalyst) is reviewed. Each therapist included his or her own self-observations in case presentations. This particular focus also included the concept of successive looks at the therapists' inner reflections as they led to their eventual critical insights that altered their earlier countertransferential experience. After these reviews, a general pattern emerged as to the overlapping phases of interventions and underlying and unconscious communications to the patients. A further reflections and self-questioning process was observed. Critical inner therapist shifts in their self-observations seemed to be related to a self-acceptance of inner thoughts and feelings, leading to a pause in the exchanges. During these pauses in which space for self-questioning and recall of earlier observations and interventions were recovered, subsequent insights emerged. Such a process might then be applied to an instructional set of guidelines and further assignments for the self-supervision process as presented in individual and seminar settings.

It is our hope that colleagues who teach, train, and administrate in academic programs will find our book a welcome addition to their work. It is intended to make clear a broad sampling of applied psychoanalytic psychology to the everyday problems that confront program leaders.

Part I

ADMINISTRATION

Chapter 2

On Thinking Organizationally, Systemically, and Psychoanalytically

Part I—Foundations

> *The effectiveness of leadership does not depend exclusively or primarily on the leader's personality. The first requirement for effective functioning of an organization—including its leadership—is an adequate relation between the organization's overall task and its administrative structure; the task has to be meaningful rather than trivial and, given the available resources, feasible rather than overwhelming.* (Kernberg, 1980, pp. 235–236)

INTRODUCTION

The roles and responsibilities of graduate psychology program administrators require a sophisticated skill set to support the institutional mission through the attainment of positive program outcomes. These skills involve listening; communicating effectively; containing untoward affects; understanding the stress points of individual faculty members; maintaining positive relationships with other university administrators (i.e., deans, provosts, president); listening to the needs of students, faculty, and staff; encouraging strategic initiatives tied to the program and institutional mission; managing budget and advocating for resources; recognizing and responding thoughtfully to symptomatic expressions of systemic conflicts; and handling the myriad of microlevel and macrolevel responsibilities that transverse teaching, curriculum, personnel, and accreditation that confront leaders on a daily basis. Management of these responsibilities engages the leader's ability to handle a wide range of stresses, including program upheaval and regression.

This chapter describes how psychoanalytic theory helps us understand the impactful and systemic pressure of subgroup and larger conflict in academic settings. The focus is on the role of the academic program leader/head as a pivotal figure in program management, who has responsibilities to students, colleagues, staff, and superiors. The program leader is subject to organizational tensions vertically from superiors and subordinates, and horizontally from colleagues. The chapter begins with a discussion of leadership, group dynamics, and the problems associated with pressure to produce quantifiable outcomes. This is followed by a discussion of the leader as a transference object and then by a review of the conflicted and adaptive aspects of projective identification as a method of systemic communication. Finally, the chapter highlights good leadership qualities and their psychoanalytic applications. These sections frame the main points of consideration when conceptualizing and formulating responses to conflict situations that impinge academic programs. Brief illustrations of main concepts are presented in this chapter and tied to vignettes in the next chapter.

LEADERSHIP, GROUP DYNAMICS, AND THE CHALLENGE OF OUTCOMES

Organizations can be understood as consisting of tasks/processes, management/structure, enterprise/identity, and contextually embedded/ecological boundaries (Armstrong, 2004). Leadership represents a complex series of interrelated activities in which different individuals assume primary responsibility for moving a group or organization toward its goals and mission while working creatively within and across organizational boundaries. By creative leadership, we include the leader's understanding of how the organization works; its core conflicts from a psychoanalytical perspective (e.g., Czander, Jacobsberg, Mersky, & Nunberg, 2002); and the creative tension between leadership and followership in which the leader can accept his or her own limits, collaborate across groups (racial, gender, ethnic), and demonstrate receptivity to the ideas of the follower, or subordinate (Berg, 1998). The leader strives to craft a vision that can be trusted and internalized (Hirschhorn, 1998), while navigating threats to leadership and group progress, including inability to inspire, resistance to change (see Thomas, 2008, for a discussion of diversity resistance in organizations in particular), need for validation, reenactment of personal issues in the work setting (Obholzer with Miller, 2004), enactment of sexual tensions (Hirschhorn, 1998), and stereotyping (e.g., Kram & Hampton, 1998; Long, 1998).

Kernberg's (1980) systems approach represents a psychoanalytic method for understanding this relationship between individuals and mission as it relates to the role of leaders (see Anderson & White, 2002; Long, 2006). Kernberg describes how a systems approach considers "the institution as an overall system dynamically and hierarchically integrating various subsystems (such as the personality of leadership, the nature of group processes, the task systems, and administrative structures of the organization)" (p. 238). He notes that there are problems associated with leaders who are inadequate and not skilled in their work, and differentiates this from other situations where problems in leadership are symptomatic of larger organizational problems.

Locke's (2003) discussion of key leadership tasks (as cited in Huffington, James, & Armstrong, 2004) presents the responsibilities of individuals who oversee academic programs and frames the tasks on which most leaders are evaluated, regardless of primary setting (e.g., business, university, hospital). These tasks include vision, maintenance of core values, structuring, motivating and team building, selection and training, communicating, and supporting change. It is clear from these tasks that there is never a quiet moment for the program leader, who must prioritize a strategic agenda that complements a larger vision, while also encouraging and ideally securing a collaborative buy-in from others who have less immediate responsibility for outcomes. The program leader is often charged with final decisions, even when leadership style might privilege collaboration, distributed responsibility, and group input. Creswell, Wheeler, Seagren, Egly, and Beyer (1990) noted that program leaders are most effective when everyone has a voice, there is an equal distribution of responsibilities, and performance expectations are stated clearly. In addition, it is critical that the program leader is accessible and faculty members have a sense of program ownership.

While these factors are important considerations in creating a positive work climate and work group, they do not guarantee good outcomes. Efforts to promote a group voice and distribution of program ownership are not without problems, including rivalrous challenges to the leader's authority. Distribution of responsibilities can lead to an increase in group vulnerability associated with a reduction in the perception of "protection afforded by more hierarchical structures" (Huffington et al., 2004, p. 71). Such protection becomes even more tenuous as advances in technology add distance to interpersonal relationships. Cooper and Dartington (2004) made this point in their discussion of the challenges of containment amid the increasing impact of technology on organizations. They noted how anxiety associated with loss of dependence on authority can increase when the organization becomes less visible to its employees, and stated: "The intersection and overlapping of tasks and responsibilities within the wider departmental, professional, and administrative structures gives rise to an experience of continual uncertainty about the actual ownership of authority" (p. 143). The diffusion of a sense of belonging to an organization, along with a purely structural approach to management that de-emphasizes the importance of personal relationships in favor of redesign, relocation, and reinventing philosophies, poses real risks to organizational integrity (Vansina, 2013).

Notwithstanding systemic influences as resource limits and personnel conflicts, the program leader is typically accountable for outcomes and for the subgroups of people who support the organization's outcome initiatives. These outcomes can take the form of enrollment initiative, securing grants, encouraging scholarship, supporting good teaching, striving for accreditation, and/or buffering superiors from program noise by cultivating a compliant, but potentially defensive, climate of good citizenship. Krantz (2013) has noted, for example, that an emphasis on good citizenship can disguise a defensive mentality where personal temperament might be privileged over skills and where maintaining the fantasy that "everyone gets along" is the priority. That is, good groups or good programs are programs where everyone likes everyone else, whether or not the program is producing scholarship and graduates/offspring to its fullest potential. As such, Bion's (1961) classification of the earnest "work group," where productivity flourishes during a period when basic group assumptions (see below) are not active, is important.

In reality, while more productive performance can inspire healthy competition that serves the organization, an increase in output might also add to the dynamic conflicts within organizational subgroupings, especially when there is disparity between people and among groups in terms of performance. Here, the leader is on call perpetually because there is always a conflict either present or lurking that has ties to group member perception of authority, as noted by Bion (1961), who identified the following basic group assumptions operating within an organizational subsystem. In the dependency assumption, there is a reliance on an omnipotent leader. In the fight-flight assumption, there is unification against a leader, who is seen as depriving. In the pairing assumption, there is a focus on the intimate relationship between two people in the group whose sexual interest in each other can magically transform, or at least carry the burden of, the group's work; this might be understood as a defense against dependency on the leader. Hopper (2012), drawing from Bion's ideas about group dynamics about dependency, fight-flight, and pairing, adds the notion of "aggregation/massification" as an additional basic assumption of groups. In this fourth assumption, the group either has too much individuality or operates as a mass with too little difference. Extrapolating to the academic setting, this might take the form of disconnect among either students and/or faculty or everyone experiencing a basic anxiety (e.g., a program at risk for being shut down or losing its accreditation standing). However, even in the most productive work groups, requests or demands for shifts in the ego-syntonic roles of group members can lead to structural conflicts around task definition and responsibilities, to interpersonal conflicts in the areas of competition, to challenges to the leader's Oedipal authority, or to what Diamond

(2012) has described as the defensive, routinized, predictable, and therefore "non-threatening" (p. 507) behaviors.

Production of outcomes is just the tip of the iceberg for the program leader. Outcomes must be measurable, quantifiable, and verifiable. Bottom-line pressures impose threats on workers, who, under the worst of conditions, operate under the specter of job loss, feel valued as less than a whole person, and are at risk for sinking into chronic negativity (Stein, 2005). There are many quantitative variables that can measure program goals, objectives, and competencies in ways that validate the program leader's effort to align the program with university and accreditation expectations (e.g., American Psychological Association, 2013). These variables might include student performance in classes and clinical placements, successful completion of qualifying examinations and research, time to program completion, and accomplishments of program graduates. Numeric variables are tied back to goals, objectives, and competencies in a way that allows the program to evaluate the fruits of its labor as these outcomes pertain to national accreditation initiatives. However, with excessive reliance on quantification, which Amado (2013) termed "quantophrenic delirium" (p. 11) as part of the "*psychic imprisonment system*" (italics in original, p. 10), comes the potentially oppressive nature of institutional controls. Amado outlined some of the risks associated with an oppressive organization, including loss of employee freedom to decline participation, focus on measuring performance competencies through ratings versus understanding processes, and catering to consumers to the degree where organizational integrity declines. When there are numeric changes related to finance, enrollment, competition from neighboring programs, and externally imposed regulations or formulas that monitor institutions and their programs, there emerge organizational strategies for change, which can often include personnel adjustments. When workers feel at risk for job loss or change in role, they can respond in a number of different ways. Hoyle (2004) identified four responses to change among workers that emerged from a health-care study: (a) sycophant (i.e., agreeable without reflection), (b) positive and challenging (i.e., open to change, but questioning), (c) negative and challenging (i.e., angry with displaced aggression), and (d) saboteurs (i.e., disruptive, nonparticipatory, and openly encouraging of conflict).

In the end, the drive toward measureable outcomes is an organizational inevitability. Here, quantitative outcomes are valued, but they are not the only way to measure outcomes. There are also qualitative processes that shape program culture and are enacted daily by faculty, students, and administrators. Examples of qualitative processes and outcomes include how people respond to each other, how conflicts are resolved, how students experience a program climate, and how unconscious communications can rifle through an organization and lead to symptomatic conflict that requires extensive conversation and, at times, reparation, in order to stabilize a shaken system. Using psychoanalytic theory to understand the nuances of organizational functioning as a systemic process (i.e., administration, department, faculty, program, students) can illuminate many of the underlying conflicts that find outward expression through various forms of enactments that belie the dynamic pressures of program leadership.

LEADER AS TRANSFERENCE OBJECT

The psychoanalytically oriented academic who serves in a leadership role aspires to Creswell et al.'s (1990) precepts of chairmanship, applicable to other forms of program leadership (e.g., director of training, dean, provost), but does so through the language of analytic theory: conflict management; affect containment and sacrifice; avoidance, when possible, of sadomasochistic enactments; and interacting in a way that does not engender nor exacerbate the unconscious transferential thoughts and feelings that are sometimes rivalrous, sometimes envious, and not always pleasurable. Freud (1921/1981) saw transference as an unconscious repetition in which the patient's early life conflicts were inevitably recreated in the analytic relationship; others (e.g., Kernberg, 1965) see both transference and countertransference as more totalistic (see Tansey & Burke, 1989, for a discussion of different countertransference definitions) and encompassing all of the patient's reactions to the therapist/analyst and vice versa. Transference is stimulated by fantasies associated with authority. In organizations, the leader's authority is a veritable "target on the back." That is, management of group regression falls on the leader's shoulders. The leader's narcissistic vulnerabilities are exacerbated by this position and, if not managed, can heighten conflict. Kibel (2012), for example, discussing a case of organizational trauma, noted that leaders can be caught up in the fame and prestige of their roles. He stated: "Praise, power, and envy that emanate from prestige, along with actual successes in the academic world at large, all combine to accentuate normal narcissistic defenses which are inherent in the human condition" (p. 8). Hirschhorn (1988) also provides excellent illustrations of organizational dynamics and their impact on the work of an organizational consultant.

The program leader's ability to understand the trappings of power and function at the level of psychologically informed group leader is a key to facilitating a positive program dynamic and outcomes for faculty and students. These outcomes are not captured easily by numerical ratings because much of what goes on in an academic program that engenders conflict, compromise, and, hopefully, cohesiveness is not always accessible to consciousness, at least not immediately. For instance, we know that students can make progress even when faculty are in conflict as a group, much like children can thrive in homes that lack harmony and/or resources, but what they internalize about the program climate and may have to repress in order to focus their resources on succeeding can sap ego resources in other ways by pushing painful feelings and associated object representations underground. It can also affect the way in which they identify with faculty attitudes and the extent to which they feel a connection to their program, as opposed to seeing the program as an obstacle. However, these identifications and connections are more subtle and frequently do not conform to quantifiable data collection.

One might surmise that the degree to which a student represents a program as an obstacle or an impetus toward growth is determined largely by intrapsychic factors; however, the interpersonal problems that a program has to contend with, and which often get centered on the program leader, can affect even the most open-minded and resourceful of students in a negative way. Freud (1921/1981) stated as much in *Group Psychology and the Analysis of the Ego*: "The leader of the group is still the dreaded primal father; the group still wishes to be governed by instinctive forces; it has extreme passions for authority; in Le Bon's phrase, it has a thirst for obedience" (p. 127). Allcorn (2007), writing about workplace oppression, speaks about the power-driven leader in terms that amplify what Freud meant by "the dreaded primal father." Allcorn noted the dehumanizing, regressive, and poorly contained experiences that characterize oppressed workers in hierarchical organizations under the direction of a power-driven leader. Oppressed workers live in fear of punishment; are vulnerable to rumor, gossip, and mistrusting of motives (i.e., "paranoiagenesis," Kernberg, 1993, as cited in Kibel, 2012); and submit to authority as a survival tactic. This mirrors an organization's vulnerability to enacting social defenses via projection, splitting, and introjection against more immersive interpersonal involvements in which a heavy task focus supports disengagement (Hirschhorn, 1988).

Kernberg (1980) has written extensively about organizational leadership from a psychoanalytic perspective and provides a synthesis of drive, ego psychological, and object relational theories when discussing the conflicted aspect of leadership roles within an institutional setting. Kernberg draws on Freud's notion of group psychology (1921/1981), LeBon's (1895, as cited in Kernberg, 1980) understanding of mobs, and Bion's (1961) writings on small group assumptions when describing the inevitable threats associated with organizational destabilization confronting the leader.

> Combining the observations made of mobs, large groups, and small groups, I am suggesting that group processes pose a basic threat to personal identity, linked to a proclivity in group situations for the activation of primitive object

> relations, primitive defensive operations, and primitive aggression with predominately pregenital characteristics. (p. 217)

Kernberg describes how the identification and idealization of the leader represent an unconscious identification with the Oedipal father, which then establishes the leader as a focal point for feelings of love, rivalry, jealousy, rage, and so on. The extent to which projections tied to the punitive, loving, and rivalrous Oedipal father when the program leader is a male are corollary to the female program leader is not clear and would be important to understand. Kernberg differentiates mobs from all groups by noting that while both have elements of irrationality and identification, small groups will expect the leader to assume a certain role, project an ego ideal onto the leader for protective purposes, and react to the leader's failure to meet the group's expectations. He further states that small groups will locate external sources of threat and also have less potential or violence, despite the presence of primitive defenses such as denial and devaluation, because of familiarity with each other. Kernberg finally notes there is a search for, and idealization of, Bion's "pairing group." In an academic setting, the pairing group might take the form of two people whose leadership is so important to the overall productivity to the small group that their relationship to each other becomes a group focus.

Kernberg also noted that membership in a large group exposed members to a state of diffusion, risk for not being heard, and loss of identity. Along these lines, Collie (2005) described the "fear of annihilation of the self" (p. 2) that besets an individual in a large organization where there are conflicts that seem irresolvable at the level of the individual. Drawing on his experience working in an inpatient facility, Kernberg outlined other considerations related to concerns that confront leaders and which we generalize to the academic program, including (a) entitlements (e.g., students, faculty, or administrators who react angrily when expectations are not met); (b) mourning and loss (e.g., program responses to students who graduate, voluntarily leave the program, or die during their time in the program; students, faculty members, and administrators who leave either voluntarily or by fiat); (c) defensive denial of aggression (e.g., fear of being perceived as retaliatory); (d) sexual acting out in a way that condenses primitive aggression and sexuality (e.g., a teacher–student liaison that represents an unconscious attack on the program and highlights boundary breaking as a symptomatic expression of an institutional conflict); and (e) risks associated with ascendance of individuals with narcissistic or antisocial character features into positions of leadership or voice (e.g., an administrator who manipulates budget for personal gain; a student who repeatedly and enviously denigrates a faculty member on a public website in response to a minor slight, such as a low grade; a faculty member who uses power to instigate students against the organization's mission). Significant problems in any area can lead to group fantasies of "curing the leader" (p. 238), possibly as a last-ditch effort to deny systemic problems by focusing psychic energy on one person; as a reaction formation against the wish to punish the leader, who is seen as a toxic representative of larger organizational conflict; or as hypo-manic efforts to direct the leader to bring about change, rather dealing with the guilt, loss, and mourning associated with accepting the depressive position's ambivalences toward the leader as the symbolic love object (Klein, 1975).

Kernberg (1980, pp. 243–244) elaborates on the regressive pressures associated with leadership. He outlined several such pressures, each of which requires the leader's ability to think through conflict situations, reflect on organizational systems, and consider a reasonable response that seeks to neutralize tensions by which the system threatens to be absorbed and the symptomatic responses evoked institutionally: (a) loneliness, (b) absence of "spontaneous and unconstrained feedback from peers" (p. 243), (c) uncertainty of decision making, (d) Oedipal fears of failure and defeat, (e) frustration of dependent needs, (f) activation of conflicts around aggression, (g) organizational pressure to solve problems, (h) continual demands to work, (i) threats to leisure time, and (j) threats to freedom of fantasy life. These threats compromise what Winnicott (1965) described as the secure holding environment that was modeled on the mother's ability to contain the infant's anxiety. The leader has a similar responsibility to his or her immediate group but is not always successful in doing so.

The following example illustrates this point. Assume that the program leader has to make decisions about a curriculum matter that involves requiring a senior-level faculty member to take on a class for which he did not volunteer and is not interested in teaching. What follows is a series of e-mails in which the faculty member feels controlled and disrespected, scours university handbooks in search of evidence of wrongdoing by the program leader, and is inclined to contact his union representative. The faculty member knows that the leader has tried, albeit unsuccessfully, to come up with another arrangement or "solution" to the problem; however, the leader's effort and empathy are met with the expressed resistances of "not having done enough." Is this a matter of poor leadership? Or, is it a symptom of organizational conflict? Or, is it both? What follows for the leader are a few nights of fitful sleep, avoidance of conversation with the faculty member, a sense of defeat, anxiety about a contagion spreading among faculty members in which the leader is perceived as disempowered, and the emergence of a fight-flight basic assumption (Bion, 1961) and paranoid–schizoid splitting (Klein, 1946), itself a reaction to, and in dialectal relation with, the dreaded ambiguity of an autistic-contiguous state (Diamond, Allcorn, & Stein, 2004).

As such, faculty encamp in two opposing positions: those who understand the leader's dilemma and those who feel that the leader could have stood firm and feel alienated in response to his actions. The leader feels uneasy venting to anyone, lest there be a perception of joining in the split, while feeling immobilized and alienated from the group.

The leader's personality style will also affect the way in which the conflict is experienced. The preceding example illustrates a leader who might be exhibiting what Kernberg (1975) terms a more neurotic structure, organized around depressive-masochistic features, with prominent Oedipal concerns, guilt, conflicts with aggression, and introjective defenses with reparative efforts. Oftentimes, this is the best that a leader can do: identify the conflict, own his or her part in it, recognize the projective identifications, display empathy, and work creatively toward resolving the regression. This is what Halton (2004) termed "reparative creativity" (p. 111), which involves showing care and concern in working to resolve conflicts associated with aggression. This approach might be considered a relatively adaptive and higher-functioning style compared to leaders whose character pathology infuses the work setting with fear, panic, depression, and more primitive paranoid anxieties. Among leadership types (Kernberg, 1980) at risk for power abuse and destabilizing a program or organization are individuals who present with (a) authoritarian, (b) schizoid, (c) obsessive, (d) paranoid, and (e) narcissistic personalities. The authoritarian leader is bossy and punitive to subordinates, but obsequious to superiors (i.e., as in an identification with the aggressor). The schizoid leader is isolated and detached. The obsessive leader is insecure in judgment and consumed with detail as a defense against aggression. The paranoid leader sees slights everywhere and projects mistrust. The narcissistic leader is flamboyant and self-serving, moving the group ahead, but consumed with personal successes, and/or ruthless, cold, and dismissive of any challenges to his or her power base. The underlying threats to ego integrity in each case lead to rigid and maladaptive character structures that threaten to implode under duress (e.g., outbursts for the authoritative leader, acute anxiety for the obsessive leader, dismissive hatred and antisocial behavior for the narcissistic leader). Kets de Vries (1977) describes another type of leadership—"charismatic leaders"—who are seen as saviors, emerging during periods of organizational crises with the promise of bringing cohesion to the organization. Charismatic leaders are often seen as transformative and eager to have people change in ways that are unique. These leaders, however, have the potential for paranoid regression under stress, when there are threats to their authority undermining a sense of omnipotence and delusions of grandeur, challenging the existing order, but also projecting aggression and persecutorial anxiety, which can make dependent subordinates fearful of asserting themselves. Allcorn (2008) classified organizations, not its leaders, into pathological subgroupings, including narcissistic, dependent, and avoidant, and offered accompanying vignettes to illustrate how the overall psychopathology of the organization operates in what becomes a self-defeating cycle.

PROJECTIVE IDENTIFICATION AS A SYSTEMIC COMMUNICATION

Projective identification is the primary method through which psychological conflicts resonate in an organization and has an extensive psychoanalytic literature base (e.g., Grotstein, 1981; Kernberg, 1987; Ogden, 1981; Tansey & Burke, 1989). Ogden (1981) described projection identification as "a set of projective and introjective fantasies in dynamic interplay with a set of object relations" (p. 318). In projective identification, the subject projects unwanted parts of the self into the object. There is pressure on the subject to act, think, or feel in ways that correspond to the projected part. Through this process of inducing psychological pressure on the object, the subject seeks to control the object, avoid separation from it, repair it, seduce it, communicate with it in nonpathological ways, and so on. Projective identification also evokes a response that permits identification with the split-off, or projected part of the self. Grotstein (1981) discussed projective identification at length, seeing it, in its adaptive aspect, as a conduit for empathy but otherwise as a defense. Grotstein defined projective identification as "a mental mechanism whereby the self experiences the unconscious phantasy of translocating itself, or aspect of itself into an object for exploratory or defensive purposes" (p. 123). Waska (1998) defined projective identification as "a fantasy dominated experience and a dialectical process within both interpersonal and intrapsychic forums" (p. 366) that can be received in an open and caring way, not received, received but not understood, and received but reacted to with outrage. Shur (1994) described how projective identification, which Kernberg (1975) identified as a primitive defense, can resonate throughout a hospital system, leading to countertransference conveyed through counter-projective identifications and conflicted enactments, and create tension among staff, therapists, and administrators. Diamond (2007) used Ogden's (1994) concept of the "analytic third" to illustrate how the dialect between organizational constituents gives rise, through projective identification processes, to organizational identity, which itself represents a third subjectivity emerging from creating tension. The main point here is that projective identification is a communication, unconscious, motivated by any number of factors, and represents a compromise in which the subject seeks to convey something of importance to the object that has the potential to result in a deeper understanding of conflict, or a rejection of a disturbing thought or feeling that gets projected back into the subject.

An example of how projective identification can resonate through an academic program is as follows. The hypothetical example involves a committee member who was continually late for committee meetings. The committee member would burst in with a flair and fast apology, but appear harried and out of sorts. A recent meeting was no different—lateness followed by an apology that left others wanting more information about why their colleague was chronically late. The room became tense as eyes shifted in ways that reflected unspoken anger. The committee leader opted to stay on task and work through the meeting agenda rather than address the affect in the room. However, the committee leader also recognized that the committee member should explain what was going on and why he was late, given its disruptive impact on the meeting. The committee leader's initial impulse was to put the committee member on the spot and demand an answer, but the committee leader opted not to do this and instead continued with the agenda. Following the meeting, three committee members came into the committee leader's office without an appointment, expressing anger about their colleague's lateness and insisting that the leader take a more vocal stand. The leader replied back that no one had said anything after the late committee member offered an apology, but was then reminded by the two other committee members that she (i.e., the committee leader) was the one who decided to move to the next item on the agenda. At this point, the leader felt on the spot to deliver an answer and somewhat responsible for the committee member's lateness; that is, by not creating a space to talk about it, the situation persisted. Thus, the committee leader was on the spot but unable to reflect on her feelings.

The fact that the three committee members came into the committee leader's office without an appointment, similar to how the committee member who was late burst into the room, did not escape the attention of the committee leader, who opted to refrain from commenting, lest the focus now become the subgroup pairing who claimed to be speaking for other committee members. During this discussion the committee leader also realized that talking about the committee member, without the committee member present, did not address the problem directly and also wondered if the lateness was symptomatic of a larger issue.

The committee leader agreed to open the next meeting up for discussion. The committee member who had been late arrived on time for this meeting. With an open agenda, the discussion shifted to how some committee members were feeling about having to now share office space with each other in order to support another department's needs. No one from this other department was on the committee; hence, the openness of affect around this issue under the guise of confidentiality within the committee about communications was not recorded in the meeting minutes. The committee member who was late was in one of the departments whose office space was redistributed. Strong emotions were voiced. The committee member who was late then spoke up, apologizing again for his lateness to previous meetings, and wondered if his previous lateness was a way of expressing frustration over the situation. That is, his office space had been compromised, and he reacted defensively by displacing anger and taking himself away from the group via the lateness. He felt disempowered and unable to have a voice with administration but, as a senior faculty member, felt displaced by another department. Further discussion led to committee members expressing empathy for what he shared, but also concern that he would deprive the group of his knowledge by coming late to meetings and unsettling everyone. At this point, there was a shift toward the expression of envy toward the other department, that seemed to be garnering resources and earning "favorite child status" from administrators.

This case vignette highlights how projective defenses bring upheaval to group dynamics in academic settings. Here, the committee member who was late felt displaced by changes in the office arrangements and took out his frustration on colleagues. Ultimately, aggression was directed toward the leader. The committee leader's ability to contain the aggression, rather than retaliating by taking an authoritarian stance toward the committee member and respond with an intervention derived from an understanding of projective processes, allowed for an open forum where feelings could be expressed; an appreciation for the larger meaning of the lateness could be acknowledged; and constructive steps could be taken to address the larger issue of access to administration. This is but one example illustrating the challenge of remaining poised, patient, and accepting of ambiguity, which Huffington et al. (2004) felt was the hardest part of leadership.

EFFECTIVE PROGRAM LEADERSHIP

Kernberg (1980) stated that effective organizational functioning and leadership depended, mainly, on "adequate relations between the organization's overall task and the administrative structure; the task has to be meaningful, rather than trivial, and, given the available resources, feasible rather than overwhelming" (pp. 235–236). In other words, it was not so much the personality of the leader but the relevance of task, its tie to mission, and the presence of resources that supported the growth of an organization. Problems arising from limitations in any of these areas are immediately apparent. For example, autocratic directives from higher administrators to move a program in a particular direction, without allowing for input from faculty, would be demoralizing and render the program leader a target for displaced aggression. Fiscal imprudence, for example, can stimulate an organizational depression, lead to misinterpretation and rumor spreading, and create suspicion of leadership.

But what makes for a more effective work ethos? Parish (2007), speaking about her role as a Tavistock Conference administrator, describes how "gratifying needs and containing anxieties" (p. 62), "containment" (p. 63), and "invisible service" (p. 64), in which needs are met "swiftly and silently," are all powerful assets for the administrator. These are cultivated psychoanalytic skills that a talented group leader brings to the consultative process. Gantt and Agazarian (2007) outlined a systems approach when working with groups that is developmental where groups move from conflicts with authority to collaboration and to integration under the group leader's skillful direction and interventions. Bush and William (2011) add to the understanding of effective intervention skills that characterize psychoanalytic clinicians. They surveyed graduates of analytic programs and had them reflect on their experiences in analysis. Most of the graduates were analyzed by classically trained analysts, and the analyses lasted for an average of 6.5 years at four times per week. They used a survey to gather information about what their analysts actually did in sessions. Not surprisingly, the respondents had positive feelings about their analyses. What was surprising, however, was that they recalled their analysts as having used a combination of classical techniques directed toward insight, and supportive techniques, including empathy and reassurance. They found that good analysts were caring and emotionally engaged, and had positive interpersonal qualities; generated a good working alliance; and used a range of techniques that might be associated not only with classical analysis but also with exploratory and supportive analytic treatment. Results spoke to the level of personal and technical flexibility that supported positive outcomes. Creswell et al. (1990), focusing on successful department chairmanship skills, offers a similar view on what works: listening, support, active engagement, open-mindedness, attention to the personal lives of faculty members, affirmation, holding boundaries, alliance building, and dealing with resistances. Clearly, there are distinctions between analysts-analysands and chairs-faculty members, but the same basic precepts, applied differentially, hold true for sound leadership practices in both domains. For example, administrators who are empathic, are supportive, contain anger, are able to set limits in a nonaggressive manner, and can articulate underlying program issues to students and colleagues in an insightful way bring a very valuable skill set to their role as program leader.

CONCLUSION

Throughout this chapter, we addressed various external and internal pressures that tax a program leader's ability to contain, process, formulate, and respond to organizational and subgroup conflicts in an adaptive manner. Management of untoward affects, primarily aggression, and the impulse to scapegoat, bully, displace, or passively withdraw as ways of coping can lead to splintering, splitting, and exacerbation of interpersonal conflicts that threaten the group and leader's stability. In particular, the leader's ability to see a larger picture, exercise patience, and recognize the potential spiraling of the projective identification process is key to providing sensible and sound responses to conflict situations.

Chapter 3

On Thinking Organizationally, Systemically, and Psychoanalytically

Part II—Applications

INTRODUCTION

In the previous chapter, using psychoanalytic theory as a guide, a number of different concepts that frame clinical and administrative work in organizations were reviewed, with the goal of providing a conceptual foundation for making inferences about problems that emerge in academic settings. In this chapter, these and other ideas are applied to clinical material, with two goals in mind. First, two published case studies (Herrick, Kvale, & Goodykoontz, 1991; Trombly, Comer, & Villamil, 2002) are presented in order to illustrate the way in which psychoanalytic theory informs dynamics that disrupt academic programs. Herrick et al. (1991) described conflict and crises in a nursing program. We offer a reframing of the conflict using psychoanalytic concepts. Trombly et al. (2002) presented a fictitious departmental conflict, developed for workshop purposes, within a dental school. A briefer discussion of this second case, building on ideas presented in the reformulation of the Herrick et al. (1991) case, is presented. Each case analysis highlights problems that crop up in academic programs, where conflict resonates throughout the university system and cannot be contained or understood within any one member, subgroup, or academic unit. For example, while the focus of a problem might be an academic department, the department's problems have to be studied organizationally as possible symptomatic expressions of a larger, institutional conflict.

Interventions directed at the department level might be of limited value if the organization as a whole as a dynamic system is ignored. Consultations directed at helping academic units will benefit when resources permit a review of the larger structure within which the program operates. This type of comprehensive approach to consultation allows for the crafting of a formulation and intervention strategy that proves beneficial to the department and university. Second, after reviewing both cases, a schematic model is suggested for summarizing consultation data.

ILLUSTRATION OF A DEPARTMENT IN CRISES

Herrick et al. (1991) presented an extensive case study of an academic department embroiled in conflict. The case material can be extrapolated easily to a psychology graduate program. Herrick et al. described how the program's chairperson was in conflict with faculty members, where members themselves had become isolated into smaller subgroups. The consultant utilized Van Servellen's (1984) systems' model for psychotherapeutic nursing and Yalom's (1983, 1985) therapeutic factors and other group therapy concepts to resolve the conflict. The primary intervention was an encounter group, with the consultant moving gradually from directive to nondirective roles. The case study does not include detailed, sequential exchanges between group members or leader–member interactions that would allow for an analysis of content and process, but provided an excellent example of how to apply a theoretically informed approach in the diagnosis, intervention, and evaluation of program progress over time. The conflict is summarized as follows and then reframed psychoanalytically.

Summary of the Case Study

The case study stated that there were nine faculty members in a program that was five years old. The program had become accredited recently. The faculty group, led by one faculty member entrusted with overseeing the accreditation, had apparently been working hard to implement the program, and their efforts were rewarded with an accreditation designation. Then, a fracture of sorts arose when a student's promotion polarized the faculty into two groups. There was another incident in which a student challenged a grade. These events were presented separately, but the tenor of the vignette was that both events contributed to the rift in a palpable way. A second event was the chairperson's intervention and awarding of a passing grade to a student. The decision to pass the student was made against the wishes of some of the faculty members. In addition, faculty members were becoming aware of an emerging financial crisis at the school. The conflict within the faculty unit was illuminated by this statement: "The faculty response was intradepartmental conflict, manifested by anger, failure to follow leadership, and unwillingness to work collaboratively" (Herrick et al., 1991, p. 32). The communication between the chair and faculty members "was unclear and often distorted, resulting in mutual frustrations" (p. 32).

The chairperson was overwhelmed and hired a consultant. The consultant saw that faculty had fallen into subgroups: (a) a leadership group consisting of the chair, the department secretary, and the faculty member who oversaw the accreditation initiative and acted as an intragroup communicator/facilitator; (b) an enmeshed group, who had worked together for a long time and had come as a trio from another university; and (c) a disengaged group that included new faculty members who were distant from the other two groups and from each other. When the intragroup communicator resigned, the leadership group's integrity was "unalterably fractured" (p. 34). There was also a faculty scapegoat, who was anxious, distressed, alienated, and receiving negative feedback from others. Group communication broke down when the intragroup facilitator (i.e., the same faculty member who was also the designated chairperson for the accreditation initiative) eventually left. "Once the intragroup communicator left, upsetting the balance among the subsystems, the chair could no longer maintain effective, conflict free-leadership" (p. 35). The group, rather than expressing pride over accomplishments, was "in the storming stage of group development, comparable to the adolescent state of individual growth and development" (p. 35). The chairperson was portrayed as having problems providing leadership in response to strong resistance as the system's level of conflict escalated. A group facilitator ("eight 2-hour sessions over the course of a 16 week semester," p. 35) worked with faculty toward resolving conflicts. Interventions included Yalom's (1983) "Go-around" technique along with discussions of conflict to study group and individual anxiety, the leader's modeling of communication skills, role play, confrontation, use of "I" messages, memo writing, and, beginning in session 5, transitioning to a less-structured format in which leaders from subgroups led discussions. This process enabled the subsystems to become more fluid over time, with positive communications established among members. While the chairperson ultimately left the department (reasons were unspecified), a new, acting chairperson received faculty support and was able to establish a firm and respected voice as the new leader.

PSYCHOANALYTIC REFORMULATION

This case study provides a rich accounting of the interplay of departmental and institutional dynamics that can contribute to conflict in an academic program. Herrick et al. (1991) offered enough details about the conflict and the chairperson's role to allow for different ways of understanding what went wrong, why it went wrong, and why it improved. They addressed the problem through the lens of systems theory, using group interventions primarily to support the process of changing the departmental climate. Rethinking these events psychoanalytically engages a different set of concepts. In what follows, we draw on ideas from the prior chapter and offer a psychoanalytically informed understanding of the conflict.

Precipitating Event

The conflict appeared to occur on the heels of three precipitating events. The time gap between the events is not clear, but each represents a trauma of sorts to the program. Each event is discussed as contributing as a whole to the chairperson's request for program consultation.

First, there was a significant program success. The vignette states that the program had been through a positive phase, with enthusiasm and collaboration tied to the implementation and eventual accreditation of a new program. These events represent a victory of sorts in terms of being able to bring a new program to life that provides resource and other benefits to the institution, offers students a career path that serves their professional identities and interests, and provides health-care service to the public. Thus, it would seem that the new program was off to a good start.

On the surface, the fact that conflict followed a success experience might seem surprising, given the positive momentum that develops in response to a long-term work ethic that eventuates in an affirming experience (i.e., program accreditation). While a letdown might be expected after the rush of energy begins to wane, the emergence of conflict signals a different dynamic in a department. Here, psychoanalytic theory offers a perspective on the sequence of events leading to group regression.

The symbolic meaning of program accreditation is an important part of the case study. The preparation for accreditation can whip faculty (or faculty subgroups) into a manic frenzy in order to meet designated criteria, and brings about significant anxiety associated with risks of not succeeding. There is also the risk of program destabilization following the accreditation "rush," when manic defenses fade, and the excitement of a validating experience begins to quiet down. Accrediting bodies wield authority and, because of their authority, may evoke in those who are subordinate, wishes to comply, rivalrous feelings both toward the authority and among members of the subordinate groups, and fears of harsh consequence if standards are not met.

Freud (1914b/1981) described the fallout that can follow success experiences by noting how there is a price to be paid for conquest, the modeled concept of the Oedipal conflict. Freud's Oedipal conflict embeds the fantasized consequences of defeating a rival, and the subsequent internalization of the superego to assuage Oedipal aggression and mete out punishment intrapsychically for real or, mainly, imagined wrongdoings. Freud also wrote about the wreckage wrought by success, using Shakespeare's Macbeth to illustrate the self-destructive chaos that followed a presumptive achievement fueled by a deadly, narcissistic ambition. However, Freud also notes how essentially asymptomatic individuals begin to regress on the heels of success. He stated:

> So much the more surprising, and indeed bewildering, must it appear when as a doctor one makes the discovery that people occasionally fall ill precisely when a deeply rooted and long-cherished wish has come to fulfillment. It seems then as though they were not able to tolerate their happiness; for there can be no question that there is a causal connection between their success and their falling ill. (p. 316)

In his description of the consequences of success, Freud provides an example of a teacher who on achieving his wish to succeed his mentor "began to hesitate, depreciated his merits, declared himself unworthy to fill the position designed for him, and fell into a melancholia which unfitted him for all activity for some years" (p. 317). With these points noted about the dangers of success, it seems that program conflict following accreditation may have been tied possibly to the meaning of the accreditation itself and the Oedipal anxiety stirred by this achievement. The following statement by Freud appears to connect anxiety in response to achievement:

> In those exceptional cases in which people are made ill by success, the internal frustration has operated by itself; indeed it has only made its appearance after an external frustration has been replaced by fulfillment of a wish. At first sight there is something strange about this; but on closer consideration we shall reflect that it is not at all unusual for the ego to tolerate a wish as harmless so long as it exists in phantasy alone and seems remote from fulfillment, whereas the ego will defend itself hotly against such a wish as soon as it approaches" fulfillment and threatens to become a reality. (pp. 317–318)

Freud further stated: "Analytic work has no difficulty in showing us that it is the forces of conscience which forbid the subject to gain the long hoped-for advantage from the fortunate change in reality" (p. 318).

Second, the case study stated that following the accreditation, "a turnover of half of the faculty disrupted the group" (p. 32). It was not clear why they left, but mass exodus of faculty, even faculty who contribute substantially to systemic conflict, renders a program highly vulnerable. Anger, disillusionment, loss of collegial contact, student loss of mentoring and faculty contact, disruption in departmental cohesion, and a potentially profound sense of not feeling cared for, especially in a department that trains its students to be health service providers, are bound to resonate throughout the department.

Third, another precipitating event is represented by the emergent fiscal problems within the college. This third event is of particular interest because it reaches faculty awareness right around the time of their successful accreditation. It is hard to know if there was a concern about finances that had been minimized by the entire faculty (an unlikely occurrence, in our view). One might wonder if administration had been vague in communications (much as faculty accused the chairperson as being) and therefore kept faculty in the dark about fiscal matters. Another possibility is that what seemed like a manageable financial shortfall had morphed into something much larger and dangerous.

All college employees are at increased risk for stress when there is a known concern about institutional finances. This type of concern strains the expected support of a positive holding environment (Winnicott, 1965), replaces it with fantasies about institutional demise, and stimulates fears of layoffs, retrenchment, anger, and disillusionment, especially for those employees who are moving forward with successful undertakings, whether they be related to program growth or successful research grant initiatives. What does the role of the program's new accreditation mean for the institution? Does it elevate the symbolic meaning of the faculty members as having succeeded despite risks? Does it promote envy in other departments? Does it spur rivalry within the department itself? Does it elevate the department to privileged status? Are there additional expectations that an accredited program will support the institution financially during a time of need? These are other questions that emerge when one group is successful, but other constituent groups may be struggling.

Symptomatic Expressions of the Conflict

Two events were presented as immediate triggers for the disturbance among faculty. These events were one student not being promoted and one student pushing for a grade change. These events could be seen as precipitating events, and indeed they were, but, in our view, were subordinate to program success, faculty turnover, and decreased college financial resources. As noted earlier, the attainment of accreditation as a symbolic Oedipal victory represents the primary trigger for regressive conflict. Here, success stimulates anxiety in the ego as a way of signaling unconscious danger (Freud, 1923/1981), possibly associated with increased ambition or, in extreme cases, narcissistic aggrandizement of potential conquests, opportunities, kudos, and the like. As such, the two events are seen as symptomatic expressions of the conflict associated with managing success.

That faculty members could become polarized over whether or not to promote a student is a matter of intrigue. Ideally, promotion criteria are specified clearly in program handbooks or other university-based publications. Yet there are gray areas in written documents that require interpretation by program administrators, and consultation with colleagues and, in some cases, with attorneys. Moreover, there are ample examples of faculty debating the merit of student qualifications, even when it appears that the student has met criteria. When making these decisions, all involved university personnel have to weigh the consequences of holding a student back against possible fallout within the student body, public comments against the program or university on social media sites, and implications of student progression as it relates to the ultimate goal of the degree-granting university, which is service to the public. These are all factors that weigh heavily on the collective group mind when addressing matters of student progress.

The case study does not provide details about why the student's promotion was at risk or what the promotion itself entailed and would lead to, but something appeared to be amiss that prompted this particular conflict. The student was not the identified scapegoat within the faculty group but may have been scapegoated nonetheless, with student promotion disguising some other conflict, possibly around ambition, within the faculty group. Again, while these inferences remain speculative, they still lead to questions for which psychoanalytic theory offers possible explanations. For example, viewing the dispute between faculty members around one particular student's promotion might reflect a symptomatic expression of a larger conflict at work within the program that condenses "wish, anxiety, guilt, and defense" (Brenner, 1976, p. 10). In other words, the question of whether or not the student should be promoted might speak to conflictual feelings about success as manifested in symptomatic, but unconscious anxiety, guilt, and undoing of the sense of accomplishment (i.e., "should we or shouldn't we promote?"). It was not clear how the faculty resolved this decision about whether the student was promoted eventually, but the fact that it polarized the group is a significant indicator of disturbance.

The second issue involved a grade appeal. The case study provides minimal information about the circumstances other than noting that this, too, served to polarize the faculty. One can only speculate about why a grade appeal would polarize an entire faculty. Appeals are usually between student and faculty. Administrators might be brought into the dispute, depending on procedures for appeal. The decision to change a grade requires the faculty member to carefully review grading criteria, demonstrate fairness in the application of these criteria, remain open to concerns without becoming unnecessarily defensive, and manage feelings associated with feeling a challenge to authority. While the appeal was for a higher grade, it was not stated whether it was related to an examination, paper, quiz, and/or final course grade. Upward movement of a grade also speaks, thematically, to the idea of student progress and might symbolize conflict over faculty success and accreditation, manifested by guilt and undoing.

Here, then, is another example where student progression becomes a fulcrum for faculty dispute. For faculty to encamp around a grade dispute, it must signal deeper concerns: Do faculty feel heard? Given financial concerns at the college, is grade inflation an issue as a defense against loss of students? Will dissatisfied students lead to an enrollment migration or trauma? Again, details were not provided in the case study, save for the decision of the chairperson to give the student a passing grade against opposition from some of the faculty members. There is no information about the extent to which the chair consulted with others before making this decision, deliberated the matter after reviewing all documents, was under pressure from administration to change the grade, misused authority to retaliate against a faculty member, told the faculty member about the change before or after the fact, or had a countertransference reaction to the student. There may have been other reasons for the decision. It is also possible that the chair may have been the final arbiter in these matters; that is, the chair makes the final call in grade disputes as outlined in a procedural manual.

What is most striking here is the meaning of the chair's action amid a period of emerging faculty conflict. We do not know if the opposition of some of the faculty to the chair's decision would have been less had the decision been made at another point in time. However, the chairperson's action was unsettling to some members of the faculty. Did this group of faculty use the chair's action as a way of expressing other feelings about leadership? We explore the question about department leadership in the next section by drawing on psychoanalytic concepts to develop an understanding of how leadership might have been experienced in this department. Thus, despite the absence of some crucial data, we try to illustrate a psychoanalytic formulation of the departmental situation as a way of guiding program leaders and faculty in their understanding of similar organizational conflicts that transverse department and administrative levels.

Leader Characteristics

The chairperson, described as the "chief administrator of the department" (Herrick et al. 1991, p. 34), was the designated department leader, even though another faculty member was designated as chairperson for the accreditation committee. While these two titles have some overlap and could cause competitiveness and unclear role definition, it is assumed that the accreditation initiative required a point-person and that one faculty member took on this responsibility.

The department chairperson in that case would have probably overseen all activities related to accreditation but relinquished primary oversight of the day-to-day management of accreditation to the designated chairperson. In addition, the chairperson and the chair of the accreditation appeared to be on the same page; that is, both were members of the "leadership group" (p. 34).

The chair was subjected to discord among some of the other faculty members. One can surmise that the chair was experiencing subtle and overt forms of aggression, struggling with containment of harsh affect, feeling attacked, and contributing to the polarization by aligning with a department secretary and another faculty member, designated as the intergroup communicator. Clearly, allegiances, subgroups, and group assumptions are operable here and discussed in greater detail in another section of this chapter. The intergroup communicator, who was the main force in driving the accreditation forward, decided to leave the college, and this person's decision to leave for undisclosed reasons obviously left a hole in the department, which, in turn, forced the chair to look outside the department for help. There was reportedly some tension as to whether the department secretary would participate in the group process that was a core part of the consultant's intervention strategy. Such uncertainty about role may reflect a structural imbalance within the department was valued by some faculty members more than others, whereas others valued the secretary's input. In the end, the consultant opted to go with the majority decision and exclude the secretary from the group "in order to preserve rapport" (p. 34). Herrick et al. (1991) stated: "However, the secretary remained a powerful ghost, capable of evoking strong feelings" (p. 34). The meaning of the secretary's physical absence is not clear, though speculation arises about the role of displaced anger from chairperson onto secretary, and also leads to speculations about how the secretary, if aware of the meeting, felt about not participating.

The department chairperson was the only person from the leadership group who participated in the group process. Thus, on the one hand, the chair was experiencing conflict within the faculty, dealing with the loss of two trusted allies, and seen as a poor communicator by faculty members at odds with the chair's leadership, and, on the other hand, a chair who was responsive enough to the level of distress among faculty members to request an external consultation. Herrick et al. (1991) provided an empathic understanding of the chair's leadership dilemma in dealing with an unhappy faculty in the following statement:

> A chairperson, like parents, may have difficulty providing leadership during this developmental stage. Power struggles for control make leadership difficult. Resistance to group influence increases the breakdown in communication and makes consensual validation impossible. Once conflict becomes the driving

> force, the system, rather than the leader, controls the organization. Conflict must be reduced in order or reestablish leadership and prevent disorganization. (p. 34)

Still, the group had, unconsciously and symbolically, "killed off" one of its own (i.e., the secretary) and would have to deal with loss and guilt associated with this decision, even if feeling respite from the secretary, onto whom they may have displaced anger experienced unconsciously toward the leader as dreaded primal father. In the end, the secretary resigned when the department chair left for unspecified reasons. The chairperson had been concerned sufficiently about changing the departmental climate and hired a consultant. The hire occurred following the loss of the faculty member who communicated across different faculty groups.

Thus, the department chair was clearly under siege. Kernberg's (1980) description of the pressures experienced by organization leaders appear applicable to the department chairperson, especially, as noted in the previous chapter, isolation (i.e., the chairperson's two closest colleagues have left), negative feedback, uncertainty about how to communicate, fear of failure, frustration of dependency, and pressure to solve problems. There is not sufficient information about the chairperson's personality to generate inferences about character typology, but strengths are noted by the fact that the chair was involved in the process of change, open to feedback, able to identify vulnerabilities, and sought outside help. Together, these qualities argue against the more disturbing narcissistic, paranoid, or schizoid qualities in leaders that severely compromise program integrity. Instead, the program is in conflict and the chair is struggling to maintain order amid surging tensions about leadership.

The timing of the chairperson's decision to resign might be related to any number of considerations about which no specific information was offered, though Herrick et al. (1991) speculated that the resignation may have been related "slightly" (p. 38) to positive changes in the group. These changes, however, were considered primarily an "outside factor" (p. 38) in the overall scheme of the group process during the intervention period. That is, there was the presumption of only a minimal relationship between the chairperson's decision to resign and positive changes in the group. Indeed, it is conceivable that the chair had been looking to move, and the timing of resignation coincided with being offered both a new position and the change in climate. It is also conceivable that the chairperson's decision to move was fueled by other motives, including frustration, a response to stress, and a wish to rejoin two colleagues who had also departed. The main point here is that this type of event activates key questions drawn from the concepts of psychoanalytic theory.

Group Dynamics

The case study noted that, in addition to the leadership group, there was one subgroup of closely knit faculty and another subgroup of new faculty who appeared to be disengaged. Although there is no information about the length of time spent by new faculty members in the department at the time of the case study, one might assume that they were relatively recent hires and therefore designated as new departmental members. Developmental considerations might have made it harder for newer faculty members to feel included as equal members of the department at a point when other faculty members were experiencing success related to a successful accreditation decision. The third faculty group consisted of a cohesive group hired at the same time from "another educational system" (p. 34), which has a vagueness to it (i.e., did they come as a package deal with certain promises?). They impressed the consultant as "enmeshed" (p. 34) and not able to function autonomously. It is difficult to discern the nature of their relationship to each other; for example, were they bound by certain research interests, ideals, and/or other professional qualities that were appealing to the department? The chairperson's challenge of bringing these three groups together speaks to a polarity of sorts that can create considerable tension in an academic department where some members feel polarized, isolated, and fearful (also see Klein's, 1946, review of the paranoid–schizoid position).

Regarding basic group assumptions, Bion's (1961) model sheds light on departmental dynamics. Bion's ideas, with some modification, are applied to the available information. As the case study unfolds, the consultant learns, at a one-year follow-up, that the chairperson had left, along with one member of the disengaged group. The secretary had also resigned. The department eventually uses the consultant's intervention to move toward a work group, where everyone is working productively toward the same end goal under the new, acting chairperson's direction and with faculty support. That is, faculty member interactions had improved "to the point that faculty were able to problem solve in order to accomplish tasks" (p. 39). Prior to this shift, one might speculate about the likelihood of a dependency assumption, suggested by reliance on the leader and/or the faculty member who chaired the accreditation initiative; a fight-flight assumption, suggested by a united front against the leader; and a pairing assumption, suggested by the possible focus on the department chair and the accreditation chair having a special relationship that had the potential to bring forth new progeny through the establishment of an accredited program. To these assumptions, we also consider Hopper's (2012) massification/aggregation assumption. Here, the college's financial stresses may have contributed to an unconscious, aggregated group massing of fragmenting anxiety/panic within the department, leading then to a massing of sorts in which most of the group seems to be organized against the chairperson but at the cost of a loss of individuality in the service of mind-meld.

Transference, Countertransference, and Projective Identification

Transference, countertransference, and projective identification are identifiable in the case study about the department's dynamic, though the absence of information about each faculty member's history and detailed exchanges among members were limiting factors. The following inferences are suggested in light of these constraints. The gender constituency of the department faculty members was not totally clear; however, the chairperson was identified as female toward the end of the case study, the intragroup communicator was female, and one might speculate that the secretary was also female. Members of the other two groups were not identified by gender, though at least one other member, identified as "resistant" (Herrick et al. 1991, p. 37), was female. Thus, the leadership group was most likely all female, and the department was most likely predominately female.

Given this hypothesized predominately female gender emphasis in the department, speculation is that the predominant transference theme directed at the female chairperson was one of anger directed toward a maternal figure during points of heightened stress (see Long, 2006, for a discussion of gender and leadership, and Parker, 2008, for a discussion of race, gender, and leadership). Relevant data points include the chairperson's decision to modify a grade in the absence of full faculty support and the response this engendered within the group. The chairperson may have also been the displaced target of the larger, institutional transference, with all faculty members feeling anxious and endangered by the college's resource limitations. Another source of possible transference displacement lies within the scapegoated faculty member, who was the apparent recipient of negative projections. The impact of this feedback on the faculty scapegoat—it was unclear if the scapegoat was the secretary or a faculty member who was scapegoated—might lead to the impression that elements of what Kernberg (1993, as cited in Kibel, 2012) described as paranoiagenesis were present in the department whereby at least one person became highly symptomatic as increasing pressure was imposed through interactional projections by other group members.

Examples of transference, countertransference, and projective identification can also be inferred from the eight-session Encounter Group process that was effective in building back a sense of trust and support for leadership within the department. The consultant started with a directive style that was supportive, reassuring, focused on the goal of recapturing group cohesion, disputing irrational thoughts and examining catastrophic thoughts, role plays, practicing, homework, communication styles, and building hope. As the group progressed, there was a shift to a less directive style in which faculty members led the discussion. Here, problem solving, consensus building, and methods for dealing with future conflict were among the topics covered. Herrick et al. (1991) reported that the first meeting included a high level of tension and open resistance among some members to participation, even though this tension did lessen over time. Perceptions of the group leader were not provided, but speculation is that in addition to anxiety about the early phase of group, some members may have been viewing the group leader as an extension of the chairperson, who requested the consultation, and representing an obstructionist viewpoint in the group that mirrored problems in the department. There was a refuting of the fantasy that faculty may never be able to work together—we assume, by the group leader—manifested in "high levels of anxiety, manifested by pressured speech, refusing to talk and crying" (p. 37). The group leader's active stance in this manner contained, confronted, and calmed the anxiety, in addition to other interventions that appeared to work with departmental conflict in a nonjudging way. Such a positive response to a group process experience may, to use Halton's concept of "reparative creativity" (2004, p. 111), lead to in which the group moves finds new directions by analyzing conflict and learns to live with the ambivalence of conflict analogous to Klein's (1946) depressive position. As their process evolved, the group experienced a "catharsis" of sorts and had begun to move forward insightfully and collaboratively as a work group in response to a positive group experience. Fallout was still present, however, despite the overall positive outcome. The chairperson and secretary left the department, as did a resistant group member, for reasons that were not clear. The case study included a follow-up meeting with the faculty, but it did not include details about how the group processed the leaving of four members (the intragroup communicator, chairperson, secretary, and a resistant faculty member) or the college's finances. Both areas would have been helpful to clarify as they relate to loss, guilt, fantasies of new hope and change in response to loss, and shifts in perception of feeling supported in relation to the college's available material resources.

ILLUSTRATION OF A CONFLICT WITH FACULTY AND BETWEEN FACULTY AND ADMINISTRATION

Trombly et al. (2002) presented a fictitious case study involving a dental school's effort to increase its financial resources. They described hiring decisions that impacted faculty relations and conflict between faculty and administration. In their introduction to the case, Trombly et al. (2002) advocated for transparency, open discussion, cautious use of confrontation, and active listening as techniques for resolving conflict. They viewed conflict as having the potential for positive outcomes but also recognized that it could breed negativity, if not handled sensitively. The case study, summarized here, illustrates fractious exchanges that polarize a faculty group and also polarize faculty against administration around the issues of equity, governance, and resource allocation.

Summary of the Case Study

The dental school was facing financial challenges. In order to increase revenue, they hired nontenure-track clinical faculty who provided clinical services through outpatient dentistry. The department chair of Restorative Dentistry, who himself was traditional academic (i.e., primarily teaching and research), was conflicted about the dean's pressing for continued support of clinical-track faculty. The dean saw clinical faculty as being able to offer services that would generate revenue for the entire dental school. These clinical faculty members generated additional revenue but were perceived as "second-class citizens" by tenured faculty members, who valued scholarship, which was not the role of clinical faculty, and who also questioned differences in workload. Clinical faculty members were in the clinic more often than tenure-track faculty, who were limited to one day per week. There were intra-program jealousies and morale problems. For example, a tenured faculty member complained to the chair about a clinic-based faculty member who was permitted weekly time for planning and administration and perceived as taking advantage of clinic work to add to his income: "It's your job as chair to keep him in line, and it sure doesn't seem like you're doing it" (p. 536). Over time, however, the traditional role of faculty had changed, with now one-third of the faculty on clinical tracks. The chair supported the hire of clinical faculty into two open positions.

The clinical faculty members, in response to the complaints leveled by tenure-track faculty members, felt angered over their lower base salaries. They were also upset because they were also earning less money than colleagues in private practice. Clinical faculty members wanted to be compensated because of their years of experience in private practice and less flexible schedules. The conflict between faculty groups was illustrated by a tenure-track faculty member stating "They can just go back to their old offices. I for one wouldn't stop them" and a clinical faculty member stating "I wish I had several hours per week to decide which carousel of 1985 slides to use in my course" (pp. 536–537). Clinical faculty members were also upset over committee recommendations that they pursue more serious scholarship and noted that these committees were loaded with tenure-track faculty members, who were less impressed by posters and abstract presentations at conferences, and "interpreted the guidelines to read that there is an implied scholarly commitment in all academic appointments" (p. 537).

Adding fuel to the fire was the distribution of faculty salaries by a clinical faculty member to all members of the faculty as a way of showing the difference in their salaries; however, in distributing this listing of salaries, the clinical faculty member omitted practice incentives built into the earning capacity of clinical faculty. Thus, the list did not honestly represent the true earnings of clinical faculty and was intended to show discrepancy at the level of base salary. Further, this particular clinical faculty member had also met privately with the dean to express feelings about compensation differential. Clinical faculty members were concerned about their future roles in the department because their fate rested largely in the hands of committees comprised of traditional faculty members. Rumors of "mass exodus" (p. 537) of clinical faculty were circulating. As such, there was palpable anger, deception, and envy between the groups. Thus, when the tenure-track faculty member brought concerns to the chair and pressed for an immediate reply, he was understandably frustrated (i.e., left pounding his fist on the chair's desk) when the chair thanked him and stated: "I can't really get into a meaningful discussion right now. I'll look into the situation and get together with you to discuss it further" (p. 537). The chair then wondered if this would be a good time to take a vacation!

PSYCHOANALYTIC REFORMULATION

Precipitating Event

The precipitating event appears to be the school's financial stress. The school's management team was anxious. The fear of insufficient funds arouses fears of annihilation (e.g., Collie, 2005) that can lead to extreme measures. The school opts to generate revenue by creating new faculty tracks, and the intent was a good one; however, as Trombly et al. (2002) stated: "It is likely that the central and department administration's management approach was poorly executed in either the timing of the communication of the communication method itself. The 'old-guard' faculty members have not bought into the concept of new faculty tracks" (p. 538).

Regarding the actions of the chair on whom the notion of clinical faculty tracks had been thrust without proper time for full deliberation, they stated: "The fact that he acted out of desperation to solve the faculty resource issue indicates that he felt there were considerable downsides to use of clinical-track faculty and/or that these negatives had not been properly addressed to allow for success" (p. 538).

Symptomatic Expression of Conflict

Symptomatic expression of conflict is evidenced by the chair's acquiescing to a faculty model about which he has considerable ambivalence, and the competitive dynamics manifested in the heated back-forth exchanges between the tenure-track and clinical faculty members. Symptoms are intensified when the clinical faculty member presents misleading data about income to all faculty members. One other example of a conflict indicator was the absence of a deliberative period during which old-guard faculty members have an opportunity to voice concerns, rather than having a new model seemingly imposed forcefully without the courtesy of a meeting to discuss proposed changes.

Leadership Characteristics

The case study provides information about the chair's leadership style in a crisis situation. The chair attempted to contain the rage emerging in his department and shows an interest in hearing both sides of the argument as presented through the warring faculty factions, but also feels overwhelmed, defeated, isolated (e.g., Kernberg, 1980) and without much say in the direction of change, and noncollaborative. Here, the chair had consented, atypically, to the dean's position but eventually questioned his judgment in making this decision. Still, by acting on this judgment, the chair appeared to fit Hoyle's (2004) "agreeable without reflection" defensive retreat from conflict. There is also a perception of the chair withholding his thoughts and feelings, even when beseeched to communicate by the tenure-track faculty member.

Basic Assumptions

The raw competitiveness within the faculty factions was characteristic of sibling rivalry for the attention of a beleaguered parental figure (i.e., the chair). The basic group assumption here was fight-flight against the depriving leader (Bion, 1961). The department was in a paranoid–schizoid mode (Klein, 1946), with faculty members feeling alienated, persecuted, deprived, and envious, with oral aggression associated with loss of basic emotional and material supplies, and without the guilt characteristic of the depressive position.

Transference, Countertransference, and Projective Identification

Transference themes are present throughout the vignette. The chair is portrayed as seeing the dean as a source of Oedipal danger where questioning of authority seems out of the question. The chair is seen by faculty members as a frustrating parental object showing favoritism and unable to deal with conflict in a constructive manner. The faculty members show features of a sibling rivalry. The projections go through the dean to the chair, and from the chair to the faculty members, in a cycle of projective identification driven by a nonreflective attitude toward countertransference.

In sum, the case studies of the nursing and dental schools provided enough information to show how a psychoanalytic approach to understanding organizational conflict can be applied conceptually to academic programs. While not all concepts equally fit any single case, psychoanalytic theory does bring an explanatory power to behaviors that disrupt organizational flow that can be utilized when negotiating the often-treacherous events that can compromise success in the academic setting. In the next section, the two case studies are summarized in a schematic model of psychoanalytic organization consultation to academic programs.

A MODEL FOR ORGANIZING CONSULTATION DATA AND INTERVENTION

A psychoanalytically informed consultation to academic programs can follow the path of many consultative approaches that lead to helpful interventions. Such a consultative approach might include contracting with the institution; learning about program and institutional history; clarifying parameters of confidentiality; identifying the presenting problem(s) and attempts at problem resolution; discussing data collection, intervention, and follow-up methods; and reviewing expectations for who receives feedback and what type of report, if any, is expected. This information can be organized within a psychoanalytic framework that provides a guidepost to final formulation, intervention, and outcomes. Information can be modified as the consultation unfolds, with the schema providing a model for capturing main data points that support the consultant's unfolding understanding of the process. The model also provides the consultant with a way of capturing information in a simplified manner in order to communicate main points to consultees. These points can then be titrated, reframed, elaborated, and integrated with other aspects of the consultation, such as program history, prior efforts to solve the problem, and methods of data collection.

Table 3.1 reviews key points from our case examples that evoke institutional transferences and countertransferences, which, if not recognized, contained, and managed, can lead to significant conflict that resonates within a department and can impact morale, productivity, and the type of collaborative commitment needed to support student progress.

Table 3.1. Conflict Identification and Management Strategies

Data Points	*Academic Program*	*Dental School*
Primary precipitating events	Accreditation, faculty turnover, financial	Financial
Symptomatic expressions	Polarized faculty over student promotion and grade appeal	Polarized faculty over differential treatment
Leadership	Empathic, overwhelmed, isolated	Dean: controlling, anxious Chair: isolated, acquiescent
Basic group assumptions	Dependency, pairing, fight-flight, aggregation-massification, and work	Primarily fight-flight; paranoid–schizoid
Transference, countertransference, and projective identification	Perception of chair as reactive; chair feels overwhelmed; the loss of faculty members takes a toll; displaced anger toward the chair; transference to the group consultant	Perceptions of chair as withholding and displaying favoritism; chair feeling uncertain; projective identifications from dean to chair; chair to faculty
Program identity	Fragmented	Fragmented
Core conflict(s)	Ineffective leadership	Administration versus faculty
Interventions to strengthen the program	Interviews with faculty; group process; consultation, which required considerable buy-in from faculty and administration	Recommended collaboration; negotiation; addressing inequities

CONCLUSION

Academic programs are continually at risk for conflict. Events that can precipitate programmatic conflict may include large-scale resource risks at the university level; enrollment decline; exodus of key faculty and/or supportive administrators; student–faculty conflict around grades, promotion, research, or behavioral enactments; unclear policies and procedures; differential faculty workload within and/or across departments; faculty–faculty personality clashes; and other similar incidents that begin to fray the program's edges that neither self-regulate nor respond to routine intervention. When conflict occurs, trust diminishes, private concerns managed previously by a good-enough work climate become public disputes, and leadership is questioned. A psychoanalytically informed understanding of these problems studies both conscious and unconscious motivations, and offers a formulation and intervention strategy that seeks to reestablish a collaborative work group by studying the organizational climate to strengthen faculty collaboration so that they focus on the collective work and goals of the group as a whole. Specifically, we recommend a psychoanalytically informed method of consultation as a way of supporting programs where conflict may require outside intervention.

Part II

TRAINING

Chapter 4

Normotic Elements in Professional Discourse and Practice

Implications for Professional Identity Development

> *Depressive society, written into the movement of economic globalisation that is transforming people into objects, no longer wants to hear talk of guilt, or of personal meaning, or of conscience, or of desire, or of unconscious. The more it imprisons itself in narcissistic logic, the more it is running away from the idea of subjectivity. So depressive society is only interested in the individual for the purpose of calculating his or her successes and only interested in the suffering subject for the purpose of regarding him or her as a victim. And if depressive society is always seeking to put the deficit into figures, to measure the handicap, quantify the degree of trauma, this is so that it will never again have to ask itself questions about their origin.* (Roudinesco, 2001, p. 29)

INTRODUCTION

In Part I, we focused on how to understand educational systems and processes psychoanalytically, with special attention to the nuances of transference and countertransference. In Part II, beginning with this chapter, we focus on the experience of clinical training in relation to professional socialization processes that impact student learning and faculty experiences.

Here, we offer a psychoanalytically informed perspective on professional identity development as it relates to training graduate students (e.g., primarily doctoral-level clinical psychology, but also with relevance to counseling psychology, clinical mental health counseling, social work, and, to a lesser extent, psychoanalytic candidates). We draw from a diverse literature in our attempt to describe how graduate training in professional psychology has struggled to find its own voice amid growing pressure form compliance with stringent education and training regulations. Thus, in a systemic way, these regulations are promulgated to discipline-specific accreditation agencies by higher educational commissions, thereby creating a hierarchical grid in which academic programs are responsive to a much larger ethos of education and training regulations and governmental structure to which they may have limited input. In particular, we focus on the experience of the psychoanalytically informed educator, whose training prioritizes individual narratives and unconscious processes. Indeed, the psychoanalytic-educator, much like the psychoanalytically oriented clinician, is somewhat of an outlier in the training of professional psychologists, as noted in Heatherington et al. (2012), and has to find ways to blend multiple psychoanalytic identities (e.g., teacher, clinician, clinical mentor) within the parameters of accreditation-driven program initiatives that demand measurable, quantifiable, and linear outcomes.

This type of impetus toward quantification of teaching, learning, and student development requires sophisticated program methodologies for accountability. However, as we discuss, it is precisely this type of numerical emphasis that can pose a challenge to the teacher/mentor who processes, formulates, and experiences the world subjectively and privileges this type of subjectivity in conducting psychoanalytic treatment. We discuss how these type of stresses have impacted the socialization, identity, and strivings of psychoanalytically informed educators and mentors, and how it affects their work as with students.

Aspects of psychoanalytic theory inform psychoanalytic educators but also pose points of internal conflict. Academics trained extensively in the psychoanalytic psychotherapeutic method must navigate the nuanced roles and divide between an understanding of theory as applied to treatment and differentiating treatment from education, both of which are discussed in this chapter, while maintaining fidelity to a psychoanalytic way of thinking about their work as academicians.

American psychoanalysis has, from the outset, been associated with an underlying conservative narrative that has tended to situate discourse in an elite, removed, and esoteric position. The development of psychoanalysis as solely the province of medical professions throughout the bulk of its history in the United States certainly contributed to this. With its *elite* and privileged status undermined sorely in the contemporary pantheon of the mental health professions, and no longer under the hegemonic aegis of the medical psychoanalytical establishment, beleaguered by the commodifying and corporatizing deformations of contemporary health-care delivery systems, a medicalized psychoanalytical movement has nonetheless retained its mysterious and esoteric aura, and even much in the way of its conservatism. We would suggest that this phenomenon owes, in part, to the impact of a particular *molding* of ego psychology in the United States with an overemphasis on the system

Cs; the functions of the ego; the desexualization and de-aggressivization of those components from psychoanalytical theory; and, instead, an emphasis on *adaptation* to societal norms, values, and definitions of health and success. Concomitantly, there is a de-emphasis on the system *Ucs*; studies on the nature of the id; and serious foci on the vicissitudes of the drives, as articulated originally by Freud (1900/1981).

Psychoanalysis in the United States, as a uniquely *American* construction, is further structured by various "normalizing" tyrannies of the *Diagnostic and Statistical Manual of Mental Disorders* (5th edition; DSM-5; American Psychiatric Association, 2013), an emphasis on coercive professional regulatory proscriptions such as the *Tarasoff* (e.g., Bersoff & Parker, 2015) decision that, with the state's intrusion into the ostensible "confidential" psychotherapeutic space, deforms the profession into a constabulary (Bollas & Sundelson, 1995). Added to this is the fact that, in the main, in the United States, practicing clinical psychoanalysts overwhelmingly come from the ranks of health-care professionals, as opposed to other countries where practicing psychoanalysts may also hail from backgrounds in the arts and humanities. As such, psychoanalysts generally owe fealty to their "host" medicalized, mental health professions, under which the professional educational and training catechisms scripted by standardized bodies of epistemic knowledge are, in turn, related to the demands of accreditation entities, which are, themselves in turn, sponsored by the pieties of contemporary rightist political ideologies.

Within this health-care matrix, certain ways of thinking, thinking about thinking, definitions of health and illness, "effective" practice, and even what constitutes "knowledge" and "evidence" to (de)legitimize said practice are increasingly becoming enshrined in accreditation standards, in professional association standards, and, of course, in the industrialized insurance registers that underwrite so many mental health practitioners' (including psychoanalysts') clinical work and livelihoods.

Within the academy, certainly a mirror of the culture at large, we see evidence of what Bollas (1987) has termed "normotic illness." Stating that psychoanalysis addresses sectors of experience that problematize living creatively, normotic illness is a manifestation of an extreme desire to be normal, "typified by the numbing and eventual erasure of subjectivity in favour of a self that is conceived as a material object amongst other man-made objects in the object world" (Bollas, 1987, p. 135). If we but substitute this term for Roudinesco's (2001) "Behavior-Modification Man," of the "Depressive Society," of which she speaks, we have a further elaboration of this. As Bollas (1987) notes, such an individual is "abnormally normal. He is too stable, secure, and comfortable, and socially extrovert. He is fundamentally disinterested in subjective life and he is inclined to reflect on the thingness of objects, on their material reality, or on 'data' " (p. 136).

To put this in other terms, emphasizing the complexities of the situation, the accreditation commission, *in part because of its own reporting requirements to a higher federal governmental body*, in many respects rewards program conformity to different domain-based program expectations and discrete implementing regulations, which in turn has implications for how faculty teach and train students. This type of conformity, even if necessary for a structured review of mental health programs, can be especially challenging for educators with a psychoanalytic bent, where outcomes are not always quantifiable, and the stringency of structure can be at odds with psychoanalytic philosophical-theoretical preferences.

If, as we might note, each culture constructs its own version of psychoanalysis, as a projection of its own collective unconscious, we begin to see the contagion of such "normotic" trends in the academy on the broader reproduction of the various schools of psychotherapy—graduate programs in psychology inscribing future generations of clinical practitioners with the logic of increasingly prescriptive/proscriptive, programmed texts—with the accrediting body insisting on more derivative, "contemporary" texts published within the past three to five years, as opposed to supporting the logic of advocating the inclusion of primary, seminal, "classical" texts that have been the hallmark of education from the founding of universities. Indeed, we should therefore not be at all surprised that this is in evidence even the professional lexicon that is transmitted and sanctified, and contributes to the professional identifications by professionals-in-training: the emphasis of statistics and the bell curve; the randomized control trial experiment (RCT) (a positivistic form of discovery that has largely been called into question in other fields while paradoxically being ever-more exalted within the field of clinical psychology, where the strictures associated with it may not readily lend themselves to articulating less-reductive theoretical and treatment modalities as in humanistic/existential and psychoanalytical paradigms) with implications for defining normality and the "(un)common"; our penchant for phasic definitions of *appropriate* development; and now an emphasis for *defining* so-called best practices, certainly related in turn with *measuring* "outcomes"—which, of course, is freighted with many political implications and, once more, instantiates the primacy of adaptation to society's standards (particularized definitions of "cure," a "successful" life, etc.). This is, of course, all very curious, given Freud's rather more humble, sensible position that psychoanalysis was doing quite well if able to transmute neurotic suffering into ordinary unhappiness (Freud & Breuer, 1893–1895/1981).

An unquestioning obeisance to such trends forecloses on efforts from within or without the mental health professions to explore the deleterious impact of such dynamics and trends on the nascent philosophical leanings and emerging clinical proclivities of professionals-in-training, increasingly scripted and pre-thought for the passive vessel that is now constructed as the right and proper nature of the "learner" and inheritor of this rich legacy of questioning, thinking, thinking about thinking, and critical enquiry. This calls to mind the interpretation of such ideological and technique-focused trends that they spawn (Kavanaugh, 1999), noting that this ideology is promulgated and privileged by the "Psychological Haves," deigning to "help" a class of people determined to be in *need* of psychiatric/psychological care (or, in increasing frequency in the United States, the onerous and revealing term "*behavioral* health"), whether they are aware of this or not—and to be "treated" in arriving at positions of *correct* thinking and behaving—that is to say, as defined by a technocratic professional class, itself an articulation of the broader ideology of the political elite's view of health and healthy *values*. This group of consumers acted upon by the de-skilled, technician-providers Kavanaugh (1999) terms the "Psychological Have-Nots." This type of thinking, left unchallenged, creates or at the least reinforces in the mind and resultant emergent practice of the clinician-in-training an orientation potentially not unlike that described by Goffman (1961), in what he articulates as "The Medical Model and Mental Hospitalisation: Some Notes on the Vicissitudes of the Tinkering Trades," in the final chapter of his book, *Asylums*. Here, Goffman equates psychiatry with a repair service industry and patients with the damaged or broken parts of society that require fixing. We offer, instead, apropos to our work as educators, administrators, and psychoanalytic clinicians the title of the late Joyce McDougall (1980) books: *A Plea for a Measure of Abnormality*.

A CULTURE OF SURVEILLANCE—OR, THIS IS HOW THE END BEGINS

Even more powerfully embraced, if not recognized as such, is, as Foucault (as cited in Lüdemann, 2012, p. 1) frames it, the status of contemporary psychiatry and other mental health professions that "place individuals in a field of surveillance [and] also situate them in a network of writing; they engage them in a whole mass of documents that capture the power of the pen/discursive power and fix them." That this is nothing especially new has also been well articulated by Foucault, who asserts that we have an ingrained propensity to view madness as essentially "other," with the asylum representing the break in the "dialogue between reason and unreason, and society and the disturbed on the other." Gilroy (1987, as cited in Rogers & Pilgrim, 2005) aptly extends the discursive elements of "otherness" as a new form of racism, as it were one that is concerned with those whom should be included or excluded from the mainstream of societal life—or, in other words a symbolic order—the system of words, narrations, and associated socially constructed and sanctified meanings: "The new racism is primarily concerned with mechanisms of inclusion and exclusion. It . . . advances reasons for the segregation or banishment of those whose 'origin, *sentiment*, or citizenship' assigns them *elsewhere*" (emphasis added) (as cited in Rogers & Pilgrim, 2005, pp. 80–81).

The mad, conscripted within the discursive elements of otherness, find themselves subject to a unique form of subjective disenfranchisement. This often involves the sense of loss of one's personal narrative, a coherent binding of the self within the frame of one's lived experience as communicable to one's self and to the Other. Here, Lüdemann (2012) cites Mauric Blanchot's *La folie du jour* (*The Madness of the Day*). This is a first-person account of an individual who, through some accident, had lost his capacity for memory, and hence, one of the symptoms included the ability to narrate. His retrospective account of his interrogations by his physicians seems emblematic of the present insistence on the gathering and ascertainment of the *facts* [*sic*] of the so-called case. In fact, per Lüdemann, this is an exemplification of the subject *become* case that is valorized in mental health training programs today, extolling the virtues of normalization through the process of pathologization, such as the degradation ceremony described by Goffman (1961) in his seminal work, *Asylums* (also cited in Lüdemann, 2012).

> I liked the doctors quite well, and I did not feel belittled by their doubts. The annoying thing was that their authority loomed larger by the hour. One is not aware of it, but these men are kings. Throwing open my rooms, they would say, "Everything here belongs to us." They would fall upon my scraps of thought: "This is ours." They would challenge my story: "Talk," and my story would put itself at their service. In haste, I would rid myself of myself. I distributed my blood, my innermost being among them, lent them the universe, gave them the day. Right before their eyes, though they were not at all startled, I became a drop of water, a spot of ink. I reduced myself to them. The whole presence of me passed in full view before them, and when at last nothing was present but my perfect nothingness and there was nothing more to see, they ceased to see me too. Very irritated, they stood up and cried out, "All right, where are you? Where are you hiding?" (p. 7)

As Lüdemann asserts, the patient is subsumed to the point of disappearance under the auspices of the doctors or what she terms the "tyranny of the Universal" (2012, p. 7). Subsumption under this nosological universal spreads to the singularized narrative itself as well: the narrator, in the end, can no longer tell his story, because it is no longer a story. Rather, it is a symptom of the illness (the *inability* to tell a story), and the subsumption of the story under the pathological general is thus conflated.

Here, we are speaking in the language familiar to today's clinician-in-training, often eager and yearning to actually *be* the "expert"; to be "The One Who Knows"—the dispassionate *scientist* instituting intellectualized treatments according to manuals "validated" in randomized clinical control trials with artificially derived patient/subject samples for psycho-diagnostic "purity"—one could easily imagine them in a white laboratory coat. (Indeed, a new term for a new form of psychological "helping professional" has emerged: that of the "clinical scientist" [Treweiler & Stricker, 1998]. Such individuals generally have very little actual clinical experience during their doctoral programs.)

Often, in addition to employing, literally, "workbooks" in the "psychotherapy" of patients, such clinicians have erasable white boards in the consulting room, approximating a didactic exercise (e.g., such is the case in the community psychological clinic consulting rooms operated by the doctoral program of one of the authors of this text). On the white board are scripted diagrams depicting "triggers" of the patient, which sponsor irrational thoughts, and the sanctified nostrums that are to be inscribed in place of them in the thinking mind of the objectified subjectivity of the patient. At times, patients are noted to refer to their appointments as "lessons" or "classes." Such "techniques" are redolent with themes of indoctrination, intrusiveness, and control.

TRENDS TOWARD NORMALIZATION

So far we have been commenting on themes that must only be termed "pathological," or trends that are "pathologizing." How does this relate to an ostensible subject of a normotic or pathological concern with the normal? Of course, they by necessity constitute a dialectic—a circle of which one necessarily presupposes the presence of the other trend.

It is of note that the late Hans Strupp (2001), one of the progenitors of psychoanalytically orientated psychotherapy outcome research and treatment manuals, should also call our attention to the unsavory alliance between proponents of evidence-based treatments and corporatist entities and the egregious conflation of psychotherapeutic efficacy and profitability that defines this allegiance. As a researcher, he noted, "I take exception to the manner in which research has been used, if not to say co-opted, as a tool for justifying the rationing of [psycho]therapeutic services and putting [psycho]therapeutic techniques into a straitjacket" (2001, p. 606). This extends into the specious development and utilization of treatment manuals—originally developed to aid researchers in their addressing certain specific symptom clusters within micro-moments of treatment with the intent of elucidating cause and effect relations and intervention strategies—a laudable-enough endeavor, to be sure—but have ultimately been adopted into becoming *the* modality for implementing totalistic clinical treatments, proper, as well as the rubrics by which insurance carriers will reimburse for psychological (read: "cognitive-behavioral") treatments.

This form of manualization not merely forecloses upon the unique vicissitudes afforded by the free associations of the patient, but the psychotherapist's potential for various acts of freedom uniquely afforded and indeed necessitated by the not-to-be repeated moment-to-moment unfolding of unconscious processes worded within the psychotherapeutic bi-personal field. Each participant is conjoined in a process of suppression and de-linking that collapses enquiry into rote prescriptions and proscriptions for correct thought and behavioral management and control. Indeed, a manualized "treatment" goes further in that it utterly negates anything other than a passive and scripted process of pre-thought knowns and a received wisdom being enshrined in the patient through an active, coercive, and impinging agency represented by the intermediary proxy of the psychotherapist-cum-technician. A normotic treatment sponsored by a normotic biobehavioral technician schooled—or, rather, "trained," one should think, is the operative term leads to laundering the self of all untoward idiosyncrasies associated with subjective experience deemed "inappropriate" by the culture at large (Bollas, 1987; Fink, 2011; Kavanaugh, 2012). Thus, the patient does not belong to the psychotherapeutic pair as the one who knows—entering this space as self-as-subject, authoring their own narrative of lived experience. This negates and displaces the individual sufferer as the author of desire—the desire to question and to come to know—as well as the associated work of wording of self-experience in the patient's own idiom through the relative ignorance and enlightened desire to understand as brought to the fore by the psychoanalyst/psychotherapist who, in being the one who does not know, embodies an ethic of desire for self-discovery and knowledge. As powerfully articulated by Kavanaugh (2012, p. 162), this is now undermined by the dynamic and political-economic forces at work above. As he states:

> In many respects, the identity of the analytic educator and practitioner as a health-care professional has become his or her strongest weakness: As a member of the health-care profession, he or she is subject to the on-going industrialization and commercialization of the health-care professions taking place through the increased centralization of information, authority, and decision-making power in various educratic entities, national committees, and other health-care interest groups. (Kavanaugh, 2012, p. 162)

Certainly, within psychoanalysis, Kernberg (1996) is well aware of the pernicious and deleterious nature of such normalizing pressures and associated dangers as articulated in his article, "Thirty Methods to Destroy the

Creativity of Psychoanalytic Candidate," as this may come to sponsor the professional ambitions and inclinations of those individuals seeking to enter the mental health professions, including psychoanalytical studies. Kernberg speaks of such matters as an insistence on the dogmatic and unquestioning internalization of key progenitors of psychoanalytical theory and practice (instituting a master–disciple relation to knowledge, instructors, and the psychoanalytic institute); hierarchical power relations that constitute what a Chicago psychoanalyst, Christine Kieffer, has articulated as the profession's "Laius Complex" in relation to new generations of psychoanalysts and the manner in which they are often subject to a form of institutional suppression (C. Kieffer, personal communication, August 2009); discouragement of original contributions by candidates; the intellectual isolation of institutes from the larger professional and academic community (reinforcing, we should add, the "almost" complete expulsion of psychoanalysis from the curricula of doctoral programs in clinical psychology (Cohen, 2007)) that can approximate Goffman's (1961) discussion of entry into a career as a mental patient; a neglect of enlightened examination of the controversies regarding psychoanalytical theory and practice; and so on.

Of course, we need search no farther for a way out of the apparent cul-de-sac than a certain nineteenth-century positivist, who first discovered the limits in the promises of psycho-physics and attempts at measuring the ineffable and, in effect, normalizing/pathologizing in the positivistic, medicalized manner again so very much *en vogue*: Freud (1895/1981), in his collaboration with Joseph Breuer, resolved that it is in this centering around a conflict in which the particular and universal are mutually influenced by the other, each in its own way, that literary and psychoanalytical case studies come together. It is precisely in this that they are to be differentiated from medical or psychiatric case studies as well. It is no coincidence, therefore, that it is the literary nature of Freud's case studies that marks Freud's "departure" from mainstream medicine (well marked by his being denied the Nobel Prize for medicine which he so greatly desired, but winning the Goethe Prize for Literature, instead):

> I have not always been a psychotherapist, but like other neuro-pathologists I was educated to methods of focal diagnoses and electrical prognosis, so that even I myself am struck by the fact that the case histories which I am writing read like novellas, and as it were, dispense with the serious features of the scientific character. Yet, I must console myself with the fact that the nature of the subject is apparently more responsible for this issue than my own predilection. Focal diagnosis and electrical reactions are really not important in the study of hysteria, whereas a detailed discussion of the psychic processes, as one is used to hear it from the poet, and the application of a few psychological formulae, allows one to gain insight into the course of events of hysteria. (1895, pp. 160–161)

Fink (2011), a Lacanian, writing of this normalizing trend, rightly notes the form of *language* adopted by the field that enunciates this movement at every turn, structuralizing further elaborations upon itself, and discursive logics unfolding forthwith. He notes that clinicians are quick to speak in terms of what may or may not be "common," when asked by patients (or merely offering said "normalizing pronouncements spontaneously") as if referencing some real or imagined statistical norm. Perhaps such didactics are offered as efforts of reassurance that, possibly, are rendered in the hope that such "information" might be helpful in alleviating a given patient's concerns about a conflict that he or she experiences or some potential stigmatizing component thereof. But at what cost? Does this not foreclose on an articulation and exploration of the patient's own unique and personally revelatory phantasies and conflicts? Can we presume to know the helpfulness as opposed to the possibly patronizing and reductive impact for the patient? Indeed, can we presume to "know" the truth of the matter, at all?

This question of exemplarities versus singularities is increasingly negated in the nineteenth-century positivism that inhabits, motivates, and authors our very thinking about thinking in the psychical—or, rather, as it is terribly rendered at this juncture—*behavioral* health realm. Of course, this requires that we become less sanguine and somnolent with respect to such time-worn wordings as "appropriate"/"inappropriate," "normal"/"abnormal," "compliant"/"noncompliant," "high-functioning"/"low-functioning," "average"/"below average," "reality-testing," "poor judgment"/"good judgment"—indeed, the gamut of mental status categories and, of course, the penchant for articulating normative, universalized models of progressive, hierarchical development—from which every student of psychology (and practitioner) can thus plot deviations and maladaptations to some fictive norm. Normalizing trends have a tendency to lead to, among other dynamics, a tendency to reassure (the patient and/or the psychotherapist), while simultaneously downplaying the existence of the unconscious, and the deeper realms of psychical reality (or, "truth," if you will) that resides therein but must be deciphered through the means of *interpretation*, and not didactics. For instance, the guilt of the depressive is dismissed owing to the fine character and morals of the person and the nature of his or her exemplary life. What is negated in this process is our knowledge of the dynamic unconscious: that there is no distinction between wish and deed; there is no such thing as a negative, or a "no." In short, that the self-reproaches always have some basis for fact in *psychical* reality—the normalizing trends in psychoanalytic ego psychology and especially other contemporary models such as American-style, interventionistic thought-and-behavioral controlling methodologies—undermines the essentials of psychoanalysis (and purely psychological treatments in general), such as the primacy of the drives and the Id, although other psychological paradigms might have heretofore left off with mention of an "internal world," or of "mind" in general. But, no more. In this sense, it is seemingly lost that, as Freud noted (1900/1981), affects are "always appropriate, at least in their *quality* . . . psycho-analysis can put them upon the right path by recognizing the affect as being . . . justified and by seeking out the idea which belongs to it but has been repressed and replaced by a substitute" (p. 461).

Thus, we would argue that psychoanalytic practice runs the risk, as with all contemporary mental health treatments, of being aligned with the Foucauldian culture of surveillance, wherein as Fink (2011) asserts, it puts itself "in the service of conventional morality and norms, [with practitioners] devoting themselves to moulding patients' behaviour so that it will be adapted to modern-day working conditions and prevailing mores, for patients who display 'appropriate affect' in therapy are thought to be likely to go on to display 'appropriate behaviour' at home, in the work-place, and society-at-large" (p. 219). Yet, for how many of us have we experienced that, in the coming-into-being of the transference neurosis, and the regression of the patient, their "condition," if you like, seems to deteriorate in a manner of speaking, in the consulting room, and by self-report, only for the clinician to discover that they are functioning in a less conflictual manner elsewhere in their daily lives? Or not? Either way: more *analysis* it is, then, rather than to be the handmaiden of the state, and prescribed construals of "proper" emotional bearing and behavioral conduct.

NO PSYCHOANALYST LEFT BEHIND: HOW TO MANUFACTURE PROFESSIONAL PSYCHOLOGY NORMOTICS

The origins of a massified, educratic encroachment on liberal education as a whole, as well as the impingements on our professional education, associated professional identity development, and which has authored the revisions and restrictions in clinical practice of which we note, can, in part, be moored in an ethos of borne of Cold War–era politics. It is intriguing to contextualize the trends toward, paradoxically, de-skilling and de-professionalization, within an anti-psychoanalytical intellectual environment within this broader historical epoch.

In 2006, Eugene Jarecki's documentary *Why We Fight* arrived in movie theaters in the United States. The title derived from a series of propaganda films made by the director Frank Capra during World War II to help build and sustain a supportive attitude toward the war effort among the populace. The 2006 documentary examined the rise and proliferation of the military-industrial complex in the United States. It was, oddly enough, a moderate Republican politician (read: liberal Democrat in the current political milieu in the United States who had coined this famous term). It was very riveting to watch and listen to the excerpts of this measured, advisory speech—and warning—that has, perhaps, not been so familiar. We should like to quote at some length from President Dwight D. Eisenhower's (1961) *Farewell Address to the Nation.*

Until the latest of our world conflicts, the United States had no armaments industry. American makers of plough-shares could, with time and as required, make swords as well. But now we can no longer risk emergency improvisation of national defence; we have been compelled to create a permanent armaments industry of vast proportions. Added to this, three and a half million men and women are directly engaged in the defence establishment. We annually spend on military security more than the net income of all United States corporations.

This conjunction of an immense military establishment and a large arms industry is new in the American experience. The total influence—economic, political, even spiritual—is felt in every city, every State house, every office of the Federal government. We recognize the imperative need for this development. Yet we must not fail to comprehend its grave implications. Our toil, resources and livelihood are all involved; so is the very structure of our society.

In the councils of government, we must guard against the acquisition of unwarranted influence, whether sought or unsought, by the military-industrial complex. The potential for the disastrous rise of misplaced power exists and will persist. We must never let the weight of this combination endanger our liberties or democratic processes. We should take nothing for granted. Only an alert and knowledgeable citizenry can compel the proper meshing of the huge industrial and military machinery of defence with our peaceful methods and goals, so that security and liberty may prosper together. . . .

. . . [T]he free university, historically the fountainhead of free ideas and scientific discovery, has experienced a revolution in the conduct of research. Partly because of the huge costs involved, a government contract becomes virtually a substitute for intellectual curiosity. For every old blackboard there are now hundreds of new electronic computers. The prospect of domination of the nation's scholars by Federal employment, project allocations, and the power of money is ever present, and is gravely to be regarded.

> Yet, in holding scientific research and discovery in respect, as we should, we must also be alert to the equal and opposite danger that public policy could itself become the captive of a scientific technological elite. It is the task of statesmanship to mould, to balance, and to integrate these and other forces, new and old, within the principles of our democratic system—ever aiming toward the supreme goals of our free society (pp. 3–4).

How prescient are Eisenhower's words. Over fifty years later, we find American culture to be thoroughly militarized and the political economy to be largely colonized by unfettered corporatist-industrial claims on the society and the citizenry. As it relates to education and training, there is more and more pressure for programs and faculty to meet external standards, which has clear implications for faculty freedom, program freedom, and the socialization processes to which students are exposed and internalize as part of their graduate training.

Intellectual curiosity and critical thinking within our educational institutions are not always so readily in evidence—in the quality of students' scholarly works, or, given the crushing complex of demands imposed on faculties, seen in the work of the ostensible transmitters of (for purposes of this chapter) professional knowledge, skills, attitudes, and values. Indeed, what is perhaps more interesting about Eisenhower's speech is his attention to the broader elements of American culture and the deforming effect of such an omnipresent militarized-industrialized shadow culture. We note this with reference not only to the more glaring "erosion of liberty" in our democratic institutions but also to the corrosion of intellectual freedoms and curiosity, the rise of a technocratic elite owing fealty to the state—and the imperilment of academic freedoms—including a skewing of scientific endeavor, touching on the very nature of the research which is funded and the ontological truths which are in turn ordered and sustained. Challenges to the rhetorically unquestioned mythos of science and scientific enquiry as "neutral" in value and objective in aim are increasingly the norm at a time when we can no longer be assured of such claims. All of this and more have we witnessed, as political ideology is positioned as master to the pursuit of knowledge and the received wisdom of "evidence."

Among other recent, politically laden efforts to assail the academy, under the guise of accountability, is the Spellings Commission, named for a former US secretary of education in the Bush-Cheney administration, Margaret Spellings. The report is entitled *A Test of Leadership: Charting the Future of US Higher Education* (US Department of Education, 2006). In this report, the commission recommends that postsecondary educational institutions, such as colleges and universities, develop a national database of students, tracking their progress and linking them (and others?, one has to ask) to their academic records—in the language of the report, "allowing meaningful inter-state comparison of student learning." Assessments are to include assessments of "adult literacy, licensure, graduate and professional school exams, and specially administered tests of general intellectual skills." This is ostensibly for the purpose of permitting state officials to make "*valid inter-state comparisons of student learning* and identify short-comings as well as *best practices*" (emphasis added, p. 23). We again cannot fail to notice the propagandized appropriation of certain phraseologies which bias, deform, and privilege particular discourses and what can be said to constitute itself as "legitimate," "competent," and so forth within their logic.

Other more or less unquestioned recommendations include the call for institutions to *measure and report* "meaningful" learning objectives and, especially, *outcomes*. Such measures are termed "evidence-based" (p. 23). University officials, while tasking their faculties to arrive at "meaningful," "outcomes-focused accountability systems" (p. 23), have been served notice that they must develop them or else have them developed for and delivered to them for mandatory usage. Among instruments currently available and recommended for by the Spellings Commission are the *Collegiate Learning Assessment* and the *Measure of Academic Proficiency and Progress* (p. 23). In quantifying the results of a collegiate degree, the faculty is also being served notice that their own pedagogical effectiveness is being *measured and reported*, along particular frameworks of what constitutes said "measurement" and "reporting," which, of course, is standardized.

Rimer (2007) wrote about the swearing in of Harvard University's first female president, Dr. Drew Gilpin Faust, who, in her inaugural remarks, served notice that she is not necessarily wont to make a Faustian bargain regarding pedagogy and epistemology with regard to these normalizing dynamics. Dr. Faust, a Civil War historian, focused many of her remarks toward these trends: "A university is not about results in the next quarter. It is not even about who a student has become by graduation. It is about . . . learning that transmits the heritage of millennia; learning that shapes the future" (Rimer, 2007, p. A12), She also took the Spellings Commission's report to task for enjoining universities to train a competitive workforce for the global economy—in other words, worker-consumers for the capitalist elites. According to the *New York Times*, Dr. Faust "offered a ringing defence of the traditional role of universities as 'stewards of living tradition'; as places for 'philosophers as well as scientists,' where learning and knowledge are pursued in part 'because they define what has over centuries made us human, not because they can enhance our global competitiveness'" (p. A12).

As discouraging and perhaps shocking as these developments may seem (or, perhaps, worse, "normal," "understandable," "expectable," etc.), at the graduate and doctoral levels in clinical psychology, such onerous requirements have, of course, been in place for many years. For example, the trends in accreditation that one has measured, quantitatively, a prescribed series of competencies valorized as requisite for independent professional practice in relation to an associated litany of predetermined outcomes, has been commented upon elsewhere in this volume. Add to this even more burdensome requirements for the reporting of quantifiable outcomes as mandated by the Spellings Commission, and the ostensible mission of transmitting an abiding appreciation for the theoretical and clinical calling into which the professionals of tomorrow are to be initiated is soon distorted almost beyond recognition. This noble undertaking would appear to have been taken to the undertaker to be interred as not only quaintly passé but unethical (Bryceland & Stam, 2005) and dangerous, as to do otherwise is unsupported by the research on so-called clinical best practices—that is, as sponsored by cognitive-behavioral psychotherapy research. Thus, we now are enjoined to technique-anchored emphasis that constructs some contemporary psychotherapeutic discourses into an in loco parentis agent of the state for the sanctioning of proper thought and behavior as befitting a citizen worthy of inclusion in some prescribed societal substratum where his or her labor and station are useful.

In the accreditation self-studies (American Psychological Association, 2013, 2015) submitted by programs in clinical and counseling psychology as part of the accreditation process, there is scant interest in and hence no space allotted for delineating an abiding theoretical and philosophical position as we would commonly view this. This is predetermined by the Orwellian Newspeak of an educational discourse commodified by the nomenclature of the corporate boardroom and the health-care-industrial complex. Programs whose identities rest on sound philosophical moorings, and wish to both note and be appreciated for these moorings, are quite unable to do so. Programs whose identities rest on sound philosophical moorings that find themselves at variance with this prevailing demand will find themselves at peril of losing accreditation or not being accredited at all if they should push the envelope of the established parameters—and phraseology. Programs that have defined themselves as principally psychoanalytical or humanistic-existential-phenomenological-hermeneutical have experienced difficulties in asserting that the programs rest on an empirical basis or "evidence-based" "scientific psychology," at least of the sort that privileges a form of reductive logical positivism that has gone out of favor with even the so-called hard sciences, such as physics, yet remains *en vogue* within clinical psychology.

Accrediting bodies and professions that can be experienced as anti-psychoanalytical are in a position to define ontological integrity and punish and sanction those "others" for heretical adherence to ostensibly nonempirically supported tendencies, further contributing to the deforming of the mental health professions by privileging an industrialized rubric, philosophy, orientation, and lexicon to the often-ineffable psychotherapeutic enterprise—formerly termed an "art," but now is termed, if not a "science," essentially *a technique* that is anchored in the "research literature" available in one's "toolbox" (as it is actually called!) of "empirically based practices." A *scientized* visioning of the profession is what is sought even if what it renders is utterly *sanitized*—that is, devoid of substance of the very subject it ostensibly offers to elucidate. What cannot be effectively rendered in the visual equivalent of the audio sound bite of a PowerPoint-driven lecture, or statistically driven, reductive, "empirical" research paper, appears not to be worth much consideration at all.

So rampant is the self-possessed rush to demark and delimit what constitutes "competence" (and, by implication, the opposite) that a certain evangelical arrogance seems to have funded the entire endeavor. Rhetoric of grand aspirational sentiments and proclamations regarding protection of the public (among other nostrums) aside, one cannot help but consider this self-righteous "movement" as an effort at securing for psychology an even more solid footing with respect to the insurance industry that, in effect, underwrites the living wages of psychologist-technicians in the present corporatist milieu. In this rush to legitimize this latest "mission," we witness the dutifully produced position papers that propose modifications to curricula, pedagogy, epistemic and ontological discourses, and assessment practices for quantification of *outcomes*, which are an essential element of a successful program accreditation review.

Indeed, an entire volume of the American Psychological Association–sponsored journal, *Professional Psychology: Research and Practice* (October 2007), is devoted to this cause célèbre. Further articulations are included in Kaslow et al. (2009), in which the authors argue for a "shift to a culture of competency" (p. S27). The fallacious reasoning put forth in such a propagandized phraseology is that all the while the profession has been promoting a culture of incompetency. In effect, by promoting a so-called culture of competence, there is the underlying assumption that competence had been absent or a secondary consideration, but has suddenly become a "buzzword" designed to support measurable, quantifiable, and not process-oriented outcomes, in part because of some emergent panic that "if you cannot count it, it cannot be happening or exist." One effect is the deformation of the educator or mentor into a trainer or accountant/auditor. Through this logic, one is either "for" or "against" competence—and, by implication, a "competence" promoted by the members of the task forces, working groups, and authors within the hierarchies of the American Psychological Association.

Kaslow et al. (2007) noted that principles guiding competency assessment "are applicable to the education, training, and credentialing of professional psychologists, and to practicing psychologists *across the life-span*. The principles are built upon a review of competency assessment models, including practices in both psychology and other professions. These principles will help to ensure that psychologists *reinforce the importance of a culture of competence*" (emphasis added, p. 441). Other papers proceed to delineate how assessment can proceed from definition, all behaviorally anchored of course; and even the lexicon must shift in accommodating the new order. As one can determine, only certain defining characteristics of so-called competence are proffered, and these hold for every professional psychologist-in-training (and, "training," indeed, it is), as well as every practicing psychologist "across the life-span" (p. 441). Once encoded, naturally, sanctions will be developed for failure to adhere to and comply with these dictates.

We must assume that, sooner or later, what is good for colleges and APA-accredited doctoral clinical or counseling program will become mandatory for the freestanding psychoanalytic institute. In a word, we have the machinery already in place for "No Psychoanalyst Left Behind." Add to this the emergent trend in licensing psychoanalysis as a health-care profession as seen in some jurisdictions in the United States such as New York and Vermont, and these seeming digressions potentially assume a more center stage position, worthy of our attention. Moreover, the psychoanalytical candidate will have matriculated through a university or college wherein the notion of a liberal arts education has been mutated beyond recognition into that of a vocational-technical school. Further still, they will have then entered the technocratic factory of graduate school to receive and mimic a complex of pre-thought givens predetermined to constitute a professional identity and competence to practice—indeed, the very mode of clinical practice.

Now the big assumption is that such individuals will even present at the doors of a freestanding institute of psychoanalytic education with the desire to become one of "Them." Assuming that they do, and mindful of the trends that are becoming legally codified, psychoanalysts engaged in any pedagogical activity, including supervision, need to be asking themselves the following: "What are the *competencies* you are *training* your students to master? What are the *outcomes* that have been determined to be requisite for entry-level practice (and beyond), and how are these *quantifiable* and therefore independently verified by external audit?"

Things just get "curioser and curioser" as Alice lamented in Wonderland. Now, perhaps it is obvious, this none-too-subtle secret: "Why We Fight" is a bit of a double entendre: we have given a very lengthy prelude (and more) as to the dangers afoot in the culture at large, including, or especially it would often appear, within our professional ranks of fellow psychologists, psychiatrists, social workers, nurses, and licensed professional counselors for whom psychoanalysis is a thing to be gotten rid of. Yet this does not touch on the question of the internecine strife and warfare waged by psychoanalysts against one another and psychoanalysis against itself—what Bollas (2006–2007) might term "the violence of the everyday" or "ordinary destructiveness." These I shall now take up in turn.

THE VIEW OF PSYCHOANALYSIS FROM THE OUTSIDE-IN: DON'T HATE ME BECAUSE I'M BEAUTIFUL

American academics in psychology are in thrall of quantification. Reducing the ineffable to a numeric that stands in place of that which it ostensibly represents as a process of substitution by reification is privileged above the more difficult pathway of drawing a bead on that which has no name, place, or verifiable existence. To number it is not only to name it but to tame it and know it—and, ultimately, to dispense with it—to be done with it—in short, to "no" it. It is no accident that radical behaviorism should have taken such a grip on the psychological field in the United States with its emphasis on prediction and *control*. That there should be a psychical corollary of the geographical "eminent domain" in America's "manifest destiny" is not surprising. No terrain is too great to conquer. It is all a psychical extension of the country's sense of entitled "imminent domain."

The mark of a good theory is noted by many factors: its empirical elements, its rational appeal, its pragmatism, and, interestingly enough, its aesthetic qualities (Viney & King, 2003). The elegance and beauty of psychoanalytical theories and their valiant effort to conjecture about and *word* the nuances of the intrapsychic life of the subject—especially the murmurings of the unconscious—are nothing short of awe-inspiring. The seeming impossibility of the task seems only to have, across time, inspired psychoanalysis to undergo nothing short of periodic revolutions, resulting in a profusion of psychoanalytical perspectives, including, but not limited to, the neuro-psychoanalytical position that takes up the Freudian "Project for a Scientific Psychology" (see Freud, 1895/1981) armed with the recent advances in the cognitive/neurosciences, neuroimaging, and the so-called psychopharmacological revolution; psychoanalysis as a hermeneutic endeavor; applied psychoanalysis; gender studies; developmental psychoanalysis, with its long and important legacy, along with the entire panoply of theoretical and associated clinical perspectives—the familiar "camps" that populate the psychoanalytical landscape—Freudian, neo-Freudian, Kleinian, neo-Kleinian, Bionian, Winnicottian, Object-Relational, and so forth. However, does the clamor of our elegant pantheon of theories with their accumulated wisdom make an impact if there is nobody listening?

In the spirit of Wundt, Titchener, and Helmholtz, American psychology has taken umbrage with information that cannot be quantified easily (see, e.g., Yalof, 2015, for a review of psychoanalytic psychology in relation to undergraduate psychology education). The sound of psychoanalysis in the academy is one-hand clapping because psychoanalysis is generally absent. So colonized by an experimentalist ethos, the academy in America has managed to take some of the best movements born abroad and eviscerate them of their more subversive, revolutionary, illuminating, and compelling elements. In the case of psychoanalysis, its embrace by departments of psychiatry proved disastrous as it became aligned with a conservative, medicalized discourse and an elite for whom adjustment and adaptation to societal dictates was the sine qua non. The seeds of its marginalization were sown at the very stroke that it reached its zenith of popularity in the United States, and much of its more readily accessible (and often pejorative) terminology co-opted into the fabric of the everyday. Nonphysicians who could have been called upon to truly house and fund broader and deeper psychoanalytically oriented academic and clinical cultures and pedagogies were deemed unsuitable for framing. The academy was left to the quantitative experimentalists who continued devotedly to measure micro- and epiphenomena and confabulate from the part to the whole that something of significance lay in their SPSS, ANOVA, MANOVA, canonical correlation spreadsheets; or brain scans, genetic and twin studies; and RCT responses to various chemical compounds (and "psychotherapeutic" interventions under investigation). Small wonder that such mutual antipathy has arisen among psychoanalytically oriented clinicians and scholars/researchers, and the rest of the academic and clinical fields—or why so many psychoanalysts hold the idea of "research" in such low regard. Yet we discard and disregard empirical and quantitative research at our cherished profession's peril.

Indeed, we would do well to recall that the term "empirical" actually has a meaning rather different from the generally accepted modern connotation. Historically, the term references an epistemic system as derived from experience, learning, and direct observation. Historically, this has depicted the mind as a tabula rasa. It has traditionally been counterposed with a rationalist view, emphasizing a priori knowledge, the existence of innate organizing principles, and the concept of an active mind (Viney & King, 2003). In this sense, the assaults on psychoanalysis are specious and posed through fallacious reasoning. Psychoanalysis is most certainly anchored within an empirical tradition; yet it embodies rationalistic elements as well. The knowledge produced by psychoanalysis is as difficult to pin down as it is to claim any one school as *the* psychoanalysis. For example, simply viewing Freud from a *philosophical* perspective, Chung (2003, p. 5) notes that he is "now considered to have taken an approach characterised metaphysically by materialism, neurologically by reductionism." It is noteworthy that dual-aspect monism refers to a mind–body position which emphasizes the applicability of two languages to describe the same phenomena—for example, the language of physiology versus the language that employs mentalistic concepts. This position assumes that both refer to the same underlying reality and is one manner in which the mind–body split may be bridged (Viney & King, 2003). Such is the status of philosophical musings about this wonderfully complex concatenation of ways of knowing and knowledge we term "psychoanalysis."

Yet as Division 12 (Clinical Psychology) of the American Psychological Association has claimed a particular, political rendering and appropriation of the term "empirical," as a method of *scientific* enquiry and *the* way of knowing (not simply *a* way of knowing, among many others), psychoanalytical communities (and humanistic-existential communities as well) have been put on the defensive. However, an immersion in psychoanalytical theory and practice is an immersion in an empirically supported treatment approach. Psychoanalysis sponsors a way of knowing that is different from that promulgated by the bedfellows of logical positivism—and the so-called evidence that is privileged in an academic, cognitive-behavioral discourse. That this has not captured the favor of third-party payor systems within the medicalized, corporatized industrial-health-care matrix is not at all surprising.

The corollary of the fate of an experiencing subject within a psychiatry captured by a biological franchise is a logical extension of the same epistemological, ontological struggle for conceptual, economic, political, and pedagogical dominance. So long as psychoanalysis cedes the field and abjures its own storied legacy within the domain of scientific enquiry, it shall be (dis)placed and lodged in the defensive position of naysayer, unable to determine and define the terms of the battle. The empirical findings of psychoanalysis over the past 120 plus years will be adjudged as inferior and the stuff of a pseudoscience. Of course, this is yet another libel that psychoanalysis has had to bear. Popper (as cited Viney & King, 2003, p. 20) has defined a "true science" as a discourse guided by a "hypothetico-deductive system by which a theory can be tested and rendered falsifiable. . . . Regardless of the number of positive instances of an observation, one is still not justified in drawing a universal conclusion."

A BRIEF COMMENT ON THE TRANSMISSION OF PSYCHOANALYTICAL THEORIES AND PSYCHOTHERAPIES IN THE ACADEMY

A vast majority of the literature extant on psychoanalytical education involves the post-terminal degree training that leads to certification as a psychoanalyst. In 2011, there was a very interesting series of papers regarding psychoanalysis and the university (Kernberg, 2011; Sonnenberg, 2011; Wallerstein, 2011). While intriguing, in the main, these important papers also concerned themselves with some of the problematics of psychoanalytical *institutes*, which, by virtue of their freestanding nature, are divorced from centers of higher education, attendant with many of the troubles associated with institute-based training: political, ideological, and intellectual isolationism and orthodoxy; lack of resources for scholarship and research-based investigations into psychoanalytical ideas and theories; and less-than-transparent hiring, advancement, and termination practices, and so on. Institutes of psychoanalytical training are also composed of part-time students (candidates) and part-time faculties and administrators, further diluting the potential investment and involvement of all participants in the workings of the institute and its educational mission.

Problematizing any relationship with a university, and especially within a department or school of clinical psychology, at least in the United States, is the legacy of exclusion from formal training in psychoanalysis, enforced by institutionalized psychoanalysis, of nonmedical candidates—a unique "arrangement" arrived at in the beginning years of psychoanalysis—an early example of "American exceptionalism," if you like. Aligned with medicine—particularly psychiatry—against Freud's (1926/1981) explicit wishes psychoanalysis became marginalized from the mainstream of academic discourse and ceded the field to behavioral and cognitive-behavioral perspectives in psychology. However, departments of psychiatry became increasingly biologically orientated, depriving psychoanalysis of its traditional academic "home" and access to potential new adherents. It is interesting to consider how the lawsuit brought against certain psychoanalytical organizations has, paradoxically, ensured the survival of the traditional psychoanalytical organizations named in the lawsuit, as nonmedical candidates are now the majority in many such institutes.

The "siege mentality" of psychoanalysis is well known. Freud's own positive view of the effects of his "splendid isolation" on the development of psychoanalytical thought notwithstanding, it has been disastrous for the inclusion, if not acceptance of psychoanalysis—as well as psychoanalysis' own necessary evolution and, quite possibly, survival—by virtue of its active exclusion by groups hostile to its aims, when it is not actively opting out of the larger community of scholars and ideas that would otherwise be afforded by its being housed in universities. This has also led to the cognitive- and neurosciences to press-gang long-standing psychoanalytical findings into their own "new," "breakthrough" discoveries with respect to learning and memory and cognitions—of course, these are couched in the terminology of the kidnapper, and the abducted child is offered to the public as belonging to the stranger—for example, "unconscious process" or "repression" is now rendered as "implicit cognition" or "implicit memory." Clinically, students are generally in disbelief that short-term psychotherapies and what we would term "crisis intervention" were originated by the earliest psychoanalysts, including Freud—or that some of the most compelling outcome literature on short-term psychotherapy comes from within the psychoanalytical movement.

REAPPROPRIATING PSYCHOANALYTICAL VOICES AND THE PROBLEMATICS OF PEDAGOGY, PSYCHOANALYTICAL, OR OTHERWISE

We feel that it is necessary to return to and underscore the salience of the Freudian unconscious and, in this sense, the primacy of the drives. Lacan (1977), in his paper, "Aggressivity in Psychoanalysis," stated:

> In the 'emancipated' man of modern society, this splitting reveals, right down to the depths of his being, a neurosis of self-punishment, with the hysterico-hypochondriac symptoms of its functional inhibitions, with the psychasthenic

> forms of its derealizations of others and of the world, with its social consequences in failure and crime. It is this pitiful victim, this escaped, irresponsible outlaw, who is condemning modern man to the most formidable social hell, whom we meet when he comes to us; it is our daily task to open up to this being of nothingness the way of his meaning in a discreet fraternity – a task for which we are always too inadequate (pp 28–29)

And what of psychoanalytical knowledge? As an undergraduate, and at a time when psychoanalytical ideas were still transmitted in a more elaborated and respectful fashion, one of the authors (DLD) was informed that psychoanalysis consisted of three things: (a) a general depth theory of psychology, (b) a research method, and (c) a psychotherapeutic treatment. It is clear that Freud made use of the clinical moment more as an investigative procedure into the workings of the mind—especially as this elucidated the dynamic unconscious. We continue to see this as still one of the principal ways of generating new discoveries and elaborations of psychological knowledge, generally speaking. As for the matter of treatment and the education of clinicians, we need to become sensitized to *how to become sensitive to one's absorption* within the rich, metaphorical language of the unconscious as elucidated by psychoanalysis, wherein, imbued with symbol and metonymy as well, we lose ourselves from the moorings of objective reality and enter into the sometimes-inchoate and ineffable states of dream, illusion, and reverie. It is through the essential subjective otherness of the dream that Freud elucidated so many of his seminal findings. The analytical space invites the dissolution of objective truths and shared realities, and invites the deconstruction of the dreamer himself or herself in its wake. As such, the analysand allies as much with the self-in-participation of the *process* of a psychoanalysis that ever becomes *more and more uniquely his or her own*, never to be repeated, as with the *person* of the psychoanalyst, per se. Each association yields itself up to the eventual clustering of a chain of signifiers, decoded through the further associations to latent meanings that each layering of derivatives yields.

It is through a process of intensive mentorship, and self-reflection/discovery (most efficaciously enabled through one's own personal psychotherapy), that one can attain such a place of introspection and the capacity for evenly suspended attentiveness. This approximates an *apprenticeship*, perhaps, more than the rote, mechanized indoctrination in techniques that we tend to see articulated (e.g., Kaslow et al., 2009) in the toolboxes of so-called competency-based education. Despite the emphases of the model for quantification, which can lend itself toward a certain reductionism, a diverse range of assessment strategies are offered, including many which would be consonant with the strategies and aims as outlined in this text. These include case presentation reviews and review of recorded psychotherapy sessions, as well as simulations and role plays.

Such recommendations are more elaborated by Mintz (2013), who also noted the impingements of economical and business pressures into the training of physicians, "such that they view the doctor-patient encounter as a business transaction between *a provider and a consumer*" (emphasis added, p. 753). We wholeheartedly agree that, in teaching psychotherapy, we are teaching not *what* to think but *how* to think in a setting "better-suited to environments where there is room for reflection, exploration, and discussion, and much less so for large lecture halls" (p. 755). Consequently, as in the mentorship/apprenticeship model that we are proffering, the transmission of psychoanalytical praxis is best suited for the context of intimate relationships, and, as such, is more "labor intensive" than other forms of psychotherapeutic treatment (p. 755).

The daunting nature of our enterprise is elucidated by Phillips's (2001, see pp. 1–34) discussion of poetry and psychoanalysis. Phillips elegantly discusses the poethics of psychoanalysis, without guilt or seeming reservation, even reappropriating the term, the "art," as well, of psychoanalysis, of which so many have become averse. Phillips asserts that "being a good poet makes you a good psychologist" (p. 4). We can think of no better way to help stem the tide of normotic illness spreading through professional schools and departments of psychology, and infecting consulting rooms across the land (and the world, given the DSM-ing of the global mental health economy). As Phillips asserted (p. 8): "The poet is our last hope for happiness faced with the scarcity of the external world, the depredations of the Super-ego and the voraciousness of the Id. The poet is the person who can get away with it." We shall consider it a victory over the forces of normotic illness in our contemporary professional transmission of a professionalized discourse, and formation of a professional identity. Like the poet, the psychoanalytical clinician is interested in language, and the efforts at forging meaning through speech-acts, themselves in turn sponsored by unconscious dynamics. At every turn, this, along with epistemological and ontological encounters to which psychoanalysis is uniquely suited, is the turning of our "psychical ears" to the latent, ineffable, murmurings of the unconscious, where we come to occupy the interstitial spaces between the known and the unknown—or, perhaps, even, the unknowable. But even should phenomena be "unknowable," in a certain sense, directly, we feel that it is the psychoanalytical enterprise that assists in ever-more approximating this Other and elsewhere. It is for us to plumb the depths of the drives as they are inscribed on the surface features of the everyday, where others see perhaps but the "thing" itself and explore the labyrinth of existence.

Chapter 5

The *Psychoanalyst's* Capacity to Be Alone

A Brief Comment on Some Challenges in Preserving Psychoanalytical Diversity While Diversifying Psychoanalysis in the Academy—The "Position" of the Psychoanalyst in Organizational Space and Culture

> *If, however, there should actually turn out to be one of you who did not feel satisfied by a fleeting acquaintance with psycho-analysis but was inclined to enter into a permanent relationship to it, I should not merely dissuade him from doing so but actively warn him against it. As things stand at present, such a choice of profession would ruin any chance he might have of success at a University, and, if he started in life as a practising physician, he would find himself in a society which did not understand his efforts, which regarded him with distrust and hostility, and unleashed upon him all the evil spirits lurking within it.* (Freud, 1915–1916/1981, p. 16)

INTRODUCTION

Freud's trenchant observation would appear to have maintained its currency despite the nearly 100 intervening years since its delivery during the 1915–1916 academic year at the University of Vienna. These reactions toward psychoanalysis and psychoanalysts continue to bear unfortunate truths and place especially onerous burdens on the individual practitioner. He or she must not only address being the receptacle of regressive strains attendant with managing the daunting vicissitudes of the psychoanalytic situation per se but also operate within a milieu that not only may be passively nonsupportive but is subtly or even openly disparaging and hostile.

The situation for the *psychologist*-psychoanalyst may even be somewhat more precarious than the medically trained, *psychiatrist*-psychoanalyst. This owes to the exclusionary "ownership" of psychoanalysis within the medical community in the United States, which excluded psychologists from receiving training outside of a few institutes in the New York City area until the past quarter century—a history that has shaped ineluctably the expression of psychoanalysis in the United States as distinct from other countries of the world where psychoanalysis has taken root. This not only stultified the refinement of psychoanalytical theories and clinical practices by sealing them off from the possibility of being investigated through various modes of research within academic communities—it precluded any possibility of open, informed debate and collegial dialogue with proponents of diverse theoretical positions in the scholarly marketplace of ideas.

Whereas departments of psychiatry integrated psychoanalysis as well as *psychoanalysts* (at least in the past) throughout their organizational structures, departments of psychology rarely had faculty or administrations that were knowledgeable of, curious about, sympathetic to, let alone intimately involved in psychoanalysis—or, as bona fide psychoanalysts. Indeed, department chairs and faculty in psychiatry were often psychoanalysts themselves; and the best and brightest of residents were encouraged to enter psychoanalytic training institutes. The anti-psychoanalytical bias rampant in the halls of academic psychology often meant, and can still mean, that students do not receive an exposure to a fair and accurate representation of even so-called classical or Freudian psychoanalysis per se, let alone knowledge of the diverse pantheon of contemporary theoretical positions.

Certainly, psychoanalysis has enjoyed a veritable renaissance in expanding and refining theory and applications, as well as a renewed emphasis on subjecting certain constructs (such as the unconscious) to empirical "validation." Yet faculties and their students still tend to be unaware of these trends, which are extant in the contemporary psychoanalytical movement. Thus, they may receive no information on, nor training in, psychoanalytically informed and driven refinements that have so energized the treatment of severe psychopathology, the practice of crisis and short-term, *albeit clinically determined*, treatments as opposed to managerially mandated and so forth. Projective personality assessment, long married conceptually to psychoanalytic theory, has become somewhat of a lost art, despite a solid empirical foundation (Bram & Yalof, 2015), with fewer personality assessment learning opportunities available to students in graduate psychology programs (Piotrowski, 2015) in the United States.

Whatever antipathy as exists within organized psychology, which may be historically understandable as derivative of the aforementioned antecedents, new assaults have been brought to bear on the broader front of the *independent professional practice of clinical psychology as informed by theory, research, and accepted norms of practice.* The chief progenitor of such trends can be discerned by the intrusion of managed care, and the concomitant limitations imposed on confidentiality and privilege that have resulted from numerous lawsuits. Bersoff (2015) describes the trade-off when the duty to protect interferes with treatment confidentiality.

Thus, even some of the ethics of psychoanalysis, in reference to, among other matters, *absolute* confidentiality, would seem to place us at odds with growing requirements toward mandated reporting, positioning us as potentially vulnerable and alone vis-a-vis the established ethical codes of psychiatry, psychology, and social work, (though these ethical codes also are subject to legal oversight, with mandated reporting laws codified in different states). In no small measure, these organized professional associations appear to actually be *rushing* to capitulate and abjure their independent, professional authority to such entities and the political-economical forces they embody. As Bollas and Sundelson (1995) noted, in 1977, when California's state legislature was drafting a Child Abuse Reporting law that swept away any protection of the patient's confidential communications, the only concern registered by the California Psychological Association was to write to the committee so as to ensure that psychologists were *included* in the final bill as another professional group who *must* report allegations of child abuse (p. 49). The received wisdom is, of course, that conscientious application of duty to warn and mandated reporting laws serve to protect the public, and, thus, at some point absolute confidentiality must be modified in order to protect the patient and others from serious harm. The main point here, however, is to highlight the meaning of these regulations as they might impinge on the learning climate to a point where fear of consequence then becomes an internalized part of the therapist's clinical work (for additional attention to these important trends, see parker and revelli (2008)). Thus, while clinical and legal circumstances are quite different from the freedoms enjoyed by Freud, exploration of the meaning of these circumstances to the student in training may be short-changed amid urgency and anxiety to take action, or risk severe personal and public consequence. As psychoanalysts, posing the dilemmas faced in the clinical situations experienced by students in their field placements assists in bringing the conundrums inherent in such legally encoded positions into bas-relief. We have often found students to be quite attuned to the ruptures that often occur in their clinical work with patients as a consequence of the requirements to breach confidentiality, and the struggles they face, at very early junctures in their education. In our own classroom experiences, we have been impressed by the receptiveness of students to critically debate and attempt to negotiate some compromise to protect the sanctity of the confidential psychotherapeutic space—suggesting that what may be called for—but not to be taken for granted as always present in graduate psychology programs—are faculty interested in opening opportunities for critical conversations around such matters now tending toward uncritical inculcation in order for student anxieties and concerns in these arenas to be appreciated and given voice.

For many psychoanalysts (see Bollas, 2003), absolute confidentiality is a prerequisite for any form of psychoanalytical treatment to occur. In the professional milieu of contemporary practice, this poses further stress for the psychoanalyst faculty member/administrator, who must delicately address such threats, while maintaining in our communications and teachings to students an absolutely ethical position and ethos of "Do no harm." Navigating the "aspirational" and "mandatory" aspects of the ethical codes while attempting to inculcate a nonjudgmental mind-set of curiosity, openness to understanding, and nonimpinging enquiry, without the immediate leap to report or inform *à la* thought-police agents of the state, is only one prime example of this. Rather, it is only through such an eventual resonance or "knowing," which is often labored and incremental, that we may come to offer, eventually, interpretations or other interventions that are contextually embedded and developmentally indicated, for each unique patient. It might be folly to presume that there can be any circumvention of the constituent parts of such knowing—including the development of the transference, the work with the inevitable and informative "resistances," let alone elaboration of the symptom complex and associated domain of the unconscious core. Such tasks are all necessarily associated with extended periods of, and struggles with, "un-knowing," as articulated so well by Bion (1974, as cited in Casement, 1991, p. 8). Similarly, Freud, in his monograph *The Future of an Illusion*, stated, in a particularly eloquent manner, with respect to the protective and defensive function of theory and dogma, "And thus a store of ideas is created, born from man's need to make his helplessness tolerable" (Freud, 1927, p. 18, cited in Casement, 1991, p. 9).

In short, the affronts to psychoanalysis (theory, practice, and research) are numerous, overdetermined, and manifested culturally, societally, across disciplines, and across theoretical orientations. With regard to the latter, the attacks seem to have become increasingly shrill, partisan, and aggressivized. For example, we have the burgeoning pharmaceutical industry with its purchase of managed care and health maintenance organizations; the logical positivist pronouncement that psychoanalytical treatment is invalid, or, moreover, even harmful, as well as unsupported by data, that only certain cognitive-behavioral treatments can lay claim to being "empirically supported" techniques (the nomenclature being changed from "empirically *validated*" after a well-deserved hue and cry arose over the egregious and politically charged phraseology of Division 12 [Clinical Psychology] with regard to certain cognitive and behavioral treatments, as embodying the only form of "evidence" acceptable in "evidence-based treatment" which is to be claimed as "valid"). Indeed, even within psychoanalysis itself, certain subcultures question the merits of remaining within any formal health-care provision program, given the untenable compromises that have inevitably accompanied the imperatives of third-party payors. Along these fronts as well, our own thoughtful forbearance, as brought to life in the here and now of the classroom, can be a powerful experience for the learner. Such a position requires as well that *we* be in contact with our own narcissistic needs for power or influence over others, as well as Oedipally driven rebellious trends, lest we, or our student "proxies," act out unconsciously with patients, or within organizational structures, including the supervisory relationship, the school/department/program, externships, internships, or beyond.

The admittedly cursory outline of certain challenges to psychoanalysis, and tenuous support for psychoanalytically oriented practitioners delineated earlier, hopefully communicates that psychoanalysis, and its practitioners of all types, face significant impediments in instituting, guiding, and bringing to appropriate, professionally determined closure optimal strategies of care and treatment back to the clinical milieu. This is especially relevant for significant numbers of our patients who present to us seeking relief for what, simultaneously, appear to be increasingly serious degrees of psychopathology.

ON THE *PSYCHOANALYST'S* "CAPACITY TO BE ALONE": WORKING PSYCHOANALYTICALLY IN ANTI-PSYCHOANALYTICAL SPACES

It is in this regard that the challenges of working within academic settings, and communicating with our nonpsychoanalytically oriented colleagues (as faculty and/or administrator), assume a more daunting cast. However, the writings of D. W. Winnicott can be illuminating and salutary. Winnicott (1958) asserted that an individual's capacity to be "alone" is predicated on the existence of a prior relationship that has been experienced as protective, reliable, and *good enough*. The internalization of such a relationship paradoxically permits the discovery of one's self and is associated with psychical integration and emotional maturity. Such a capacity attenuates the experience of persecutory (or annihilatory) anxiety. "Loneliness" suggests the lack of internalized, stable, and abiding self and object representations that can attenuate and neutralize regressive trends that may become mobilized in the face of such dynamics. Now, it is one thing to speak of such matters as pertinent to the "analysand," but in light of the gist of this chapter, let us consider this as a most necessary accompaniment for the psychoanalyst-*academic*, and, in particular, the psychoanalyst-*administrator/educator*.

Drawing upon an extrapolation of Winnicott's (1965) notion of the *holding environment*, Stapley (1996) extends the concept to an examination of organizational life and "culture." Organizations, while fictive, nonhuman, and "as-if" constructions, tend to assume a variety of characters/qualities that become quite real for their "inhabitants." Such "realities" are, however, subject to the myriad of more-or-less distorted transference-like phenomena, facilitative, containing, impinging, or even pathological mechanisms located within individual members' psyches, as well as the collective culture of the organization itself. These vicissitudes approximate the clinical psychoanalytic situation.

At this point, we would do well to take to heart Freud's (1937/1981) cautionary assertion that no patient may proceed beyond the neurotic complexes of his or her psychoanalyst. If the academic professional training organization is indeed singularly crucial to the socialization and training of subsequent generations of practitioners—if, as part of its accrediting, "gate-keeping," clinical training functions is the perpetuation and transmission of the culture of the profession—we would submit that it is all the more crucial for psychoanalysts to not only enter educational and clinical training programs but proactively assert themselves and their theoretical/technical positions at every level of their contacts with faculties and administrators, as well as students—across baccalaureate, masters, and doctoral programming. If others on the organizational stage do not have available to them objects for identification, particularly the ability to internalize relationships and experiences (and associated remembered images) of being mentored and "held" in light of the daunting vicissitudes of the contemporary climate, another very real danger exists for the professional and personal readiness for subsequent generations of psychoanalytical practitioners (and perhaps, even, that there should *be* subsequent generations!). This includes the capacity and willingness of the psychoanalyst to "go it alone," if need be, in order to advocate for students, for a psychoanalytical presence in the academy, and so on. To remain utterly "hidden," afraid of being "seen" (and hence "targeted"?), is to communicate a most unfortunate message, one that reifies a message of danger, scarcity, and rapacious self-servativisim. In short, no organization may progress beyond the collective limitations of its faculty and administration.

Having exploded the myth of the "well" psychoanalyst vis-a-vis the "ill" patient, the psychoanalyst functioning as an administrator/faculty member must certainly shed some of our field's well-known aloofness and abstruseness, which superficially can be experienced as elitism and inaccessibility. Grandiosity can sometimes mask our own sense of inadequacy, as seen through various rescue phantasies or heroic inner scenarios, as we strive to be, as articulated by Brightman (1982), omniscient, omnipotent, and beneficent. Addressing some of the toxic dynamics of organizational life, Shaw (2006) cautions:

> Unassailable, unimpeachable perfection represents the narcissist's desperate need for control. . . . [t]he authoritarian's oppressive demands for submission are based on the pathologically narcissistic need to maintain omnipotent control and superiority. Authoritarianism, like pathological narcissism, is based on defining others as inferiors and, through whatever control methods are possible, maintaining them as such. Pathological narcissists use a kind of reverse Fairbairnian moral defence [Fairbairn, 1952]: they give someone else all the burden of the badness and always claim the moral high ground for themselves. (p. 69)

The more passive, neutral qualities of the psychoanalytical treatment enterprise that is often associated with the psychoanalytical/psychoanalyst practitioner can become still another impediment to the administrator's need to be seen and available as a very real object on the stage of organizational life. The need for active, collegial, collaborative engagement with numerous, often conflicting constituencies also requires that the psychoanalyst administrator/faculty member be capable of exercising a firm degree of action in the material and psychological dimensions of the work-space.

While our training emphasizes understanding over doing, the administrator must be prepared and able to develop plans of action that may have considerable impacts on the day-to-day functioning of the organization, based on his or her assessments. And, with the *organizational* "frame" established, he or she must be capable of confronting and managing deviations from, and challenges to, this frame. Unlike the Marvel comic book character The Watcher—a Supreme, Other-Worldly, implacable, and mysterious alien being—tall, statuesque, garbed in a toga, and equipped with a huge, bald cranium (symbolical of an associated superior consciousness)—who is forbidden to intervene (impinge) upon the course of human events—the administrator cannot always afford to be "*in*, but not *of*" the organization that he must manage.

In this regard, we need to be prepared to deal with the inevitable conflicts that will proceed from the establishment of administrative parameters. Students and faculty will necessarily have diverse and overdetermined responses to such structural imperatives. In this regard, the understanding and interpretation of resistance can be informed by our appreciation for its manifestations in the clinical scenario. That is, we should attempt to comprehend its individual and organizational stirrings, as well as disentangle our own contribution to the situation (or impasse). It would be tempting to leap to an assessment that either it is a resistance based on our own personal inadequacy, character, and so forth or it is a derivative of a disdain for psychoanalysis, envy, and so forth. In addition, nonpsychoanalytically orientated individuals will, likely, view phenomena as "things in and of themselves"—indeed, a contemporary trope is, "It is what it is" (to be certain—but, *what* after all, *is that?* The rejoinder might well be that "it" is most certainly *not* what "it" is). Such concretizations and simplifications reify a reality structuralized in relation to establishing power relations that define roles and associated divisions of labor, responsibilities, status configurations, organizational capacities, and so forth. Such a construal fails to appreciate how, much like a symptom, such structural derivatives are, in addition, unconscious outcroppings of efforts to address and defend against libidinal and aggressive drives and the dreads and anxieties associated with them. These dynamics can most certainly tax the self-esteem and sense of adequacy/efficacy of even the most dedicated and "self-sufficient" psychoanalyst-administrator—all the more reason to have some internal *and* external wellsprings of narcissistic and ego supplies to draw upon.

This can be especially powerful in the clinical training domain wherein the university administrator/faculty member is called upon to "investigate" and address issues of concern raised by students with respect to a clinical training site; and/or the clinical training facility that raises concerns against a program's student or students; or even, by implication, an academic program's curriculum, the clinical training and preparation of its students for field placements, and so forth. The university or academic representative most often charged with addressing such matters in clinical psychology programs is the director of clinical training and is often subject to multiple and simultaneous pressures to be swayed by and adopt each involved party's perspective when a conflict does arise. It is the director of clinical training who often, unique (and uniquely *alone*?) among other members of the academic family, experiences the anthropologist-like experience of participant-observer of "being *in,* but not fully *of*" any one system. Unfortunately, unlike the anthropologist, there exists every expectation for the director of clinical training or program director to exercise his or her authority, to *act*, and to *do* something—preferably compatible with the wishes of each of the parties feeling aggrieved in some manner and to fulfill a role as their respective advocate and to accordingly validate their position. Here, the requirements of gathering sufficient information, often entailing site visits, interviewing/speaking personally with all involved parties, and following established policies of due process to the letter, may be frustrating to some who would prefer more immediate action and unilateral action be taken.

In some respects, such work "on the frontier" of interorganizational boundaries and structures places the director of clinical training as uniquely alone, and in need of possessing sufficient internal resources to manage the vicissitudes of operating in such circumstances rife for experiencing grave doubts about one's self and the accuracy of one's perceptions, assessments, judgments, with associated depletion of reservoirs of healthy ego supplies.

As it can often be the case that multiple "truths" can obtain, and the compromises that are forged as solutions may feel unsatisfying to some or even all parties (a failure of satisfying the law of talion that may become activated under the aegis of regressive and persecutory-retaliatory dynamics), it may even be the case that the director of clinical training becomes an object for the displacement of hostilities and frustrated projections, rescue phantasies, and so forth. One of the authors has likened this position to that of being a "lightening rod."

ON NEUTRALITY AND RELATEDNESS

We tend to prefer a notion of psychoanalytical "neutrality" that is a more liberal rendering of Freud's (1912b/1981) metaphor of the "blank screen." Freud's (1912b/1981) other, oft-quoted provision of an "evenly suspended attentiveness" seems to be in accord with positioning one's self in such a manner as to be available, within the "potential space" offered by the paradoxically open and closed field of the organizational milieu. It is "open" in the sense of Winnicott's (1971) concepts of transitional space and phenomena, as well as the potential space wherein something unique, phantasied, and ultimately possessed by the creator (learner, student, and faculty member) may transpire, happen, or, simply, *reside*. The play between internal and external, *me* and *not-me* can proceed adaptively only in so far as the space is also "closed" or perhaps, more appropriately, "contained" (time, space, roles, responsibilities, etc., being spelled out). Thus, we may be "used" in the Winnicottian sense as "as-if," constructed, deconstructed, and transferentially distorted objects. We can expect to be "scanned" for our preferences, personal histories, biases, and values, just as in the clinical situation.

The academic environment is perhaps seductive in terms of its disingenuous retreat from such carryovers generally associated with clinical work. We are more active in a real, or at least, "hands-on" kind of way; we talk much more (and face-to-face); we may give people frank directives and hold evaluative responsibilities with regard to others duly implementing them. We hold and conduct meetings, yet at times, a more "social" and certainly egalitarian/collegial atmosphere indeed prevails. But we need to be exceedingly mindful that our own observance of deadlines, time frames, professional-yet-accessible comportment/decorum are exemplars of one's own honesty, integrity, ethicality, consistency, constancy, and concern. Our own capacity to directly manage conflict, and, especially, bring to manifest levels latent, destructive processes or phantasies that impede optimal *organizational* functioning, while necessary, often goes against the grain of psychoanalysts used to and more comfortable with private clinical practice with individual patients.

The professional work ego, as we may term it, must necessarily function along the lines of a kind of "manager" of administrators' intrapsychical dynamics but also negotiate the terms of the organization's "psychodynamic architecture," including boundary management. Here we are also referring to all manner of ego functions, such as so well articulated by Bellak and Faithorn (1981), including perception, judgment, memory, stimulus barrier, reality testing, defensive functioning, synthetic-integrative functioning, and object relations (i.e., ARISE, Adaptive Regression in Service of the Ego).

Despite the previous chapter's misgivings about appropriating normative, phasic developmental lines, as appropriating normotic channels of destiny of the individual, Kaslow and Rice (1985) delineate the developmental line associated with immersion in the clinical psychology internship year with the phases of psychical development as articulated by Mahler, Pine, and Bergman (1975) centering the vicissitudes of the clinical internship process with the process of individuating requiring the very sort of integration of Winnicottian praxis and the American Object-Relational School so influenced by Mahler and her colleagues. Beginning such a singularly formative and even transformative year in the aura of loss or even lack, the gravity associated with the evaluative elements of the internship easily stirs potentially paranoid-schizoid dreads and regressive anxieties, associated with the early emergence from symbiosis, and the entry into separation-individuation.

Holding and containing functions and resources available at this early juncture can mitigate against the more serious regressions and mobilize previous successful efforts at adaptation that have been internalized as well as foster identifications with new objects for hedonic stabilization. In one of the authors' experience, it has been noteworthy how varied and uneven sites can be, however, with such "obvious" facilitating and holding features, such as orientation meetings, arranging contacts with outgoing and incoming interns, making available programmatic literature, and information on housing. Across time, the successful titration of support, engagement, and neutrality, distance, as noted in the developmental spheres by Winnicott (1958) and Mahler, Pine, and Bergman (1975), yields an individually thriving intern capable of managing the vicissitudes of alones and who is approaching authorship of post-doctoral professional life. Optimally, "supervision" begins to be experienced more like "consultation." A new phase of termination—associated with loss and possibilities—can be addressed by clinical training staff, academic institution/faculty (especially if the dissertation is not yet completed), and intern.

WHO AM US ANYWAY?

Psychoanalysts in administrative and/or faculty positions may be viewed as some odd species, neither fish nor fowl, espied with suspicion by one's clinical psychoanalyst colleagues and nonpsychoanalysts alike. Troubling as well are reports we often receive from students indicating that they are exposed to fairly active, biased, denigrating assaults on psychoanalytical theory and practice (perhaps even psychoanalysts, as clinicians). Thus, we must at times assume a very thoughtful, reflective, and nonaccusatory stance in addressing such delicate matters (including the matter of assessing the veracity of the reports). This can facilitate the movement toward appropriate, respectful discourse and civility. Indeed, it may help to illuminate what the "real" problem is, as compared with the presenting or ostensible one, just as a psychoanalytically orientated clinician would if this were in the realm of clinical practice. For example, is it related to a faculty member's or student's sense of being slighted, not receiving validation for a job well done, or being passed over for a promotion?

It can be counterproductive and destructive, for the dean, the program chairperson, or the program director to resort to defensiveness in response to one of the aforementioned or other, significant, but possibly symptomatic, program events. To do so can be not only counterproductive but destructive as well. This could devolve into more dysfunctional forms of ego function/structure (Czander, 1993; Diamond, 1993). Conscious or unconscious pressures may act upon the psyche so as to constitute a disjunction that is ego dystonic, between one's own professional work ego and that of the pressure or "demand." The reflective psychoanalytical administrator may thus experience a crisis, between enacting something ego alien and being upbraided, reprimanded, and so forth, for a failure to "comply" with organizational requirements. A refusal to enter either sphere may risk becoming the container for hostile, persecutory, megalomanic, seductive, or other primitive projections. This, in turn, may result in (further) alienation, aggressivization, or schizoid withdrawal, depending on the psychical personality structure of the administrator.

The administrator is ineluctably drawn into pathogenic tableaus borne of a multiplicity of projections and transferential deformations, displacements, need-fear dilemmas, and the like. Jaques (as cited in Czander, 1993) noted:

> Organisations . . . provide institutionalised roles whose occupants are sanctioned, or required to take into themselves [force], the projected objects or impulses of other members. The occupant of such roles may absorb the objects and impulses—take them into themselves and become either good or bad objects with corresponding impulses—put them into and externally-perceived ally; or enemy, who is then loved, or attacked [termed "projective identification"—present authors]. The gain for the individual in projecting objects and impulses and introjecting their careers in the external world, lies in the unconscious co-operation with other members of the institution or group who are using similar projective mechanisms. Introjective identification then allows more than the return of projected objects and impulses. The other members are also

> taken inside, and legitimised and reinforced attacks upon internal persecutor, or support manic idealisations of love objects, thereby reinforcing the denial of destructive impulses against them. (pp. 112–113)

Being able to realize that such processes have been activated and to recognize the "signs and symptoms" of their movement upon the self-in-organization will, again, as in the clinical situation, enable the psychoanalytical administrator to successfully traverse these psychical terrains far more adaptively. This can proceed from a depth realization that articulates not only their presence, movement, and possible contagion within the group but also pathways toward resolution, via addressing the sources of organizational discontents through empathic resonance, transmitted via the holding and containing—maternal and paternal registers—interpretative and affectively accessible, validating—as articulated by Winnicott (1971). Such an approach permits a return to the coherence of secondary (ego) processes, and the potential space conducive to creative and symbolical thought, conceptualization, and deliberate(d) action.

Such functioning also may have the salutary effect on the person of the psychoanalyst-administrator—alone in the midst—one might say. The recognition and navigation of theses *organizational* vicissitudes can bring a very special yield, in the form of the administrator feeling lived and authored by—or, rather, *authoring*, their "true-self," as opposed to a false-self built on compliance.

FURTHER NOTES ON ATTENDING TO "PSYCHODYNAMIC ARCHITECTURE": IMPINGEMENT, REGRESSION, CONTAINING, AND HOLDING

Administrators of academic programs can be said to exist "on the border" of multiple systems within and outside of the program/university (faculty, programmatic/departmental, university at large, clinical/professional, psychoanalytical institute and/or society, national psychological organizations, national training councils, etc.), and it is instructive to consider, *psychoanalytically*, the conscious and unconscious functions of a "boundary." It is the *psychoanalyst*-administrator, we suggest, that is uniquely able to discern, decipher, retranslate/interpret, and therefore "address" the vicissitudes of what we will term the "psychodynamic architecture" of an organization. Apart from demarcating inner from outer, important psychodynamic architectures such as boundaries confer a socially validated form of the "real-ness" of the fictive, constructed experience of life "inside" of the organizational culture. Life on the inside also confirms elements of a distinctive group identity, including that of a collective ego, or ego ideal. Accrediting bodies, other university departments, programs, schools, and administration, like other external agents, may heighten regressive, persecutory anxieties by activating imagoes of an invasive, malevolent Other. Contrariwise, such agents may sponsor phantasies of rescue from an internal source of anxiety/dread by an external, beneficent, omniscient, omnipotent source of all-good supplies. Multiple vectors of organizational culture become activated in the service of self-preservation and identity maintenance, and appeal to other potential allies in asserting their claims to legitimacy.

Winnicott (1952) suggested that impingement embodies qualities that work to inscribe a false-self structure in the developing ego of the infant. When the surround is unresponsive to or misinterprets the spontaneous (generative) gestures sponsored by the infant's emergent capacities for coherent activity, under the aegis of its desire, the subject retreats into compliance with demand. As increasing pressures for professional "standards" are transmitted across bureaucratic frontiers and become framed in technocratic and even legal statute (e.g., competencies, duty to warn), the holding and containing functions of program administrators to manage pressure "from above and below" as well as "inner and outer" proliferate. That accrediting bodies and university administrations, like the culture at large, privilege particular forms of "evidence" in treatment paradigms may be especially alarming to programs inclusive of non-cognitive-behavioral approaches. This dynamic may stimulate (sibling/subgroup) rivalries that threaten the interior harmony of the program during accreditation.

In one sense, we are discussing an organizational equivalence of the need for securing and maintaining, in the language of self-psychology, a cohesive self (Kohut, 1971). This falls to program administrators, who, in many respects, function as group ego, modulating pressures from the group id or superego. In many respects, it is, interestingly enough, the latter pressures that are often activated by the accreditation and site-visit process. That is, faculty, students, or associated contributors may demonstrate pressures to appeal to site visitors as some form of organizational "Complaint Department"—some beneficent, omniscient, and/or omnipotent Other—to compel certain programmatic elements—often administration—to "live up to" ostensible promises or expectations. It is often not realized that this is incredibly self-destructive, as accreditation site visitors are attuned to these concerns. Thus, such eruptions are often interpreted as indicative of programmatic disarray, lack of broader institutional support, or corruption.

This is a reason for the administrator to establish, in the core of the program, a capable administrative team for gathering and managing data, and monitoring the executive functions (e.g., curriculum; clinical training [site development, placement, maintenance]); committee structure that empowers faculty and further delegates authority; as well as student governance that also empowers students and fosters inclusion in the organization of the program, such as faculty committee structure, continuous liaison, so that potential disruptions to the internal and external harmonious functioning of various systems can be monitored and ensured.

Stapley (1996) notes that each organization may assume certain qualitative elements that assume the potentialities of personality or character—albeit in a collectivist sense. As we consider the vicissitudes of organizational personality, we can note how the different "languages" of psychoanalysis can be instructive—stressing again the need for the psychoanalyst-administrator to be well versed in a multiplicity of theories. For instance, from the perspective of Lacan (1977), we may note that the paternal and maternal registers are activated—and that one feels "created" in the virtual imaginary field of the other, pressurizing the frame toward some conformance with the image through action. We need to be attuned to the signifiers that order the sequence of unconscious logic into the symbolic register and resist efforts at seductions and corruptions of the frame just as in the clinical simulacra. Here, we may find the language of Winnicott (1965) and Bion (1967) with emphases on holding and containing functions—within a transitional *milieu*—to be instructive in creating a potential space (Winnicott, 1971) in which destructive passions can be neutralized and generative functions working toward mobilized.

A BRIEF COMMENT ON SOME CHALLENGES IN PRESERVING PSYCHOANALYTICAL DIVERSITY WHILE DIVERSIFYING PSYCHOANALYSIS IN THE ACADEMY

Psychoanalysis in the United States is imperilled not only from without, in terms of admittance to departments and programs of clinical psychology (a major exception being professional schools, offering the doctor of psychology [PsyD] degree), but from forces within the psychoanalytical movement. The term "movement" is deliberately appropriated to connote the broad range of perspectives that constitute psychoanalytical theory and associated applications. As we have seen organized psychology largely capitulate to "market forces" with respect to so-called evidence-based treatments, not-so-tacitly (in many instances) privileging cognitive-behavioral paradigms, so does psychoanalysis appear to ever-increasingly opt for the less paradigmatically freighted appellation of "psychodynamic." In doing so, there is a decided effort to compete on the same terms of cognitive-behaviorism and a nineteenth-century logical positivism. Other epistemological and ontological frameworks—even in programs open to psychoanalytical perspectives—are in danger of being negated.

Various pressures for such trends—a narrow definition of "evidence," "science," and so on, are easily discerned—not the least being perceived anti-psychoanalytical forces in accreditation. However, in the rush to "validate" psychoanalytical theory, the same dynamics that have so deformed the practice of clinical psychology to that of the de-skilled technician can easily be seen at work in diminishing psychoanalytical theory and practice. Such trends are discerned in a more here-and-now discourse, jettisoning of the drives from theory (desexualization, de-aggressivization), a retreat from emphasizing longer-term treatments in favor of a valorization of short-term "psychodynamic (psycho)therapy," and so forth.

In the laudable efforts to secure a place for psychoanalysis in US psychology, one of the challenges before us is to ensure that emphases on the warp and woof of psychoanalytical paradigms, modes of treatment, clinical populations, treatment issues, and *theory* do not become casualties of the commodification of professional education and clinical practice.

There are, to be sure, pitfalls instantiating psychoanalysis in the academy, abandoning its "splendid isolation," as Freud termed his creative period. Immediately, psychoanalysis/psychoanalytical studies would have to compete with other programs for its share of the university and/or departmental or school budget, and amass data demonstrating its viability—in attracting and retaining students, generating grants, funding research (i.e., research of a particular design). This environment is increasingly competitive, and we know only too well—historically and contemporaneously—the suspect regard in which psychoanalytical theory and practice has been and is held—and how its methodologies do not readily lend it to the research protocols and funding agency requirements that sponsor much of the research being published today. Furthermore, as noted elsewhere in this text, the historical *absence* of psychoanalysis/psychoanalysts from academic psychology, owing to the history of the psychoanalytical movement in the United States, has problematized the creation of generations of psychoanalytically oriented academics, even as full training in psychoanalytic institutes in the United States opened to nonmedical clinicians. One result is that psychoanalytical discourses that are pluralistic in nature are more likely to be found in departments of the humanities than in clinical psychology programs.

This then, is another challenge, and one that is further complicated by trends in the culture at large. A *New York Times* article (Schulten, 2013) cited some noteworthy schools, such as Stanford University, where only 15 percent of the student body has declared a major in the humanities. To be sure, Stanford's reputation in the sciences is duly noted in this regard, but the trend is noted for a number of other private and public colleges and universities, from Harvard to Bard. "College is increasingly being defined narrowly as 'job preparation,' not as something designed to educate the whole person," according to Pauline Yu, the president of the American Council of Learned Societies (2013, p. A17).

These pressures for audit are not lost on university administrations, still highly dependent on tuition dollars and, increasingly, external grant revenues. As such, in bringing psychoanalysis into the academy, we are cautious about the survival of *psychoanalysis* as an intellectual *and* clinical practice *movement*, if and when this goal were to be more fully achieved.

Once introduced and more fully established in the university, which a growing number of so-called *psychodynamically* oriented thinkers and practitioners are increasingly prepared to do, will this movement survive in the variegated and diverse expressions of what we have come to consider it: that is, the various "schools" of Freudian, Kleinian, Self-Psychological, Object-Relations, Lacanian, and so on? Given the appearance and content and lexicon of short-term psychoanalytical treatments, replete with acronyms, it seems plausible that the resultant "psychoanalysis" will approximate that of the manualized behavioral and cognitive-behavioral treatments. Indeed, they already exist—and we are pleased that they *do* exist. However, in extending the pantheon of the psychoanalytical movement, and in the service of simplification, so as to better subject its premises to certain forms of research enquiries, and replication, we are concerned that the many other traditions will be sacrificed in the rush to "scientize"—and thus only through this one narrow perspective, legitimize—psychoanalysis as a *health-care* profession, to the exclusion of other possible incarnations.

"What" psychoanalysis *is* or is *not* may or may not preoccupy many of us. But for those individuals beginning their careers—for those of us hoping to see it continue into the future—and seeing the many forms of psychoanalysis as a unique healing process—this issue becomes something about which we cannot be sanguine. In many respects, the university exerts just as much of a deforming influence on culture and the transmission of culture as the corporations that they now so closely resemble, with greater dangers of turning away from a rich liberal arts tradition—necessary, we would argue, for anyone practicing a healing *art*—into a kind of vocational-technical school, with de-professionalized theories and lexical topographies as ample evidence of a de-skilling of professional selves and knowledge-in-use (for a rich discussion of this transformation review, see William Deresiewicz's, 2015, "How College Sold Its Soul," in the September 2015 issue of *Harper's* magazine). For example, citing the political and cultural attacks on the moral foundations of education, Deresiewicz (2015) asserts, regarding the neoliberal assaults on traditional educational values:

> It is not the humanities per se that are under attack. It is learning: learning for its own sake, curiosity for its own sake, ideas for their own sake. It is the liberal

> arts, but understood in their true meaning, as all of those fields in which knowledge is pursued as an end in itself, the sciences and social sciences included. . . . As for the moral purpose, the notion that college might prepare you for life by inciting contemplation and reflection, it is typically dismissed. (p. 27)

This constitutes a considerable challenge for students and early-career professionals who cannot imagine beyond the permissible of state-sanctioned identifications, let alone the *possible* that might exist beyond a discourse of surveillance, of thought and behavioral control (a young colleague of one of the authors lamented that, in working with children, the cognitive-behaviorally oriented treatment team was practicing something they evidently now term "thought replacement," redolent with intrusiveness and coercion).

Psychoanalysis functions as any society's veritable "canary in a coal mine," in relation to its dedication to free speech, among other values. If, as Edith Kurzweil (as cited in Horstein, 2002, p. 481) writes, "every country creates the psychoanalysis it unconsciously needs," the US bird is looking rather wan. Many years ago, after a presentation in one of the authors' classes, a student asked the late psychoanalyst and theoretician Peter Giovacchini, MD, if psychoanalysis would survive. "If the culture is to survive, it will," he replied. At the time, the thought occurred to us that this was a bit grand and melodramatic, but we have come around to the wisdom of this prediction. Our challenge is to keep psychoanalysis chirping along—although, the authors, coming from Chicago, sometimes suspect that we may be back to a version of the old (illegal) speakeasy when it comes to spreading our subversive psychoanalytical ideas.

ON THE IMPORTANCE OF BEING A PSYCHOANALYST IN AN ACADEMIC SETTING

Interestingly, psychoanalytic training may provide excellent preparation for assuming administrative and program leadership roles. For example, organizations are replete with manifestations of the symbolic-metaphoric-derivative spheres. The psychoanalyst is trained to attend to the uniquely and collectively constructed meanings of an organization that become reified. Micro- and macro-transferences and their vicissitudes and management of parental and sibling transferences, splitting, and secrecy versus openness are among some of the typical issues that one encounters. The psychoanalyst must redefine the meaning of "patient" to include systems and remain aware that multiple legitimate needs and agendas must coexist within larger systems. There may not always be a concordance among the goals and aims of the individual system or entire organization. The psychoanalyst must then attend to the tension between organizational cohesion and goals and individual needs, desires, and goals.

While challenging, such work is also highly stimulating and rewarding. Such interdisciplinary discourse and student contact has the broad potential to enrich all parties. By creating and maintaining a place for psychoanalysis within the academy, we ensure the ongoing evolution of psychoanalysis and its relevance for the treatment of a diverse range of psychopathologies. In addition, if psychoanalysis is to survive, it cannot continue to be seen as solely a unique treatment methodology (as exemplified by psychoanalysis, proper). Our training prepares us to function effectively as educators, consultants, and administrators as well.

Chapter 6

Locating the Subject Matter in the Matter of the Subject

On the Education of Mental Health Professionals in a Cookbook Culture

> *Hark ye yet again,—the little lower layer. All visible objects, man, are but as pasteboard masks. But in each event—in the living act, the undoubted deed—there, some unknown but still reasoning thing puts forth the mouldings of its features from behind the unreasoning mask. If man will strike, strike through the mask! How can the prisoner reach outside except by thrusting through the wall? To me, the white whale is that wall, shoved near to me. Sometimes I think there's naught beyond. But 'tis enough. He tasks me; he heaps me; I see in him outrageous strength, with an inscrutable malice sinewing it. That inscrutable thing is chiefly what I hate; and be the white whale agent, or be the white whale principal, I will wreak that hate upon him. Talk not to me of blasphemy, man; I'd strike the sun if it insulted me. For could the sun do that, then I could do the other; since there is ever a sort of fair play therein, jealousy presiding over all creations. But not my master, man, is even that fair play. Who's over me? Truth hath no confines.* (Melville, 1991, p. 178)

INTRODUCTION

This quotation from Melville's Moby Dick is Captain Ahab's poignant commentary on an inner life in a moment of reflective turmoil. At this juncture, it is perhaps all too easy to minimize or even neglect the powerful insights of the founder of psychoanalysis, Sigmund Freud. Even if psychoanalysts/psychoanalysis tacitly acknowledge(s) his discoveries, and use(s) his works as a veritable touchstone, it opens the door for misunderstandings and a presentist perspective on our development as a profession, and, in parallel fashion, our development as individual psychoanalysts and psychoanalytically orientated clinicians. Indeed, Freud's most radical discovery, and associated theories, regarding the dynamic unconscious, infantile sexuality, and so on, via the radical methodology of free association, has, in many psychoanalytical paradigms, been displaced from its primacy in the discourse of phenomenological, etiological, or treatment considerations. The important contributions of the British Object-Relations School, the American Relational School, Psychoanalytical Self-Psychology, Intersubjective Psychoanalysis, and Constructivist perspectives aside, there has been an emerging tendency to view clinical phenomena as occurring in a mutually co-constructed, here-and-now, relational matrix that, it is suggested, potentially forecloses on the patient's own wording of his or her experience and associations that eventually elucidate the unconscious, inner world/life.

This chapter endeavors to describe the effort to create and maintain a space for an intrapsychic focus and subscribe to a psychoanalytical ethos—amid the attendant impediments owing to the emphasis on so-called evidence-based or empirically supported treatments that privilege social reality over intrapsychic reality. We feel that the ideology of the marketplace has supplanted a professionally anchored discourse and that this has been hastened and abetted by our professional organizations, leading to the growing proletarianization of our field (Deresiewicz, 2015).

The cascade of problems attendant with such collusion with or capitulation to the market forces and corporatization by organizations ostensibly working to protect the sanctity of psychotherapy as a profession, across the transmission of professional knowledge, skills, clinical/professional values, and attitudes, is well in evidence and pervasive. Indeed, while senior clinicians' practices are adversely affected by the devotion to simple, mechanistic treatments dictated by the health-care industry, and a popular cultural myth regarding the nature of "*behavioral* health" (as premised by an address to overt and "maladjusted," "irrational" thoughts and associated behaviors, through a series of directive, psychoeducational *interventions*), this is increasingly shaping and driving the desires, interests, experiences, and worldviews of individuals who are applying to programs in clinical psychology, and setting about *beginning* their clinical practices. Such individuals, who are at an early nexus in their careers, may find it difficult to establish a space for speech (here we refer to the Freudian method of "free association") given the impediments, impingements, and strictures of managed care, as well as the active, interventionistic, psychoeducational, and technique-focused "best practices" currently being held forth as the centerpieces of that which constitutes solid, ethical psychotherapeutic treatment and practice in the world of academic psychology.

Indeed, the epistemological and associated pedagogical paradigms offered in most PhD programs are decidedly quantitative and experimentalist. Even within PsyD/professional school programs, there is a growing need for student demonstration of competence in conforming and performing to "evidence-based" treatments—note, again, the propagandized appropriation of certain terminologies and phraseologies that predicate what may be legitimized or delegitimized—premised upon discreet formulations of the experiencing person as malleably constructed into correct behavior and cognition through a series of prescribed therapist-sponsored activities—all of which must be numerically encoded, quantified, and monitored. Such an approach is absolutely encouraged, and indeed required, by the ever-growing requirements of accreditation, and a proliferation of accrediting bodies, sponsored by various governmental bodies at federal, state, and local levels. Increasingly, this is encompassing the domain of not only the psychotherapeutic disciplines at masters and doctoral levels, but the post-licensure, postdoctoral training associated with psychoanalysis, proper (Parker & Revelli, 2008). Such accrediting bodies are intent on programs demonstrating during the arduous accreditation process that their students have mastered discreet *competencies* that the program (or, more accurately, perhaps, which the accreditation bodies) privileges. Epistemologically reductive structures and didactic, coercive pedagogies now proliferating within professional schools and departments of clinical and counseling psychology supporting such views are prescriptions for psychological authoritarianism (and, ultimately, cultural and political authoritarianism—trends that seem to be all too in evidence at the present historical moment), rather than democracy, as this finds its expression ever more in the orientation of the newer generations of practitioners and their clinical work now being imposed on their patients. For instance, in some organizations, such as Veterans Administration Medical Centers, only specific "evidence-based treatments" are permitted, specifying cognitive-behavioral, dialectical-behavioral, psychotherapies, and so on. Here, one must ask the question, "If it does not exist in the culture, how can it exist in the mind?" referring to alternative ways of knowing, practicing, defining what constitutes "evidence," and so on.

Indeed, recent papers explore these trends in detail (e.g., Messer 2004, 2006; Messer & Winokur, 1984), and what the authors of one term a growing "mono-culture" regarding the education and training of future generations of practitioners across mental health professions toward behavioral and, especially, cognitive-behavioral theoretical and treatment orientations (Levy & Anderson, 2013). This follows upon an earlier paper outlining the distinct trend of a narrowing of theoretical orientations articulated in doctoral psychology programs in clinical psychology (university-based PhD and university-based and "specialized" or freestanding/independent PsyD programs) by faculty members (Heatherington et al., 2012), in which the predominant theoretical orientation of faculty educating and training the clinicians of the future is overwhelmingly of a cognitive-behavioral orientation.

While this is not the focus of this chapter, and the literature too large to adequately summarize, it is important for the reader to be aware of recent meta-analyses, and summations of the research of psychoanalytical treatments and their efficacy across a variety of clinical conditions. Despite this large body of empirical, quantitative, and qualitative research to support the efficacy of psychoanalytical praxis (e.g., Leichsenring, Leweke, Klein, & Steinert, 2015; Leichsenring & Rabung, 2008; McWilliams, 2013; Shedler, 2010, 2015), for more generalized reviews of the effectiveness of psychoanalytical treatments and efforts to redefine what constitutes evidence (e.g., Gottdiener, 2006; Gottdiener & Haslam, 2002, 2003; Karon & VandenBos, 1984), the reader is directed to the studies of Milrod and colleagues regarding the psychoanalytical treatment of panic (Milrod, Busch, Cooper, & Shapiro, 1997); our task can be all the more daunting given the fact that psychoanalysts and psychoanalytically orientated practitioners today are treating, even in private practice settings, patients that are more primitively organized than in the past. Indeed, faced with patients whose histories of severe trauma are veridically sound on many fronts and are not to be regarded as mere intrapsychic phantasies, as well as the attendant strain on the psychoanalyst to "provide" *symptomatic* relief in the face of clear and intense suffering, it might seem quaint at best, and ludicrous or unethical at worst, to recommend the maintenance of a purely intrapsychic, interpretative focus (Klerman, 1990; Stone, 1990), knowing, from our practice as psychoanalysts, that symptomatic change comes as a *by-product* of making the unconscious conscious and of personality/structural change.

Nevertheless, such pressures would seem to be a derivative of the potential breaking through not simply of a patient's unconscious conflicts, and associated enfeebled emotional-behavioral controls, but possible enactments that, in the contemporary psychotherapeutic setup (double entendre intended), preclude exploration for their unconscious meaning structures, and bringing these derivative expressions into language. These pressures inevitably lead to further enactments: to provide active suggestion, correctives, educative exhortations, and so on, as demanded by manualized, evidence-based approaches. Such processes, in short, do not augur a departure from Freud's (1912b/1981) "rule of abstinence," or abandoning a position of "evenly suspended attentiveness." Rather, what is called for is quite the contrary—such pressures and dynamics rightfully become subjects of analysis in and of themselves. For example, might this be a *parallel process*, reflecting the degree to which the psychoanalyst does not feel "held" by his or her profession, or the cultural surround, and thus unable to create a potential space for the development of a psychoanalytical treatment to unfold itself?

In short, by maintaining, intact and untrammeled, the principal rule or ethic that conjoins the members of the Freudian pair (the fundamental rule of free association), we, as psychoanalysts, potentially afford our patients that most increasingly rare "commodity" (and, indeed, a commodity such a space for freely speaking *and* freely listening has, indeed, become, assuming that such a space *can* be found, for purchase in the psychotherapy marketplace): a space for the democratic exercise of *free speech*—and offers to the analysand a more unburdened space (even of the psychoanalyst's own impinging subjectivity, at least in so far as we offer a mode of practice) for self-discovery borne of the "play" in the transference that Freud (1912a/1981, 1914a/1981, 1915/1981) cogently wrote about and Winnicott (1958, 1965, 1971) embodied in his writing and professional work. At this point in time, we might do well to consider the simulacrum of the "speakeasy" of Chicago during Prohibition, where one, if given the codes for entry, might repair and have access to other forms of the forbidden, excised from polite society via various forms of censorship, legislation, and penalties. To be certain, we need look no further for evidence of the "subversive" and "dangerous" nature of free speech than to look at the various and often-extreme ways and means by which various groups and entities go to censor, curtail, and outlaw its exercise. Again, Bollas (2011) lends his inimitable voice to the articulation of these trends:

> However, if these [psychoanalytic consulting rooms] offer a special form of *jouissance* for their participants, both analysand and psychoanalyst know the price they must pay for this secret bliss. They suffer the persecutory anxiety of being seen to participate in some form of soon-to-be banished, forbidden activity. And in spite of all the efforts to sanitise the appearances of psychoanalysis through verbal dry-cleanings—"evidence-based practice" or "competencies"—the psychoanalyst is still regarded as someone dripping of the unseemly. He is still the Freudian, hanging out with sexuality and aggression; still the figure who encourages discussion of that which culture insists should be forbidden. (p. 250)

In this regard, the stereotypical images of the cold and unavailable (i.e., "Freudian") psychoanalyst often come to mind, and with it a perhaps quaint but outdated and potentially ineffective or even harmful form of treatment. Such criticisms generally come from outside the psychoanalytical movement, and from sources uninformed about and inimical and often overtly hostile to psychoanalytical theory and psychotherapy. We would argue that such criticisms, by no means novel, are unwarranted, given what actually unfolds—or may unfold—in a psychoanalytical treatment. Theoretically, some of the research points to the overriding curative factor as being moored in the treatment relationship (e.g., McWilliams, 2013). The deep and abiding paradox here is difficult to convey but begs a deconstruction of the concepts of "relational" or "related." (As in "What, exactly, 'is' 'The' '*Relationship*'? and 'Related to *what*? [or to *whom*?' "] Is it the Some-*Thing*-ness of the analysand's unconscious, unseen, unknowable, except derivatively? Is this a reference to a construct of some fictive "Third" coalesced out of the speculative reach for populating the treatment with the "Otherness" of some personage or personages to which or to whom the appeals for symptomatic relief or an effacement of what has been the life of the patient/analysand can be directed? Of course, one can rightly answer, "It all depends"—opening, again, rather than closing, something that announces itself as a question and must therefore be analyzed.) The authors of this text argue from an integrationist perspective with regard to theory and the psychoanalytical movement, that is, to become steeped in the traditions of the British Object-Relations School, Self-Psychology, Freud, and Lacan, influenced by and respectful of a diverse array of psychoanalytical discourses. Still, for some of us, it has been of exceptional value to further professional development, and seems to have been of salvific value to patients, for a (re)turning to Freud, and through this, to the discourse of a psychology of the unconscious—in order to carry out precisely the sort of treatments with severely ill patients that Winnicott (1958, 1965), Searles (1965, 1986), and others have so evocatively written about, and for which there is, as always, such pressing need—as well as to consider for premising the transmission of theories and clinical practices across the pantheon of the psychoanalytical movement.

WHY FREUD, AND WHY NOW?

It is with the above in mind that we have purposefully positioned the thought of Sigmund Freud at the center of this chapter, as exemplar, sine qua non. In our estimation, his work epitomizes the revolutionary possibilities embodied within the psychoanalytical movement and simultaneously signifies the centering of the culture's antipathy for psychoanalysis, itself, as well as its foundational ethos. We will also endeavor to illustrate my assertions through an elementary exposition of my teaching of basic courses in psychoanalytical theories and psychotherapies at the doctoral and master's levels. At the center of these courses resides the students' immersion in psychoanalytical treatments that one of us (DLD) conducted during a predoctoral clinical psychology internship and early postdoctoral years of practice—this "immersion" centers, situates, and locates the *student* in the position of being not only the psychotherapist within the very subject matter of the treatment but the matter of the subject of the course itself, as an experiencing subject/participant.

These questions "Why Freud?" and "Why now?" are important to pose and not merely rhetorical. Indeed, there have been a number of heralded "Returns to Freud"—perhaps most famously or infamously associated with the teachings of Jacques Lacan (1977) and his followers. In some psychoanalytical institutes, very little of Freud's theories may be taught, or exposure given over to his primary texts. Of course, in general, with respect to undergraduate and graduate psychology programs, students are exposed to only the most skeletal of outlines, perhaps along the lines of the structural (Freud, 1923/1981), tripartite model of id, ego, and superego—with notes as to its quaint and outmoded utility—in other words, reduced to the level of curious historical footnote. Interestingly, it is often within programs devoted to filmic or literary criticism, English, philosophy, anthropology, or gender studies that Freud survives at all. It is with this in mind that my bracketing of "(re)turning to Freud" highlights the double reading as it implies a "turning to" Freud by many, with the primary texts perhaps being considered for the very first time, as opposed to an outright "return" to that which has been left or lost and is now rediscovered.

Yet, in arguing for (re)creating a space for Freud in psychology programs, it is not my intention to propose an uncritical, potentially transference-based discipleship to Freud. Particularly at this point in time, when psychoanalysis has been in the bloom of burgeoning developments and refinements of diverse theory-building and associated clinical researches, the political movement that is also psychoanalysis has been finding itself confronting the unique strains of an increasingly diverse set of agendas and associated tensions—for example, the familiar discord between purists from the various theoretical camps that comprise contemporary psychoanalytical thought and practice, and, increasingly, strains between and among the researchers and the practitioners.

In addition, divisions exist among the practitioners who feel that the questions regarding the efficacy of psychoanalytical treatments promulgated by other mental health disciplines and theoretical perspectives, third-party payors, politicians, and other policy makers, must be addressed and, indeed, assert that psychoanalysis must adapt to the exigencies of contemporary culture if it is to survive—and those that argue (e.g., Bollas & Sundelson, 1995; Kavanaugh, 1999, 2012) that if it *is* to survive, psychoanalysis must remove itself from the health-care matrix that commodifies the theory, the practice, and the psychoanalytical pair to the level of technocratically controlled, de-skilled, and regulated marionettes. This, it is asserted, makes psychoanalysis and psychoanalytical treatment, with its emphasis on free association, the interpretation of the transference, a *clinically* determined length of stay, for multiple sessions per week, authored by the whims of de-skilled "regulators" who will de-professionalize the Freudian "talking cure," decentering the patient from the central position as both the subject and the author of analysis that they should rightly occupy. Here, impingements regarding the length of treatment are only one element of many with which we are concerned and are accompanied by justifiable trepidation over the privileging of the confidentiality of the content and process of the treatment (Bollas & Sundelson,

1995; Kavanaugh, 2012). Like the conformism and mediocratization rampant in the culture at large, the eviscerating co-optation and normalization of psychoanalysis and its subversive elements follow a trend as theory and clinical method. In this mode, psychoanalysis becomes its opposite, emphasizing adaptation and facilitating the development of "normotics" or "normopaths" (Bollas, 1987; McDougall, 1980, respectively, as delineated in detail in chapter 5)—defining health in terms of the patient's *compliance* to the desires and demands of the society at large, even if this means the installation of a pathological "normalcy" (ineluctably associated with the co-optation and the normalization of psychoanalysis itself, in betrayal of its revolutionary promise of subverting the order of things).

Yet we know that in times of considerable flux and change, ambiguity becomes a threat to the psychical well-being of the person and of the group. In this regard, by (re)turning to the writings and theories of Freud, is there not the risk of asserting a different fundamentalism in a context that is fraught with so many fundamentalisms—especially, it would seem, of the religious and political types? Is there also not the risk, then, of further promoting division, rather than dialogue and rapprochement among the various streams of psychoanalytical practice and thought?

As Bollas (1995, 1999), Reisner (1999), and Roustang (1976) have variously noted, theory-building is fraught with such dynamics. In this respect, any attempt to idolize, idealize the theory and/or person of one such as Freud, Lacan, or Jung, who is thus the Creator or Master, is to submit to the Him or His established representative as "the one who is supposed to know." In effect, this is to become the passive vessel of pre-thought constructions and a received wisdom that forecloses one's own ability to speculate, theorize, and author one's own experiences. We can also, in the process, create, so as to justify such mental gymnastics, the Humanistic Freud, the Relational Freud, and so forth.

However, there are a number of ways out of this apparent cul-de-sac. Reisner (1999) notes that "Freud's greatest contribution was psychoanalysis itself: a way of thinking about our ways of thinking and being . . . its commitment to progress through questioning, and its mindfulness of what gets left out of any discourse—even its own" (p. 1038). Thus, I would suggest, the language of a Freudian psychoanalysis invites its own destruction, rather than an entrenchment in absolutes. Within the theories of the different psychoanalyses extant today are the seeds of their inevitable demise—contradictions of which Freud himself took note and led to his constantly revisiting and revising his works. This subversive element of Freud's psychoanalysis, which holds the most revolutionary promise for the advancement of an understanding of cognition, affect, motivation, behavior (indeed of psychoanalysis itself), has been termed by Casey (as cited in Reisner, 1999). Here the text "complicates or qualifies itself in such a way as to put into question a thesis already announced expressly in the same text" (p. 243). This is not so much the Kuhnsian sequence of thesis, antithesis, and synthesis but a process by which "multiple vectors of thought and language arise, disappear, and reappear transformed, progressively expanding our understanding of *how we think and the terrain of what can be thought*" (Reisner, 1999, pp. 1046–1047, emphasis added). If ever there was a pathway out of the extant normalizing, scripted, manualized techniques that now comprise the "toolboxes" (yet another all-too-revealing term "du jour" underscoring the technocratic and mechanized foundational principles undermining and underlying contemporary psychological practice) of the contemporary mental health clinician *cum* technician, such a perspective as this would be "it."

Roustang (1976) situates this deconstruction within the transference one has to theory and to the Master. Much as the clinical psychoanalyst attempts to relieve the patient's distress by evoking, through the neutrality of the psychoanalytical setting, the transference, the student of psychoanalysis (whatever the point this may be in his or her career and relationship to psychoanalysis) "must first stop being fascinated by theory and analyse the fantasies and desires that gave rise to it; one must analyse theory as the text of a dream or myth" (p. 58). To do otherwise eviscerates the radical possibilities that psychoanalysis holds for articulating the psychodynamics not only of individuals but of cultural phenomena such as war, religion, art, and science to which Freud, across the arc of his professional life, pointed the way.

Failing this, psychoanalytical thought devolves into dogma, intellectual totalitarianism, and symptom—protection and defense from the knowledge that one does not know. And in pursuit of knowing, and the finding in the theory and/or the Master, such premature "knowing" (which ultimately leads to foreclosure or "no-ing"), one must, at some level, be prepared to accept one's status as disciple—which is rather different from merely being "one who does not know"—the latter being a truthful-enough and honorable position to occupy on the way to knowing, never reached, and clinically, one might add, quite necessary in bringing the analysand to the point of being an experiencing and desiring subject who *desires* to know and can come to speak themselves to the psychoanalyst who can receive this. Contrariwise, it is the disciple, who has foreclosed on theorizing for themselves, that may assert that they do, in fact, "know."

Thus, by refusing to view Freud as "The One Who Knows," but who nevertheless articulates a way, a method, a process out of this seemingly insoluble dilemma that binds us to him as the Master, that is, by making use of the pre-thought "knowns" as mere starting points for one's own process of thinking and eventual discovery, we accept, in name, the process with its weltanschauung and associated logic of discovery as "Freudian." This leads to the possibility not of foreclosure but an attunement to and the privileging of the murmurings of the unconscious, that is, the privileging of the *patient*'s unconscious and through this an acknowledgment of a "Third," or absent Other, which opens the possibility for an escape from the collapse of the psychoanalytical space and enterprise into the symbiotic or narcissistic claustrum that otherwise might obtain from the overreliance on the psychoanalytical pair that in effect holds up the here-and-now co-constructed relationship as mirror to often nothing other than itself.

In this claustrum, the psychoanalyst potentially offers an entanglement or engulfment either in the belief of a provision of the sort that Balint (1985) termed "primary love," but which ultimately comes to be experienced as seductive or persecutory, or both. Among other matters to consider in the psychoanalyst-analysand dynamic is the presumption that we (the psychoanalysts) can presume to know to whom the patient's speech is directed and, indeed, who is speaking to the patient (or, for that matter, the psychoanalyst).

This focus on the Third is consistent with Freud's three-body psychology, which includes derivatives of the Oedipus complex. While acknowledging the intersubjective field that, *in part*, constructs a psychoanalysis, Muller (1999) notes, quoting from Freud (1940), that the analyst offers to the patient an *analysis*, through an *interpretative activity* of what Freud termed "material influenced by the [patient's] unconscious. Our knowing is to make up for his unknowing and to give his I back its mastery over lost provinces of his mental life. This pact constitutes the analytic situation" (p. 173). Muller (1999) asserts that it is through the intersubjective field that the mutual pact can function as a Third if it incorporates "the entire structure of language, culture, and horizon of understanding that is largely unconscious" (p. 517). Such a pact emphasizes the patient's communications and recommends a cautionary stance with respect to the use of self-disclosures by the psychoanalyst. One is reminded of Winnicott's (1955) admonition, with respect to working in the area of regression to dependence that the psychoanalyst "stay awake; stay alive; and behave himself."

This also echoes Bion's (1967) recommendation to approach the patient encountered in each session without the psychoanalyst's memory or desire being imposed on the analysand. To do otherwise is again to open up the possibility of a cure by transference, persuasion, or exhortation—the imposition of one's will (the stronger and more knowledgeable, influential, and authoritative—omnipotent, omniscient, and beneficent) and the acting upon the other that becomes an all-too-personal echo or construction of the psychoanalyst's subjectivity and/or desire, supplanting that of the patient's. Rather than working toward the dissolution of the transference, it becomes put to use in an unanalyzable field of relativized and mutually co-constructed experience states.

As Bollas (1999) notes, "Freud's insistence that the bearer of memory, instinct, pain, and trauma, be the patient; leaving the analyst free to think about these matters from an unbiased, emotionally unmoved place" (p. 18) is instructive. This means that for Freud, the patient's speech becomes privileged above all else—regardless of what it is that the analyst may think or feel. It is the psychoanalyst's silence that helps to evoke this speech. As Bollas proceeds to explain,

> We may further wonder if the creation of neutrality bears the curious truth of the impossibility of transferring the self-analytic experience to the self-other relation. Turning to contemporary interest in the field of the inter-personal, we would have to find a place for neutrality as a representation of an essential feature of all human relations: that the other is beyond hearing and knowing—speakable to but impossible to hear from. Neutrality is, then, an indispensable part of the psychoanalysis. Too inter-personal a relation, one that socialised neutrality and displaced it, would refuse this truth. (p. 13)

Muller (1999) asserts that such a stance amounts to the psychoanalyst's capacity to sustain "an emptiness so that he can make room for the Other . . . in order to be able to resonate with the Third, the [Freudian] unconscious" (p. 518). In this respect, we can conceive of a certain space within the psychoanalytical process whereby the analyst exercises his or her interpretative function that can be reflectively anchored within the ongoing requirement for self-analysis regarding one's immersion in and contribution to the countertransference/transference matrix. What is called for is to disentangle self-disclosure from "self-display" and alert us to when "self-disclosing is self-imposing" (Muller, 1999, p. 519).

As we become absorbed within the rich, metaphorical language of psychoanalysis, imbued with symbol and metonymy as well, we lose ourselves from the moorings of objective reality and enter into the sometimes-inchoate and ineffable states of dream, illusion, and reverie. It is through the essential subjective otherness of the dream that Freud elucidated so many of his seminal findings. The analytical space invites the dissolution of objective truths and shared realities, and invites the deconstruction of the dreamer himself or herself in its wake. As such, the analysand allies as much with the self-in-participation of the *process* of a psychoanalysis that ever becomes *more and more uniquely his or her own*, never to be repeated, as with the *person* of the psychoanalyst, per se. Each association yields itself up to the eventual clustering of a chain of signifiers, decoded through the further associations to latent meanings that each layering of derivatives yields.

Bollas (1999) and Kainer (1999) note that such self-states are the precursors for the eventual transference to come. That is, the experience of being held in the mind and psyche of another, as well as finding oneself situated within a living, evolving *clinical* process, necessarily comes to be fixated on the person of the psychoanalyst and his or her presumptively shared experience that is not merely presumed to be coterminous but co-existensive with that of the patient's. Whether the patient is able to make use of such transference states, or tends to relate more to the person of the psychoanalyst, is of lesser importance than the psychoanalyst's maintaining a position of neutrality, receptivity (evenly suspended attentiveness), and a graded silence that yields itself only to an interpretative mode.

Again, following from Bion (1967), we must even question our desire to be helpful, especially as this may proceed from a pragmatic, symptom-focused perspective, and wonder instead after the meanings of these significations of the symptom, which brackets and labels and potentially lives the patient, may embody. Certainly, we each have experienced firsthand the powerful, salutary impact of free association, in and of itself. Such "unconscious freedom," as Bollas (1995) terms it, also incorporates a corollary to the analysand's free association: the psychoanalyst's evenly hovering attention, or, as Symington (1983) termed it, "the analyst's act of freedom"—an acknowledgment of separation from the analysand. It carries with it the possibilities for the relaxation of the analyst's immersion in secondary process, in being helpful, and so on, allowing for the emergence of the analyst's own associations, oscillating with those of the patient—for, as Freud described, it is possible for the system *Ucs* of one person to pass through to another, entirely without registration in the system *Cs*. This becomes the "intermediate area of experiencing" that Winnicott (1971) discussed and the entry into reverie that Ogden (1999) describes. As Bollas (1999) explains,

> When Freud divided the analytical couple in two—the one to free associate and report dreams, the other to evenly hover and then interpret—he cannily exploited an ordinary partition between subjective and objective states of mind, oscillating between . . . subjective renderings of reality and . . . objective reflections upon prior subjective states. . . . . This oscillation between the self immersed in its complexity . . . and a more reflective self subsequently objectifying those states is also the structure of inner speech: split as we are between the speaker (the I) and the addressed (the you). . . . When the analysand speaks freely he does so not just to an historic object from the transference, but also to the rhetorical other: the you who never replies. (Only the I speaks in inner speech). The analyst's silence allies with the rhetorical you of intra-psychic discourse. . . . *The subject is summoned to think about his life because he is confronted by its mystery*. (p. 8, emphasis added)

TRANSMITTING A PSYCHOANALYTICAL ETHOS OF PRAXIS

Enter the realities of the contemporary professional, epistemological, pedagogical, theoretical, and clinical contexts. In essence, psychoanalysis is the veritable "canary in a coal mine" for this, or any society's, valuing of free speech. In the present corporatist, technocratic, and scientized milieu, the psychoanalytical endeavor, including its very premises, is being challenged and increasingly marginalized. The American way of destroying something is not quite as ham-fisted as outright suppression. Such a thing can be accomplished more subtly and with greater "legitimacy" through so-called market forces, including the economical dictates of managed care organizations. In addition, the ever-present/simmering antipathy of organized psychology (historically, always more behaviorally, cognitive-behaviorally, and empirically [i.e., quantitatively and experimentally] constructed) as well as the re-medicalization and biologism of organized psychiatry have all conspired to the ever-increasing marginalization of psychoanalytical theoretical and treatment paradigms. Oddly enough, perhaps these trends and patterns represent the greatest "Return to Freud"—that is, psychoanalysis today faces some of the very same challenges and affronts to its legitimacy as that which was faced by Freud himself, and the movement he founded, in its earliest beginnings.

This reordering of the cultural mazeways and mores is having the effect of limiting our perceptions of the possible—and the permissible. This is especially so for young professionals-in-training, for whom no other (legitimate) alternatives exist. However, many of the difficulties we face are self-inflicted. Complicating matters, psychoanalysis has been encumbered with its quasi-religious devotion not only to The Founder, but other Masters. This has, in turn, been associated with the creation of subcultures and associated disciples within psychoanalysis. Across the history of the psychoanalytical movement, such trends have sponsored a subservience to one or another doctrinal stance and excommunication of dissidents, a highly esoterized ("terrorized"? considering the fates of those such as Tausk, Adler, Ferenczi, and Rank who would dare to question the oracular voice of The One Who Knows, such as supervisors, one's psychoanalyst, professors, consultants) and ritualized passage into the elite inner circle of The Chosen. As such, psychoanalysis may be said to have developed a siege mentality (only heightened and problematized by the very real efforts to devalue and abolish psychoanalysis) that has historically made the profession regard empirical investigations into the support or refutation of its theories with hostile or phobic disdain or alarm (there are, however, growing references of psychoanalytically oriented researches that are being carried out and, indeed, have been for decades to dispel such myths).

"Empirically validated treatments" was the term adopted before the hue and cry ultimately led to the more benign-sounding "evidence-based treatments" and an ostensibly theoretically neutral fig leaf for foisting mandated cognitive-behavioral theoretical and clinical approaches to psychological treatment onto *all* doctoral programs seeking accreditation. A doctoral program's survival depends on its securing APA accreditation. Such site visits and reviews authorized and sanctioned by the APA through its Commission on Accreditation are increasingly sensitive to the existence, in the core curriculum, of such evidence-based treatments—and the documentation of the quantification of adequate mastery of the competencies associated with particularized forms of evidence.

While not a simplistically straightforward and unmitigated positive, it is the case that many programs of professional psychology, offering usually a doctorate of psychology, or PsyD degree, have, on average, maintained a presence of psychoanalytical thought and theory (one drawback is that, again, PsyD programs are often seen as problematical on a number of fronts by traditional PhD clinical psychology programs—including, but not limited to, their emphasis on transmitting diverse psychotherapeutic theories and associated clinical practice, as well as psychological assessment)—therefore, these potential *academic* "havens" for psychoanalytical discourse can be dismissed or deprecated owing to their perceived "poor standards" for admission, lax academic requirements, and perceived general lack of scientific rigor or ostensible exclusion of research requirements in the core curriculum.

However, once again, the findings of Heatherington et al. (2012) and Levy and Anderson's (2013) surveys regarding the contraction, reduction, and outright banishment of psychoanalytical praxis from academia and resultant mono-culture of cognitive-behaviorsm are a harbinger of dire times ahead—for the "science" of psychology, for the advancement of knowledge, for intellectual enquiry, and for *effective* treatment options available to the public (see also chapter 4 of this text on "Normotic Elements" impinging on the profession). This can only be expected to increase across time, uncritically, as cognitive-behaviorists fill more and more faculty positions—even within practitioner scholar programs such as professional schools of psychology—and transmit a praxis solely from this perspective to yet still other future generations of clinical faculty and practitioners.

In general, however, the complaints of the rigorous scientist-researcher trained clinical psychologist-practitioner regarding applied psychoanalytical treatments can be dispelled. (NB: The modal number of postdoctoral publications from *all* doctoral programs in clinical psychology [PhD and PsyD] is zero.) As Luborsky (2001) noted, regarding psychotherapy outcome studies:

> The major findings are that: (a) Each of the different types of psychological treatments shows benefits; (b) The amount of benefits from each type of therapy shows mainly non-significant differences; (c) These non-significant differences are especially evident when the researcher's therapeutic allegiance is taken into account; (d) Both short-term and long-term treatments show some positive benefits for some patients; and (e) There is a tendency for longer treatments to show more lasting benefits. (p. 583)

Psychoanalysts must endeavor to reposition themselves within an inclusive community of scholars and ecumenical debate if psychoanalysis is to survive—and much depends on the survival of psychoanalysis, as determined by *psychoanalysts*, and not by those who would denigrate or deprecate it, or otherwise construct it to conform to their definitions, capturing it within some scientized/sanitized/normalized *vision* of what might constitute a *version* of an eviscerated corpus that would appease the medicalized, DSM-valorized arbiters of a mental health service delivery establishment that holds hegemonic sway in the American health-care discourse. Miller (1996a, 1996b, 1996c) and Strupp (2001) argue that the *rationing* of care and the *managing* of costs must not be confused with the *managing of care*. It is of note that Strupp, one of the progenitors of psychoanalytically oriented psychotherapy outcome research and treatment manuals, should also call our attention to the unsavory alliance between the proponents of so-called evidence-based treatments and corporatist entities and the egregious conflation of psychotherapeutic efficacy and profitability that defines this allegiance: as a researcher, he noted, "I take exception to the manner in which research has been used, if not to say co-opted, as a tool for justifying the *rationing of therapeutic services and putting therapeutic techniques into a straitjacket*" (2001, p. 606, emphasis added). This extends into the specious development and utilization of treatment manuals—originally developed to aid researchers in their addressing certain specific symptom clusters within micro-moments of treatment with the intent of elucidating cause and effect relations and intervention strategies—but has been adopted into becoming *the* modality for implementing totalistic clinical treatments, proper.

Such manualization not merely forecloses on the unique vicissitudes afforded by the free associations of the patient but the psychotherapist's potential for various acts of freedom uniquely afforded and indeed necessitated by the not-to-be repeated, moment-to-moment unfolding of unconscious processes worded within the psychotherapeutic bi-personal field. Each participant is conjoined in a process of suppression and de-linking that collapses enquiry into rote prescriptions and proscriptions for correct thought and behavioral management and control. Indeed, a manualized "treatment" goes further in that it utterly negates anything other than a passive and scripted process of pre-thought knowns and received wisdom being enshrined in the patient through an active and impinging agency represented by the intermediary proxy of the psychotherapist-cum-technician. Thus, the patient does not belong to the psychotherapeutic pair as the one who knows. This negates the wording of self-experience in the patient's own idiom through the relative ignorance and enlightened desire to understand as brought to the fore by the psychoanalyst/psychotherapist who, in being the one who does not know, embodies an ethic of desire for self-discovery and knowledge.

A BRIEF COMMENT ON THE TEACHING OF PSYCHOANALYTICAL THEORIES AND PSYCHOTHERAPY COURSES

We have researched a number of papers reviewing psychoanalytical education in the preparation of this chapter. This includes the efforts of Auchincloss and Kravis (2000), who offer their experience in teaching some of the primary texts of Freud to undergraduate students. In a similar vein, Blass (2001) offers her account of situating a course on Freud centering on the Oedipus complex in a department of psychology in Israel. She acknowledges that the situation in Israel remains rather more "friendly" and accepting of psychoanalytical percepts in this country as opposed to the United States. But what is important to note, from both accountings, is the spirited discussions and papers born of considered, critical thought that these courses catalyzed in students. Examples from ordinary life—and not just the clinical domain—assisted in making these readings relevant—again—in the twenty-first century.

What follows is a personal accounting of one of the authors (DLD), who describes a teaching approach and training model that privileges the process of understanding and discovery through bringing the unconscious into the field of speech—in a basic graduate-level course in psychoanalytical theories and psychotherapy—that has been taught for many years to graduate students. This course has utilized audio-recordings and transcripts from a twice-weekly psychoanalytical treatment conducted during a portion of my clinical training. The patient afforded me, as the clinician, a need to learn outside of myself and go beyond the texts of the British School (e.g., Winnicott, 1958, Winnicott's 1958 *Collected Papers*) and Self-Psychology (e.g., Kohut, 1971) that had constituted the bulk of my readings and associated clinical preparation to that point, and to better familiarize myself with Freud. One of the many things learnt from this patient was the essential power of free association and my own capacity for silence in the midst of rich, evocative narratives that constituted treatment sessions with this person.

The first few class sessions are devoted to more "Freudian" perspectives, and students read most of Freud's papers on technique and a case study of the Rat Man. I also show a very fine dramatization of the Rat Man's treatment done many years ago by the BBC and Time-Warner. This has been especially enlightening for students, for whom Freud's ideas were never explicated beyond the arid and simplistic reiteration of the structural model. (Thereafter, class sessions cover a variety of theorists, including Jacobson, Hartmann, Anna Freud, Erikson, Mahler, Kernberg, Fairbairn, Klein, Winnicott, Kohut, Lacan and/or treatment-related and theoretical arenas such as dreams, sexuality/gender, working with ethnically/racially diverse patients, and termination). In addition, special attention is given to such central tenets of psychoanalysis as the Oedipal complex and the transference, as they have been so diluted and normalized as to be fairly trivialized and so nearly lose any precise and accurate meaning. This has been associated with a resultant loss in the explanatory power of these constructs and a deeper (if nascent) appreciation for their derivative and more manifest expression and psychotherapeutic role by professionals-in-training.

Across the course, students are required to compose several weekly case conceptualizations, from the perspective of the readings of that week. Each conceptualization requires a discussion of the content of the session (for which audiotapes and transcripts are available), detailing developmental, and personality/structural matters; unconscious processes such as wish and associated dangers to the self; defense; and analyses of the treatment session. In terms of the latter, to what extent does the session mirror, or not, the theory or topic under discussion for that particular week? What changes in technique or focus would be indicated to make the session more concordant with the theory and associated practices discussed? Students are also required to comment on the transference and countertransferential matrix as evidenced within each session. This mode of conducting the class has enabled students to, in effect, work alongside of me, complete with a review of my many missteps, gaffs, empathic ruptures, and efforts at rectification. The praxis afforded has made an all-too-esoteric set of theories "come to life" for students and affords them the opportunity to view, hear, and reflect on faculty members' work rather than always testing their mettle. They also are able, across each class's unique makeup, to continue to reveal to me and our learning collective/clinic novel aspects regarding the remarkable person who presented for a treatment, and to appreciate more fully theory-in-use. Importantly, I believe, it offers an in vivo decentering of the instructor and psychotherapist/psychoanalyst as "the one who is supposed to know."

It has been expressed by students in class after class, across academic programs as well, that they lack access to actual case material that is not staged or contrived in some way. Furthermore, as PsyD and MA students, who hope to be clinicians, it is my desire to provide a forum of openness whereby the work of seasoned clinicians, including myself, can be viewed for its usefulness not only in learning a form of psychotherapy but also in transmitting an ethos of ongoing learning, expanding professional development, openness to criticism, and the helpfulness of professional consultation. Thus, I permit my own displacement as "The One Who Knows" and further debunk the notion of "learning" anything instructive regarding a totalistic treatment endeavor via a contrived, formulaic, rote, manualized format. By not requiring in vivo role-playing, students could be more productively focused on the learning of various treatment philosophies and associated methodologies (interestingly, the power of unconscious communication as afforded by something as "basic" as *free association*), which are clearly alien to them, given the tenor of the curriculum for them to this point in their education and clinical preparation, as opposed to managing anxieties attendant with performing in class.

For one of the classes, in short-term psychotherapy and crisis intervention, the students are required to complete a role-playing assignment submitted as a video-recording. Other anxieties, associated with the desire to be instructed in "correct" *technique*, could be brought into the foreground and discussed. The recording and associated case conceptualization paper that are required could be leveraged in a manner as to afford the student optimal control and comfort over their own work, by practicing across the term with their partner, and thus come to approximate a short-term treatment. Thus, the class room approximates "clinic"—and the "potential space" as articulated by Winnicott (1971).

To assist in my assessment of student learning, as well as adding greater structure to the evaluation process, students address certain psychotherapeutic elements within the video-recorded "psychotherapy" or "crisis intervention" sessions that are required for the course, and this is done with a colleague as the pseudo-patient. In order to do this, students were required to review the *Analytic Process Scale*, developed by Sherwood Waldron and colleagues (2004). Students are also required to utilize elements of the scale, further familiarizing themselves with the essential features of a psychoanalytically oriented treatment, per se, and then explore the extent to which these were present in their own work.

Students are, furthermore, required to explore the degree to which these were appropriately adapted within the context of the short-term psychotherapeutic models that were explored during the course of the term, demonstrating their internalization and mastery of essential course content. Importantly, with APA mandates for students to begin measuring treatment outcomes during clinical practica, I have, for the years that I have been teaching this psychoanalytically oriented course, been exposing students to such measures, outside of more symptom-focused, behavioral measures. These include not only the APS (Waldron et al., 2004) but the *Ego Function Scales*, developed by Leopold Bellak (as cited in Bellak & Faithorn, 1981).

While not part of my particular emphasis with respect to my teaching and discourse, these elements of the course further give lie to the notion that psychoanalysis is not based within an "empirical" matrix. The privileging of specific forms of evidence and the lack of regard for theories and associated methodologies that do not subscribe to behavioral and cognitive-behavioral paradigms is, similarly, questioned—including the evident political ramifications—something of which students generally seem to be unaware, even at this crucial nexus in their education—strangely enough.

Furthermore, by requiring works that address emerging as well as current trends within the professional practice arena—a scene with which the instructor is intimately involved—a space was opened for critically questioning an industrialized, commodified, de-professionalized, proletarianized, and, in many ways, *coercive* ethos and associated clinical treatment pantheon, which increasingly holds the profession in sway. As such, students are encouraged to critically appraise the received wisdom of such a system and their own potential participation in what Thomas Szasz (1998) termed the "Therapeutic State." They become aware of not only the philosophical antecedents of the clinical and scientific elements of short-term professional practice but the myriad of political and economical forces that are authoring and shaping the profession today—further preparing them for eventual practice in a contemporary landscape that is in considerable flux. By opening this space for critical exploration, students seem to register, paradoxically, a hope that they can maintain a space for a *professionally and clinically determined* treatment as opposed to one that is mandated by administrative, political, and economical pressures and priorities. This reshapes the debate on the ubiquitous call for short-term treatments and the ostensible empirical evidence for the same, within a critical-dialectical context that questions the *clinically based* usefulness of any treatment approach, as opposed to its administratively enjoined rationalization.

In this spirit, I very purposefully endeavor to ensure that there are readings that assist the students in critically deconstructing the very arguments and received wisdom that are offered to mark the *necessity for* and *superiority of* shorter-term treatments over long-term treatment modalities. In assisting the development of professionals, rather than de-skilled "technicians" that function at the behest of corporatized health-care concerns, my interest was in sensitizing professionals-in-training to the exigencies and vicissitudes of "real-world" clinical practice. Again, I endeavor to do so by example, and utilize video and audio recordings of my own clinical work—offering that there are no "sacred cows," and to demystify the process of short-term treatment, as well as detoxify the matter of audio or video recording one's work for professional development, feedback, and life-long learning.

Across time, additional readings specifically augmenting exposure to the subject matter of psychoanalytical thought and theory have been central. This also was very consciously decided, so as to position *theory* at the center of the course—and to dethrone *technique* from its position of primacy—accompanied as it seems to be with a relative denigration of *theory* (or, at least, what *I* consider theory, which may well not have immediate clinical/methodological relevance, but, when all is said and done, most certainly does). These readings also offer different models for assessing suicidal lethality, as well as intervening in suicidal crises in other than the coercive, impinging, technique-focused modalities that often have, at the core, an imperative to protect the clinician, the treatment facility, and so on, from litigation (in this case, the title of the psychoanalytical text from which additional readings were derived is entitled, fittingly enough, ***Relating*** *to Self-Harm*—emphasis added)—important in terms of contemporary practice trends, when clinicians are avoiding treatments with patients suffering from more severe and chronic forms of psychopathology. such a trend betokens the patient as becoming a phobic object, leading to disconnexion, as opposed to relatedness.

While chary of ascribing to psychoanalysis a cure, if not a method, for all of the ills that ail us, I know of no other mental health discipline that is so concertedly and simultaneously jousting with itself, while extending into novel, diverse theoretical and practice arenas, across such a diverse range of populations, with such varied and passionate agendas. Far from making a virtue out of a necessity, some are confronting head-on the specious arguments in favor of evidence-based psychotherapies, manualizing treatments. Dr. Kevin Hartigan noted many years ago: "Therapy by manual has as much relation to psychotherapy as paint-by-numbers has to art" (as cited in Bollas & Sundelson, 1995, p. 136).

With this in mind, we reference the perspective of Peter Fonagy regarding the "*scientific validity* of psychoanalysis" (as cited in Chung, 2003, p. 14). Fonagy is, of course, no stranger to empirical research and has contributed much to the literature to support the efficacy of psychoanalytically oriented treatments to severe psychopathology, among other things—much needed in the present-day milieu, and stated:

> I see no reason why psychoanalysts should care if psychoanalysis is a science. I can see how they might benefit were this to be the case, but I cannot see that any amount of playing with categories, demarcations, and boundaries of science would make it so. The questions which should concern us are about the nature of mental life, the process of cure, the efficacy of analysis as therapy. Naturally, these entail critical methodological issues concerning which procedures might be most likely to yield pertinent data. . . . I do not think we know enough about what psychoanalysis is to make a meaningful attempt to link it to an, in any case, ill-defined and heterogeneous category of enterprises which we currently call scientific. For some of us psychoanalysis is principally a clinical matter with some generalisations concerning technique and theory. I would prefer to see it as a body of knowledge which is applied to a currently somewhat constrained set of psychotherapeutic situations. (p. 116)

Psychoanalysts must endeavor to reposition themselves within an inclusive community of scholars and ecumenical debate such as that afforded by universities if psychoanalysis is to survive—to be transmitted to successive generations—and much depends on the survival of psychoanalysis, as determined by *psychoanalysts*, and not by those who would denigrate or deprecate it, or otherwise capture it within some revisionist paradigm within the health-care-industrial complex. As a partial remedy, we would argue that psychoanalytical institutes need to consider affiliating with universities.

Winnicott (1971) noted that the psychoanalytical situation provides a setting separate from, but related to, the world at large, and in this way so too can the academy—along with protections such as academic freedom, grievance procedures, institutional and programmatic *Policies and Procedures*, and even accreditation bodies (potentially good for something after all). A major challenge is to preserve the integrity of students' professional development in a similar fashion. By securing a frame, a container, faculty and administration can titrate upward the students' exposure to various pressures, diverse discourses, and external impingements as this relates to the internalization and ultimate discharge of their professional responsibilities. By constituting itself as a "holding environment" or "potential space" within a culture that is suspicious and hostile toward psychoanalysis, the university structure that supports psychoanalytical discourses creates conditions that maximize the growth and unfolding of students' capacities. Unless this occurs, psychoanalytic institutes will not have suitably prepared candidates—or, perhaps, candidates at all—desirous of seeking additional training in this tradition with its rich legacy.

"The ones who know" and who would incarcerate and therefore deform not only the discourse but the practice of our profession into a commodified, proletarianized, "evidence-based practice," divested of its unsettling, unseemly, subversive, and liberating elements, have privileged the "damaged brain" (complete with "irrational thoughts" that must be debunked and removed) above all other explanatory paradigms and with this a "physico-chemical-genetic machine" over an experiencing subject—one who submits himself or herself passively for cognitive and behavioral *adjustment and programming*—better *adaptation* and fit to society's norms. As Kavanaugh (1999) states, "Standards standardize—regulations regulate—and institutions institutionalise." I would emend this to include the following: "Standards stabilize—regulations pulverize—and institutions mediocritize." The clinical psychologist as the de-professionalized, de-skilled *technician*, aided and abetted by our professional associations and accrediting bodies, is already upon us. However, more than ever, practitioners and professionals-in-training are challenging the received wisdom of a technocratic construction of "brain-and-behavior man"—and wonder of wonders, quite on their own, without being mandated to appear before a psychometric technician for prediction and control of behavior—people continue to seek themselves—to wonder after the marvelous—to ponder the thought that thinks itself—in the presence of ones who only know that they do not know.

In this vein, I will end with a quotation highlighted in a book given as a gift by a student at the point of that individual's graduation from doctoral studies. It underscores in a most evocative fashion the ethos that I endeavor to transmit (and, hopefully, to approximate in my own professional and personal life). It is by Rainer Maria Rilke (2000, p. 35):

> You are so young. You stand before beginnings. I would like to beg of you, dear friend, as well as I can, to have patience with everything that remains unresolved in your heart. Try to love the questions themselves like locked rooms and like books written in a foreign language. Do not now look for the answers. They cannot now be given to you because you could not have lived them. It is a question of experiencing everything. At present, you need to live the questions. Perhaps you will gradually, without even noticing it, find yourself experiencing the answer some distant day. Perhaps you are, indeed, carrying within you the potential to visualize, to design, and to create for yourself an utterly satisfying, joyful, and pure life-style. Discipline yourself to attain it but accept that which comes to you with deep trust, and as long it comes from your own will, from your own inner need, accept it and do not hate anything.

Part III

TEACHING

Chapter 7

How Psychoanalytic Perspectives and Processes Can Inform the Curriculum and the Teaching of Self-Observational Skills

To be a teacher is to have a thousand selves, for the image of the teacher is, in part, the creation of the learner. (Field, 1989, p. 852)

PERSONAL REFLECTIONS: AN EARLY DOCTORAL LEARNING EXPERIENCE

In an early experience as a doctoral student, I was privileged to participate in a seminar in psychoanalysis with Dr. Bruno Bettelheim. I was presenting my first case as a new child care worker in an adolescent residential center. Since it was my first presentation, I thought it appropriate to discuss the schizophrenic process of Eric (pseudonym), a teenage client. I wanted to first present this boy's demanding behavior as a prelude to a discussion of diagnosis. As I was into my account, I had described what I felt were this boy's unreasonable demands for an ice cream bar following a trip to the doctor. Therefore, after we were leaving the doctor, Eric spied an ice cream bar dispenser and started to demand I purchase a bar. I told him "no" in a somewhat intense and mildly agitated way. He responded by getting louder and more insistent.

At that point in my report, as I was just illustrating Eric's demandingness, and heading toward discussing Eric's diagnosis as a schizophrenic boy, I was abruptly interrupted by Dr. Bettelheim: "Why did you refuse the ice cream bar?" His question threw me off. It seemed tangential and off the point. I had been heading toward a conceptualization of Eric's diagnosis. I was initially startled and mildly disoriented. I was intimidated by this question by a world-renowned author and psychologist. I then realized I felt blank, but I also recognized a reluctance to answer his question. My presentation was to just present Eric's pathology. Why was he stopping me and throwing me off course? I noticed a feeling of intimidation and felt embarrassed in front of my new doctoral colleagues in the room.

However, I then began to struggle to answer given his stark question and started to recall that I had been forewarned by my work peers not to say "yes" to the demanding, manipulative patient. I realized I feared their opinion of me if I gave in. What emerged in my subsequent self-observation was recognition of the degree to which I did not want to be "pushed around" by this boy, given how I imagined my new peers might feel toward me, and that I would be seen as weak if I allowed Eric to get his way. It then became clear to me that my forceful "no" to Eric was a composite of my reaction to his demanding manner and to a threat to my self-esteem in my new setting. This acknowledgment led to a further exploration of why Eric was as angry as he was. He not only didn't like hearing "no." He might also have been suspecting there was more behind it in terms of my agitated and reactive tone when I refused him.

This discussion led to Dr. Bettelheim's clarification that if my "no" had come from me, it would have had a different tone. If it had come from my actual experience with Eric (I had only been at the residential unit for a week), it would have carried less "baggage." Eric would have been mad but probably less so. His awareness that I was responding primarily to my peers more than to our relationship likely spurred him to become even more defiant. I might add that his request was also a possible testing of a new staff member. These were the understandings that came out of what one might call a somewhat challenging and surprising question. I had never thought it was anything more than a diagnosis of a disturbed adolescent and learned that being pushed to self-observe could yield so much important understandings.

I include this teaching and learning episode as paradigmatic of an example of an instructor questioning my motives behind a specific response to a patient. Whether Dr. Bettelheim was fully correct in this example, he had taught me the importance of exploring my motives around a specific clinical event. The exploratory question was actually much more meaningful and relevant to my development as a clinical psychologist than the diagnostic information would have been about Eric.

ADDRESSING THE SIGNIFICANCE OF SELF-OBSERVATION IN CLINICAL LEARNING

> I do not share the belief of many psychoanalysts that the most valuable things in psychoanalysis can be learned. They can only be experienced. . . . Nothing that does not originate in an experience can become an experience for others. (Reik, 1956, p. 264)

My interpretation of Reik's quotation was that an important part of learning about psychoanalysis should come from a curriculum that addresses not just intellectual and conceptual models. His belief was that the experience of one's own therapy is foundational in the development and enhancement of one's own self-reflection capacities. However, as therapists, we also know there are particular self-observing skills that also can benefit from training in targeted self-observations.

Preliminary challenges for the graduate and postgraduate therapist: the absence of recordings and the need for independent, observing skills in professional practice. Zimmerman (2005) noted the following: "Few teachers effectively prepare students to learn on their own" (p. 69). The reason for the significance of this quote is that there is a special need for students to develop self-supervision skills as they move into independent practice, which doesn't usually provide the supervisory network with a strong training structure presented in graduate programs. Postgraduates in independent practice and in particular graduate training settings do not routinely allow the recording of psychotherapy sessions.

This loss of outside supervisory presence is one that is not usually discussed explicitly in graduate programs. However, psychoanalytically oriented faculty do frequently include those skills in particular courses and psychotherapy seminars. The actual presence of opportunities that are available in a range of teaching activities has potential to deepen student self-reflection that is part of what is typically addressed in many graduate programs. Rather, the implicit assumption is that a skill such as self-reflection will primarily be promoted in individual therapy and less valued as a graduate learning task that can be transitioned into postgraduate practice.

The following chapters are in part designed to concentrate on instructional tasks that can make such a transition more complete in the domain of self-observation. Zimmerman and Bandura (1994) reinforce an attached and implicit problem: "One of the fundamental aspects of self supervision is to get oneself to do it. . . . This means mobilizing and listening and sustaining one's instructional efforts" (p. 845).

Zimmerman and Bandura's reminder is to alert the readers to the resistance and ambivalence in graduate students, who are overwhelmed with the pressures of program demands and instructor expectations. All faculty engaged in such graduate education are well familiar with this understandable reality for students. In these problem contexts, the instructional tasks would benefit from conceptualizing the integration of self-observing skills throughout a program curriculum. In doing so, I am hypothesizing that engagement of students and recognition in the value of these instructional and curricular tasks will, in part, be carried into postdoctoral practice, whatever it might be.

FIRST TASK: COLLECTING DATA

These chapters are devoted to guiding instructors in facilitating a basic professionalizing value. In pursuing this focus, the students first must acquire the clinical data necessary for subsequent observations of the self and the patient. It is important to find motivation, time, and meaningful ways for doing so, given the occasional absence of qualified instructors and supervisors and a recorded transcript or video of an actual session. In these contexts, the therapist then might rely on the notes taken during a session. As many analytically oriented therapists have noted, this tactic is not necessarily desirable as it may foreclose on a sense of openness in the session and be distracting the therapist's focus on the self and the patient.

In order to acquire the clinical data necessary for self-observation, it is important to find time and ways for doing so in simply remembering the material, given the absence of the usual recording supports in postgraduate private practice settings. In those contexts the therapist might have to rely on the notes taken during a session (not necessarily desirable in terms of the therapy relationship and a potentially distracting focus in the process). Or, most might choose to recall the session after its completion, when there are hopefully no distractions. Add to these conflicts, the rich debate over taking minimal or no notes, with the concern about having a biased perspective around the upcoming session. However, such a biased perspective would also benefit from some post-session observations, unless one is a particular kind of psychoanalyst or therapist.

It is clear that the absence of recording data is a loss for accessing detailed exchanges. It is likely that most private practice or postgraduate clinical settings may not emphasize the producing of complete and reflective notes in the absence of available supervisory personnel. It would seem that therapists' motivation for doing so in the face of a busy individual or private practice setting might not prioritize serious note taking, even when there might be a professional need to do so. In those contexts, one purpose of this series of chapters is to both evoke more interest in creating self-supervisory and reflective notes and learn a process of self-supervision in the absence of outside supervisors or consultants. It is an attempt to find ways to recall and self-reflect on the part of the student and postgraduate practitioner, and shift a mildly reluctant attitude to one that promotes increased motivation in creating an expanded vision of the therapeutic relationship.

In that context, I believe that the education of analytically oriented therapists should include what an experiential component is, as Reik (1956) suggests. In order to achieve such exposure, many programs require students undergo personal psychotherapy. I would add that in addition to that personal experience, programs should include a range of activities that promote self-reflection. Such instruction can be enhanced by learning tasks in which the instructor provides experiential teaching opportunities from which to help therapists find a meaningful and immediate grasp of the patient.

The channels through which these teaching connections can be found are topics centering on the facilitation and enhancement of the "observing self" of the student-therapist. This focus then organizes the direction of reviewing clinical transcripts and notes in the graduate program setting. It also implements training topics through which an instructor may evoke the identifications and emergence of clinically relevant self-knowledge in the student-therapist. In that sense, the following instructional and curricular perspectives are a representation of how a focus on therapist self and patient observations can be integrated into instructional tasks and course emphases.

This focus is already implemented in some therapy courses and seminars in which there is a heavy emphasis on engaging student affective reactions to a portion of a recorded session. The learning model is organized around developing a conceptualization that is derived from a seminar process of transcript and case review. That conceptualization is derived from the observation of themes of student self-observations. This emphasis on the value of such self-observations, and their use in developing a formulation, has been employed successfully in terms of faculty seminar teaching.

In that context and in the example just cited, a main purpose of the section devoted to teaching is to provide models for broader student learning activities within the clinical curriculum. These models would be designed to provide self-focused reflective exercises attached to the graduate educational experience. The goal here is to find extended options for student self-reflections on program-related experiences and subsequent development of extended self-awareness around such options. Teaching approaches of the clinical instructors draw on certain goals embedded in the course materials and processes that reflect analytic thinking. For example, the instructor's exploratory emphases on teaching and supervising present a type of clinician instructor figure model for our students. The clinical instructor can then be viewed as a figure that models certain exploratory qualities of a psychoanalytically oriented clinician in a range of course topics and assignments.

An example: Students were asked to reflect on their practicum experiences. Some said they were not satisfied and had a resistant attitude around certain supervisors. The instructor posed the possibility that the students might also explore the particular meanings of their reactions and judgments as well as the institutional stresses within the practicum sites. Were there other factors operating in their reactions that might enlarge their scope of understanding?

A TEACHING GOAL AND METHODOLOGY

Bruno Bettelheim (to employ him once again) once said to a child care worker, who had just presented a troubling episode with a disturbed adolescent: "Don't tell me what you made of it, just tell me what you observed." Theodore Reik (1956) amplified this statement when he wrote: "It is the problems already solved that present the most numerous and difficult problems to the inquirer" (p. 327). Both of these remarks actually echoed a fundamental teaching methodology in terms of accessing the depth of clinical processing in psychotherapists' experience though repeated observations.

Therefore, I begin with discussing various methods through which students can learn to enhance their observing skills. The idea here is that once student-therapists identify such observations, they are then able to reflect on them. And part of our observing requires we guide students in their quest to engage this process by engaging their curiosity. Bettelheim had abruptly asked for me first to observe my motivation with my patient, as opposed to just conceptualizing his pathology. While I initially had to cope with his surprising and sudden way of confronting me, his goal was to move me into a self-observing position. He ultimately helped me to see what, in part, motivated my agitation with my patient, a critical instructor task. That very concentrated focus opened me to a range of subsequent impacts on my supervisor/consultant role in addressing supervisor and peer-generated elements of countertransference reactions.

Teaching targets accessing the self-experience of the student-therapist. As noted earlier, one major focus in these chapters is on accessing students' inner reactions in response to patient behavior within a graduate training context. However, by expanding this process beyond clinical observations, students can enhance their development of observational skills by enlisting a wider range of targets. This expansion can broaden and deepen the development of student professional skills by widening the range of instructional targets in the exploration of their inner reactions to institutional experiences.

However, with respect to the clinical arena, a first essential instructor step is that students identify a clear problem area or topic on which to concentrate their explorations. This initial definition then draws from the students' question and concerns. This step is where problem definition can start as students begin their study before a clear problem and data focus is established. As Bettelheim noted, first observe before formulate. My own experience includes my having to remind my students in my seminars (when they start moving away from the data) to "look at the transcript." This shift can focus them on the data. For example, a student was disturbed by a particular patient's direct provocations in a prior session. She was initially overwhelmed by the experience and also critical of the intensity of her reaction. The instructor then requested a look at some specific exchanges between her and her client.

What was discovered was that the communications of the patient were both attacking and apologetic and indicated a need for a type of attachment to the student. The emergence of these observations shifted the student's initially angry and self-protective attitude toward her client toward one of interest and curiosity and less defensiveness going forward in her relationship.

In this instance, I am suggesting the first task is to focus on the activation of a goal and problem definition in identifying clinical targets. The aforementioned student first stated her problem in terms of the patient's attacking behavior toward her. Exploration of her reactions by the seminar followed, expanding her view of herself in relation to the patient. This was then shifted to an exploration of the actual data that captured additional exchanges between her and her patient. This was a general but important seminar process in terms of shifting from a conceptually focused approach to a data-driven approach, thus altering the student's understanding of the patient's actual ambivalence about the therapist.

In this context, it was noted that the therapist had a dual institutional role with her client, which expanded the implications of this exchange and the particular pressures on the therapist. A process then was engaged, which went beyond just the clinical elements. I shall note that this seminar process grew into reflections on the roles of students in particular practicum settings. The seminar immediately was able to connect to the theme of work, with supervisors working in sites with mixed missions and populations.

This expanding of such targets requires the instructors of therapy courses and seminars to design a range of topics as part of class readings, exam foci, experientially directed assignments, and observations of particular curricular and learning experiences. These targets are directed to ways to stimulate and then discuss student reactions and reflections around these learning tasks. These observations would also include seminar instructor follow-up, which extends these conversations between the instructors and their students. This particular step then opens up a second tier of observations and reflections regarding further thoughts between students and instructor as to implications of their first wave of observations.

In that context, teaching targets will address a range of these courses, instructor-instruction, and training activities that both extend and deepen a student's reflective repertoire. The students and instructor then are not just engaging in those learning tasks. For example, the goals in these instances are not only to expose students to the clinical and conceptual content addressed in practicum responsibilities but also to step back. The task is then to discuss and review their reactions to the practicum setting itself as it impacts student learning in that context.

More specifically, students might also have assignments and evaluations calling for their reflections and critiques of specific aspects of a course or seminar. This would include the particular meanings of the learning experiences in both academic and clinical domains. The written assignments and questions around these particular topics would provide for the development of expanded and autonomous self-observing capacities that go beyond the content and clinical topics. As stated earlier, such a broader set of topics then allows for additional practice of observing the self around the wider dimensions of program.

In short, the utility of attending to this wider set of the aforementioned targets for such observational skill training is a way to repeatedly address the critical and central status of such underlying reflective processes in students. The goal of this approach is essentially to make students more self-aware of an undercurrent of inner observations across many domains, thus exercising the activation another tier of a self-exploratory process. The more pervasive application of these skills can extend internal observing skills. This extension can extend therapists' self-awareness, empathy, and understanding around their clinical responsibilities and within their clinical settings. These activities can help provide a deeper and richer meaning to clinical exchanges and to the professionalizing process.

The role of therapist resistance to an enhanced intra-session focus on self and patient. Irwin Hirsch (2008) has described analysts' frequent resistance to practice tasks such as note taking, review of notes, and reasonable schedules that allow for reflective note-taking time between sessions and therefore "*optimal patient involvement*" (p. 18, italics in original). Various themes of being busy and keeping a full practice head the list. In that context, it is important to consider these additional activities as also evoking not just the economic interests of the analytic community, but it may also relate in part to a reluctance to review their past sessions for concerns about being reminded of interventions that were unsuccessful, or conceptualizations that are not helpful.

As to students and new postgraduate therapists, the following observations as to how to address some of the problems stated earlier might be of help in improving their professional commitments to their patients. In that context, I am suggesting the following areas for further reflection and consideration in improving the quality of attention and treatment of our patients.

Instructor approaches: mindfulness perspectives. One element of the model of mindfulness practice is devoted to learning to become more self-observant and achieve a sense of calmness as well. In order to engage successfully in such practice, time is set aside each day for a practice period in meditation (Kabat-Zinn, 2005). It is the quiet, the stillness, and the repeated shifts between repeating a mantra and then getting absorbed and reabsorbed in our daily thoughts, and then catching ourselves to recover the mantra that heightens our self-awareness and our calm. This process results in an increasing awareness of the internal flow of thoughts and feelings that can become more apparent to the meditator. Such awareness is helpful, over time, in the enhancement of our capacity to observe ourselves and relevant to becoming a therapist.

The role of the instructor in encouraging the student's creation of the inner space in which to reflect and review clinical experience. This meditative model also emphasizes finding a quiet time and space alone or in a group. It is the nonjudgmental stance on recognizing all thoughts, particularly ones that are discrepant with our inner the self-image and our superego demands. It is that awareness and the ongoing struggle with the self-acceptance of those disturbing feelings and thoughts that provide a significant part of a teaching stance toward student observations.

Bollas (1987) provides his perspective on the inner attitude of therapists regarding the creation of an inner space connected to therapeutic listening.

> The evocative mental process occurs when the mind is receptive and at rest. Khan (1977) terms such rest "lying fallow," an accomplishment which as a form of tranquility is essential to the self-analytic function . . . (p. 240). Only by carefully nurturing and sustaining an internal mental space for the registration of his thoughts and feelings can such an analyst reliably provide additional clinical space for the analysand's transference usage. (p. 251)

The instructor in that context encourages the selective surfacing of those feelings and cognitions with an awareness of the essential need for students to be as open as possible as they self-reflect around their cases. However, it is important to note that there must be important boundaries in such teaching explorations to assure that such types of self-revelations are contained and appropriate to the situation under discussion. These observations must remain contained and confidential if the student so wishes. It is also the instructor's responsibility to communicate these boundaries to students, who sometimes might be unable to manage a reasonable range in their self-revelations.

The goal here is to direct attention to the students' self-recognition of around previously hidden thoughts (especially around their work with patients). This teaching position matters most in the students gaining increased acceptance of such discordant thoughts and feelings. It is that process of acceptance being highly valued by the instructor, whether disclosed or not, that constitutes a key communication from the instructor. This model of self-acceptance, instructor interest, and openness around such reactions, as well as interest in student reluctance to communicate their reactions as a fundamental part of instructor emphases, starts to build a safe setting for the students. And it is that sense of safety that permits and encourages the students' own receptivity to their own inner experience.

POST-SESSION I: SETTINGS FOR REFLECTIVE TIME

One part of this instructor course structuring might be to discuss the student creation of a temporal setting that can provide time and "space" for reflection and freedom from external distractions. The students' allocation of quiet space in their own busy schedules can add to the reflective space of a scheduled supervisor meeting time. In circumstances in which the student or postgraduate therapists cannot have early access to instant outside consultation or regular supervision when confronted by a difficult session, the creation of such protected external and internal time and setting for review can create an independent safe space. It can become a time and a structure during which time students may then reflect, without external distractions, on the just-completed session. Obviously, in true emergency situations, when immediate or emergency decisions must be made, students and postgraduate therapists must arrange for access to consultative figures. In short, when the need for external help is not severe, this autonomous space can be helpful in gaining perspective on the problem area. It is essentially where self-supervision can happen.

When in school, such space is automatically present in supervisory exchanges and in the creation of formulations and planning for assignments. Since this chapter attempts to address some settings and postgraduate settings when such education and training structures are not externally available or the student is not accountable for achieving such self-observing goals, there is no external pressure to review, reflect, and self-communicate in the life of the therapist.

In that context it is the internal pressure and instructor support for that structure that facilitate a deepened self-awareness in the graduate and postgraduate therapists.

Interestingly, actual conversations about claiming such reflective space in student and postgraduate practice are infrequent in doctoral programs despite the self-observing foundation such arrangements might provide for independent reflective activity. While students frequently cite they have too much to do, instructor valuing of how to find time and space can enter into a reflective versus tactical discussion about the use of time. This is not only about "time management," which is a valuable pursuit in itself. It is more about reflecting on time management and being curious as to negative student feelings about particular tasks that might play a role in their being overstretched.

It also can reflect on the lower priority on protecting and establishing such space. In approaching this issue, the instructor can empathically relate student reluctance to take notes post-session as a topic for discussion and exploration. This resistance around creating and maintaining such time can be seen as a partly dynamic process. The value of exploring therapist reluctance can transfer to empathizing with a patient reluctance to attend sessions regularly. The potential for a greater appreciation of the patient's avoidant motives may come from an appreciation of one's own reluctances to self-observe around one's participation in a problematic therapeutic exchange.

For example, is the difficulty around claiming reflective time for oneself only about the amount of student responsibilities, or is there also a subtle reluctance to engage in such a self-review process? As is obvious, this question addresses the entry of a dynamic component into such a discussion. Student feedback in my individual and seminar meetings has indicated a recognition that there are anxieties about observing themselves or recalling painful moments if they do create a self-observing space. They acknowledge worrying about how they will appear to themselves and the instructor, or survive possible guilt and shame around a particular interaction with a patient.

Such a seminar or individual discussion then can be part of exploring student difficulties in finding time for what might feel like a painful or unproductive task. This type of focus can identify the value of observing one's reluctance versus saying "I am too busy." As can be seen, a safe learning climate and a trust in the instructor are then foundational in creating conditions for such topics to be discussed with an instructor.

Without establishing a time or physical setting for quiet or written reflection, doctoral and postgraduate students likely sacrifice the chance to access their inner world in ways that can advance the type of discoveries that come with reflective time and space. And, as stated earlier, they also sacrifice gaining an empathic view of their difficult patients with parallel resistances. Primarily, the deeper dynamics of this reluctance to create and sustain such a portion of time affects the establishment of a post-session reflective window for therapists attempting to access memories of a session on their own. What I would add here is the frequent lack of program expectation or interest in encouraging such types of sequestered time for those in settings where this process is not necessarily required.

Later in this chapter, this topic of autonomously created reflective space will be addressed in a discussion about the importance of note taking in the absence of session recordings, most especially when our students enter postgraduate practice settings.

Teaching methodology in the development of self-observing skills: tracking exchanges in the therapist–patient relationship. Another instructor's teaching focus is to introduce the students to the application of a tracking methodology that can be applied to observations of the therapeutic experience. This methodology is what can be internalized and practiced in the students' individual reflective space.

The model of this careful observation of the therapeutic interaction is, in part, derived from the observations of infant–mother exchanges (Beebe & Lachmann, 2002). It can also draw from the "moving on" perspectives of Daniel Stern (2004) in the tracking progression of patient and therapist exchanges in a therapy session.

The application of this tracking approach to a transcript is a way of understanding the underlying dynamics embedded in the therapist reactions in the conversation flow of a particular session. In addition, these types of sequential observations are modeled by the instructor's process for examining the impacts of each figure on the other. Such exploration modes can help unpack the onset and resolution of particular therapeutic events at a minute-by-minute scrutiny.

In this context, the instructor draws on the availability of the therapists' inner space (quiet, reflective time) to support the presence of a mindful perspective on tracking the clinical exchanges without judgment. The communication of curiosity and receptivity is part of the therapists' role in furthering a safe relationship with their students. Most particularly, it is the nonjudgmental capturing of free-flowing thoughts and ideas that can provide a type of image of the instructor's nonjudgmental stance that can surround this perspective. It is, in fact, the self-accepting component of the meditational perspective that can help frame the students' acceptance of aspects of their own experience and those of their patients. All clinical instructors and supervisors are well familiar with the hypercritical self-judgments of students as a part of their immediate recognition of a "mistake" or a disruption in the therapy relationship.

In using the opportunity that the safe individual space provides, students may then enhance their access to their underlying thoughts. These thoughts may play a critical role in understanding the therapeutic interaction. Specifically, the instructor attempts to create a safe space for students and their patients through a modeling of curiosity and interest in the students' clinical material. The goal is to make available a gradual identification of the student with the instructor's or supervisor's ways of relating to the student-therapist. As noted earlier, the instructors' personal attitudes of interest, receptivity, and attentiveness that are relevant to the work with the student can be applied to similar attitudes of the student in an extended supportive and empathic instructor/supervisory presence with the patient.

It is important to note that much of what is defined as a "safe" supervisory or instructional space comes with the personality of the instructor, who has specific personality qualities that reinforce the provision of acceptance along with the presence of the aforementioned features. Students, of course, are highly attuned to these aspects of the instructor. It must also be added that a core element in this relationship is a transference to the person of the instructor.

Like a therapeutic relationship, the transference can account both for the students' positive or negative reactions to an instructor and for the potential countertransference in the instructors' response to such reactions to their students. Within those domains, the ways in which the instructor is understanding of the early student anxieties, self-doubt, and perfectionistic tendencies can confirm or modify the nature of the transference to the instructor.

In light of the preceding discussion, mutual awareness of these emotional factors can be linked to instructor–student relationships in a classroom or supervisor's office. Class discussion and observation of these factors can help students to see the relevance of these dynamic concepts as they impact their relationships with their individual teachers. It can be noted that the tracking of such experiences with the instructor (particularly after intense reactions are in evidence in both parties) can reveal the presence of transference and countertransference experiences on both sides. For example, all instructors can relate to the occasionally demanding or "entitled" accusatory student who requests special favors around particular assignments. In this context, the encouragement of student self-observations (with those that can self-observe) and revelations in terms of their own associations can help the management of both student reactions and those of the instructor.

In a sense, this type of tracking process mirrors the fundamental rule in psychodynamic therapy that tells the patient to say what "comes to mind." The implication here is that the student-therapists will feel safe in reporting their own reactions as they attempt to capture the flow of their reactions within a safe therapeutic and supervisory exchange. For these reasons, such selective openness is important as a strong part of both the teaching and the therapy approaches of the therapist.

Quite simply, the invitation for the instructor to observe both the self and the student can generate the emergence of an associative network that can yield important findings for the student-therapists if they are receptive to their inner thoughts and feelings. That is why helping the students to establish a settled, reflective, and receptive stance and inner space is conducive to a more extensive and useful set of inner reactions.

At this point, the impact of the instructor's attitudes on student learning can help to model and create a type of "clinical process" embedded in the structuring of the course. I am not suggesting that these types of discussions during class or seminar times become a "therapy" hour. Rather, I am suggesting that there are parallel goals and processes in both domains that can be approached in a bounded fashion, where the focus in on the immediate contexts of the course versus the students' personal histories. I would add here that there are occasional references to prior learning challenges relevant to the students's current anxieties. These general disclosures can also start a student's private pursuit toward addressing these historical learning problems.

As noted earlier, the clinical instructor can model a relevant and selective "clinical" process in the structuring of class time, class discussions, class assignments, student evaluations, and individual meetings with the students. Basically, this process would include instructor interest in and follow-ups with the students, encouraging further articulation of their reactions to a range of topics in the course structure and teaching processes. Obviously, by engaging in this process, students will be exercising this observing process. In those contexts, the parallel processes of inquiry, interest, and exploration that characterize an instructor–student exchange can be selectively and strategically transposed onto the ranges of student approaches to therapy relationships.

POST-SESSION II: NOTE TAKING

As mentioned earlier, one structural location for self-reflection space is post-session time. This space can be used by students who are engaged in the note-taking process. In most cases, students are frequently under time pressure and unable to devote significant time to therapy notes. It is clear that students must meet the mandated notes required by a particular site. However, these notes, while significant, do not necessarily include instructor self-observations because of legal concerns. However, the fact is there is actually nothing to constrain more journal like notes, which record the therapists' individual reflections and observation of the underlying concerns as they record their notes. Such notes are private personal process notes versus those that record attendance, topics of discussion, and foundations for decision making and recommendations for the patient in an agency or private practice setting.

As a part of introducing more peripheral and underlying student observations of self and patient into their learning experiences, a seminar group discussion addressed student reactions to the process of post-seminar or class note taking. Typically, the reaction was one of "no time" unless it was a product of required note taking. However, the process of more engaged note taking can open yet another door to a more mindful and increased observation skills use of this often onerous and marginalized task. Lifting this element to the surface of explicit note-taking activities is especially important in particular situations, such as limited graduate training site and postgraduate private practice supervisory structures.

More specifically, instructor assignments related to note taking might communicate an open model of not just recalling crucial details in a session but also inviting the active expression of inner thoughts when reflecting on a just-completed session. This type of general assignment can help to reinforce the inner coexistence of recovered memories and associations to those memories of the session. The goal is that the process is, in part, to use the notes (for therapist only) to encourage and stimulate an approach to an inclusion of spontaneous reactions and observations and associations to critical therapeutic moments as they are remembered in the note-taking process.

In this context, a goal of such sequestering of post-session time and process for note taking is also to lift the self-censorship and endorse a structure that emphasizes the safety of reflecting freely in the process of note taking with this particular model. This type of an instructional view of the students' note-taking self-reflections is parallel to the instructor's encouragement to deepen student-therapist's self-exploration in the process of doing the notes.

There are a number of studies of the effectiveness of note-taking models that can help increase self-awareness in students and postgraduate students. These studies of college students note taking in or outside of class can inform discussion of the role of such modes of note taking in the further development of a mindfulness gained through the process of thoughtful notes and summaries in post-session reflective time. There are a number of studies that address these potential factors, and several on the generative role of the note-taking implications for the student and postgraduate therapists (Kierwa, 1989; Muller & Oppenheimer, 2014).

An addition to the general note-taking considerations is an observation that college students doing handwritten notes when tested comparing in-class versus post-class retention appeared to do better than the in-class note takers (Peper & Mayer, 1978). Another study (Muller & Oppenheimer, 2014) found that handwritten notes, while slower, were also more easily remembered than computer notes. Therefore, while more notes could be recorded with the computer model, they apparently did not have the staying power of the handwritten version.

While there are clearly good reasons for computer note taking, the aforementioned observations are worth noting. The advantage of written note taking was cited when evaluating the greater attentive immersion in the topics because the actual handwriting slowed down the recall and expressive process versus the more-rapid typing process, which, as noted earlier, did create more information. Muller and Oppenheimer recognized the influence of the pen over assistive writing technology in observing note taking outcomes from the two approaches. In such note taking, the beneficial role of written summaries might facilitate the greater integration of thought into understanding the patient and self in relation to the patient. The observations made in the Peper and Mayer (1978) article reinforced the possible advantage of the generative activity of written notes, which might all relate to improvement in the therapist's retention and engagement with the session being recalled.

Pennebaker and Smyth (2016) have written about the value of various forms of writing, as it has the benefit of articulating and expressing one's thoughts and inner reactions around traumatic events. When beneficial, it seems clear that the process of externalizing internal processes allows for greater awareness and capacity to accept and also reflect on such unspoken feelings.

Again, the main point here is not necessarily the value of handwriting but the underlying need to put time into one's notes whether written or typed. The purpose is to go slow enough to allow for the emergence of associations and ideas as the notes are being written. This post-session "safe space" concept, which includes the opportunity for written note taking, can be seen as a part of addressing the importance of developing a parallel "inner space." The space in which therapist thoughts and affects can be internally observed and reflected upon after the session could then be seen as an extended part of the therapist–patient encounter. As noted earlier, the instructors' and supervisors' encouraging attitude toward the therapists' written self-revelations can then be echoed in the students' stance toward their patients.

This extended note-taking model is intended to facilitate the establishment of an inner openness in the student-therapist. The deeper empathy coming from these self-exploratory models can add to a sense of professional commitment to the patient. Quite simply, these processes act on developing a real therapist commitment to their patients. This happens as these types of reflective activities can also provide a backdrop as the therapists recognize and accept their own conflicts in reflecting on their reactions to their patients. This capacity to experience their inner clinically focused lives in these written notes helps the students to then gain the inner experience with which to employ the empathy that has been experientially learned as a bridge to understanding their patients.

POST-SESSION III: RECOVERY OF CRITICAL EXCHANGES

In order to effectively collect the data from a therapy session, therapists most often begin the recovery of critical exchanges and themes after completion of the hour or later in the day. However, while it is best done after a given session, it can still be effective on the same day when the experience is fresh. This recovery and reflection is clearly a product of patient communications, student and graduate therapists' memory, the setting, and timing mode of the note taking. When too much time intervenes between session and notes, memories and access to one's own affect can diminish and valuable perceptions can be partly lost.

The range of delay between the session and note taking can also vary depending on the therapists' memory, therapy goals, professional schedules, clinical urgency, and institutional and clinical pressures. In those contexts, the goals of the note-taking experience are important to identify. For purposes of this chapter, the critical linkage is the contribution of note taking and note reviewing to the therapists' growth in self-observing skills and sense of professionalization. As noted earlier, this activity can heighten the therapists' ability to be sensitized to certain triggers that can occur at certain critical moments in future challenging sessions. It may depend on the number and quality of the reviews of the therapist as well.

In short, the question is how to use the note-taking activity as a way to increase therapist self-awareness and knowledge about the patient and the self in the therapeutic relationship. Again, this is most significant when the therapist is operating without regular consultation or actual recordings of the session. However, the answer to the preceding question clearly depends on the priorities and goals of the therapist, including preparation for eventual consultations, next appointments, or enhancement of understanding of patients and self. The notes may then include capsule summaries, specific charged events, critical observations of countertransference reactions, and revised conceptualizations of the case.

These approaches may then also include reporting and commenting on sequences and exchanges with particularly challenging patients. In those contexts, therapists might likely note session challenges, disruptions, self-experiences, attitudes toward the patient, evaluations of the treatment, anticipations of upcoming concerns, and detailed memories of the beginning and end of the session. While such a list can be endless, it is the increased awareness of particular hidden observations now coming to light that advantages the therapists' expanded attitudes toward their patients.

One recommendation for the graduate therapist is to find time to review the notes, spread over a period of intra-session time. The final step in this process is a review of the notes before the next session. This activity is meant not to create an agenda for the session but to have activated the prior observations noted in the previous session. In doing so, such memories remain within reach if they appear in the patient's material. In short, this process of presession review is more for the sake of latent access than for preplanning. It is a type of priming for the future appointments rather than as a planning function, although at certain times it could serve that purpose as well. In other words, the capturing of problematic and unsuccessful interventions in such a review can also help the therapist to respond more reflectively to similar communications in the patient's upcoming session.

As such, one major issue is the process by which the therapist gains an understanding of the patient in a moment-to-moment (vs. step-by-step) way. What are the observational stages and processes (not necessarily sequential) through which a therapist proceeds to achieve a level of empathy that will produce a strong understanding of the patient? What is the connection between the identified introspective processes of expert therapists and those revealed in a microanalysis of a therapeutic interaction? These questions will be discussed following the presentation of clinical material. The focus will include the inclusion of specific inner reactions to patients within a therapeutic exchange. It is a part of understanding how one "gets to empathy."

POST-SESSION IV: FURTHER BENEFITS FROM THE NOTE-TAKING EXPERIENCE

A highly significant offshoot of this revised note taking is the activation of a stronger therapist commitment to understanding the patient. In that context, the increased commitment and curiosity that comes with the time devoted to the more extensive note taking is rewarded in the patients' manifest or latent awareness of the therapists' level of interest, curiosity, and increased sensitivity in their experiencing the therapists' renewed energy and engagement in the following sessions. In those contexts, therapists most likely can reflectively note challenges, disruptions, self-experience, attitudes toward the session, evaluations of the treatment, anticipations of upcoming concerns, and detailed memories of the beginning and end of the session. Again, the list can be endless, and for that reason the therapist also needs to recognize a range of topics and intra-session events to consider that are important to remember and describe, and what might not be immediately available for immediate recall.

The significance of micro-analytic approaches to exploring self-observation processes in teaching from transcript exemplars. Before applying a micro-analytic approach to the clinical material, a word of explanation for use of this model is in order. Frequently, students question the value of focusing on limited therapeutic exchanges. Daniel Stern writes: "Life between people is directly lived at a relatively small sale: a sentence, a pause, a facial expression, a gesture, a feeling, a thought. Of course can be strung together and assembled into overarching units" (Daniel Stern, 2004, p. 149).

Course assignment to engage the direct self-observations of students: a take-home examination assignment focused on the students' self-experience of a mock problematic exchange and a model of integrating the self-observational emphasis into an examination context. This section represents a description of an assignment of a student set of self-observations, working on a micro-analytic approach (cf. Daniel Stern, pp. 157, 234–235). I will apply this model to an assignment in my course in psychoanalytic therapy. The outline of the assignment requires student attention to the moment-by-moment exchanges and inner reactions to these exchanges. I note that this assignment that incorporates real-life events into this transposed vignette is a product of our curriculum that does not introduce the analytic psychotherapy model until the second year in the curriculum, one year earlier than when the psychotherapy practicum is introduced, when students have real patients. For that reason, most students cannot access a real therapy case to discuss in light of the model presented in the analytic course until the third year. Because of that delay, I constructed a mock therapy assignment using the student as therapist interacting with a partner transposed into a therapy exchange: a real-life situation with a real person (who would be seen as the client) and the student who would be the therapist. This was based on the recall of a problematic situation that occurred versus a role play of such a situation.

A list of critical questions addressing the details of the assignment were presented to the students. They were to select a situation in which a difficult situation grew worse, presenting it as a therapy exchange, with the student being therapist and the colleague, partner, spouse, salesman, and so on being viewed as a patient. Students were expected to recall enough of a particular episode to create a transcript, with therapist's (students) reactions to a set of comments actually made by the patient (friend, spouse, etc.). They were then to respond to the micro-analytic structure by inserting their inner thoughts and reactions to the "patient's" evocative comments or behaviors as expressed in a transcript form.

The goal here was to provide a sample of an uncensored, self-observing experience in the students' real life to a mock therapy context. The mode of addressing the exchange by employing the instructions included encouragement to make their written reaction commentaries uncensored. This assignment, then, was to help students to develop and experience the type of self-observations characteristic in the work of experienced therapists. I asked for feedback as part of this examination in terms of what the students learned. What was most interesting was the fact that a high majority of students who completed this exercise found it generating insight and open up a broader understanding of the presence of latent reactions to themselves and their "clients." In that way they were introduced to the experience of self-reflection and its value in psychotherapy. This could be seen as a model for self-supervision in terms of their therapy experience in the years ahead.

This topic of accessing countertransference through self-reflection will continue to be discussed in chapter 9. As noted earlier, that chapter will include focus primarily on studying expert therapists' self-observing processes as they recognized the emergence of their countertransference reactions in their self-reflections. The self-reflection process leading toward and away from and finally toward a recognition of those reactions in their transcripts can be a teaching target for the instructors in those contexts.

Part of the instructions and course perspectives around accessing self-reflections include not only the instructor's direct teaching but also the tracking model expressed in the instructor's teaching methodology. This image of the instructor's approach to transcript material can be observed in several distinct micro-analytic and tracking approaches to the listening, reflecting, and intervening processes that constitute particular phases of the therapeutic process. For example, most helpful in learning how therapists experience psychotherapy includes ways in which therapists explore therapy exchanges side by side with their own self-reflections as presented in selective written transcripts. This process is a portrait of the sequence of therapist inner conversations and speculations through the progression of a session.

The instructor's goal is to expose students to what therapist self-tracking looks like in the capturing of specific therapists' inner thoughts and reactions during intensive countertransference experiences. In that context, the student is introduced to a self-experience of countertransference discovery, which exposes the student-therapist to a major dynamic insightful experience. Class and seminar observations about the same processes presented examining the sequence of inner exemplar observations can be another way for the clinical instructor to then demonstrate self-observation to student-therapists.

The post-session tracking of these inner processes can be focused on transcripts or close descriptions of exchanges. The attention to shifts in reflection focus can then be observed and modeled in the exemplars' self-observing work of experienced analysts. The instructor and student challenge is then to locate what happens in a sequence as it displays an important pattern of patient interpersonal functioning. These observations can help provide some guidance to the instructor and the student-therapist in thinking about the particulars of the exchanges by both therapist and patient and getting acquainted with the concept of countertransference in the therapists' inner and interventional observations. In these contexts, the learning here is a product of the instructors' specific, micro-analytic focus on the critical exchanges in both the student and expert therapists' transcript analyses and the student's actual associated reactions to such exchanges.

COUNTERTRANSFERENCE AWARENESS: A TEACHING MODEL TO INCREASE THERAPIST AWARENESS AND THE MEANING OF THE THERAPEUTIC INTERACTION

Many analytically oriented instructor and supervisor discussions about the uses of countertransference and the value of therapist self-awareness have, at times, assumed that student-therapists have already developed the intuitive capacities with which to access disturbing internal reactions to their patients. While there is some truth to this assumption, it does not necessarily preclude the importance of supplementing this foundation with teaching student-therapists a focused and systematic method of recognizing the presence of countertransference as a way of understanding different aspects of the therapy relationship.

While these natural introspective capacities are addressed optimally in individual/personal therapy, supervision, consultation, and/or continuing education, the absence of such a singular focus on particular countertransference experiences in certain settings and in private practice indicates the value of having an independent method for working with countertransference. This focus is especially critical when there is a stalemate or interpersonal crisis in the patient–therapist relationships. In this context I am proposing a more focused attention to the therapists' ability to identify, process, and intervene in ways that reflect the presence of countertransference memory and understanding. This awareness might provide the instructor with an additional and specific guide in building on established introspective skills.

This use can be relevant to understanding the therapeutic relationship and moving toward a resolution of an impasse. This chapter has already offered a way of accessing inner thoughts, derived from close-process monitoring (tracking and micro-analytic processes) of the therapy interaction. This approach can provide a range of focused introspective processes for observing and understanding the emergence of therapeutic impasses. This range helps to build a teaching model for working with countertransference in subsequent chapters.

In addressing the question of accessing and defining critical goals as a specific countertransference observation, researchers (e.g., Gelso & Hayes, 2007; Robbins & Jolkovski, 1987) identified factors such as levels of self-insight, anxiety management, empathy, and conceptualizing skills as related to effective management of countertransference. In order to identify these factors, this research was conducted asking therapists to define the presence of these qualities in expert therapists. While these factors were found to correlate with a reported reduction in the intensity of countertransference responses, the therapists' ability to successfully identify and work through their specific countertransference processes within or following disruptive therapy exchanges was not a part of this research.

Chapter 8

Additional Perspectives on Instructional Models of Teaching Self-Observation

> *Perhaps there is a universal here which applies to us all, the lesson also taught by Socrates, Freud, Proust—that a life, a human life, is not a life until is examined; that it is not a life until it is truly remembered and appropriated; and that such remembrance is not something passive, but active, the active and creative construction of one's life, the finding and telling of the true story of one's life.* (Sachs, as cited in Luria, 1987, p. xvii)

This chapter continues to identify additional models and perspectives that offer further options focused on teaching this essential skill to graduate students and postgraduate practitioners. I do so because therapeutic stalemates require additional therapist awareness beyond that required of less acutely upsetting experiences.

THE ROLE OF SUCCESSIVE OBSERVATIONS

These tentative guidelines would focus on the possible uses of successive observations of the therapeutic impasse in selected therapy exchanges. If there is outside supervision, that can be one source of successive observations. If the therapist works privately or has no ready consultant available, this independent process can then provide additional guidance, which is a potential product of this level of more detailed self-observations. In short, the utility of this process focus also serves to promote greater openness in the minds of therapists as they encounter therapeutic stalemates or enactments. The exemplars presented in the following chapter are, in effect, a demonstration of how the independent self-observing process might ideally unfold. It can be an approach that builds on the processes described thus far in these chapters. Its goal is to guide therapist awareness of the self and evoke heightened attention to the patient's experience of the therapist.

This last focus on the patient's reaction to a specific therapist behavior or comment can help to open up an additional perspective. This can be quite meaningful if it was these therapist reactions to the patient that led up to the stalemate or enactment factors in the exchanges. Theoretically, these could be episodes when the therapist is unable to contain the projective elements of a prior patient communication. In addition, the process of moving from immersion in the projective exchange to one of observing that exchange is a most important part of this discussion. The close and repeated observations of available interactional material with associated elaborations can help therapists to discover and observe the insights required in these impasses.

PSYCHODYNAMIC PHASE MODELS: ACCESSING COUNTERTRANSFERENCE AND RESOLVING IMPASSES WITH THE PATIENT

While quantitative studies, noted earlier, have identified expert therapist qualities that optimize countertransference management, there have also been descriptive models (e.g., Safran & Muran, 2000; Tansey & Burke, 1989) of process and intervention analyses in accessing and managing countertransference reactions within and following a session. These models might be defined as phase-focused, attempting to provide a general tracking approach to the process of impasse resolution in actual clinical exchanges. It can be noted that such models implicitly draw on the works of Stern (2004), Beebe and Lachmann (2002), and others. Findings from extended and careful moment-to-moment observations of the infant–mother as well as patient–therapist interactions provide a model for therapeutic interactional analysis. The value of this micro-phase level of interactional observations is evident in the productive work in attachment research and in subsequent connections to the application of these approaches to the therapeutic interaction.

One such observational model applied to the therapeutic interaction, proposed by Safran and Muran (2000), described a series of stages which offer a "resolution model for withdrawal ruptures" (pp. 142–149). The following stages are identified in this process: "Stage One: Withdrawal Marker," "Stage Two: Disembedded and Attending to the Rupture Marker," "Stage Three: Qualified Assertion," "Stage Four: Avoidance," and "Stage Five: Self-Assertion." In this model, Safran and Muran (2000) identified a type of intervention stage process to impasse resolution through therapist self-observations and metacommunications of his or her participation in the exchange. By internally defining and attending to "markers" of patient withdrawal, confrontation, and avoidance, therapists also gain further self-awareness as to the nature of their involvement around the triggers that activate these processes. In this context, awareness is enhanced through direct therapists' attention to the meanings of their responses to their patients.

Safran and Muran focused primarily on guiding the therapist through a series of interventions, initially attending to and then articulating internal processes, and suggesting ways to present those observations in metacommunications to the patient. Stages, then, are described primarily in terms of successive interactional strategies that emerge from patient and therapist behaviors, and include therapist observations of his or her immediate action and intervention inclinations. In one example (Safran & Muran, 2000, pp. 164–174), a description of several interactional sequences between patient and therapist demonstrates the types of specific self-disclosures the therapist makes in efforts to describe his or her reactions to the patient's challenging communications. These explicit disclosures of therapist confusion, sense of being maltreated, and feeling "stuck" are parallel to such reactions in therapists who do not disclose but observe those reactions within themselves as they attempt to find a way to articulate their discoveries from either interventions or altered understanding of their patients.

The Safran and Muran (2000) model does provide ways in which therapists might begin to access their countertransference reactions and interventions by using the concept of "rupture markers" to identify moments of rupture. The model then focuses on specific moments for therapist self-observations, which in themselves offer a point of entry into increasing the self-awareness of the therapist in relation to the patient. It also offers a range of recorded clinical data versus recalled data in the written accounts that further locates the key rupture moments in the exchange, with its goal a development of a very general road map for therapist interventions.

In contrast, Tansey and Burke (1989), in their phase model, focused primarily on the evolution of internal stages of awareness that eventually would culminate in an intervention to the patient. These stages are optimally observed to lead to a shift in the therapist's countertransference attitudes toward the patient and emergence of subsequently useful options for intervening. Their concept of phases and subphases through which greater awareness and movement toward impasse resolution are achieved is meant to be seen as a fluid rather than a rigidly stepwise process.

Tansey and Burke (1989) include the following subphases organized around reception, internal processing, and intervention. Subphase 1: Mental Set: Therapist "mental activity immediately before and during the session" (p. 72). Subphase 2: Interactional Pressure: "Therapist begins to experience the emotional pressure of patient's interactional communication" (p. 77). Subphase 3: Identification-Signal Affect: Therapist notices "modification of his self recognizing the signal affects emanating from within that alert him to the possibility that an identification has been made" (p. 82). Subphase 4: Containment-Separateness: "Therapist required to contain (Bion, 1959) and tolerate in consciousness his thoughts, feelings, and impulses having to do with himself, his patient, and their interaction" (pp. 85–86). Subphase 5: Working Model: "Therapist focusing separately on the self- and object representation components of the 'interactional introject'" (p. 88). Subphase 6: Empathic Connection: "First category involves a concordant (matching) identification in which the immediate self experiences of both participants are similar in some significant way, . . . the second category of interactional fit results from the patient's influencing the therapist to identify with an internalized object representation of the patient's as opposed to a self representation . . . the third category of interaction fit identification in the therapist . . . the third category of interactional fit involves elements that are both concordant (matching) and complementary (counter identification)" (pp. 94–95).

As such, one major emphasis in this model is the process by which therapists gain an understanding of the patient and in a fluid moment-to-moment versus step-by-step rigidified way. What are the internal observational stages and processes (not necessarily sequential) through which therapists proceed (sometimes back and forth) to achieve a level of empathy that will produce a stronger understanding of the patient? What is the connection between the identified introspective processes of expert therapists and those revealed in a microanalysis of a therapeutic interaction? These questions will be discussed in the next chapter following the presentation of clinical material demonstrating specific reactions to patients within a therapeutic exchange. It is a part of understanding how one "gets to empathy."

UNFORMULATED EXPERIENCE

Donnel Stern (1989) has written extensively on the elusive process of capturing "unformulated experience." His writings chronicle in some detail his own thought processes that led him to discoveries that were not available to him before he engaged in observing a series of internal observations in his retrospective recall of those reactions he had registered during the session. One of those processes will be demonstrated in chapter 9 when he works over a series of reactions to one of his patients, and discovered a meaning to what had formerly been overlooked, though Reik (1956) vividly addressed this same issue.

The focus on note-taking post-session is particularly suited for the search for the hidden meanings of patient and therapist exchanges. There are several important quotations here that can be part of discussing the importance of the recalling and reflecting processes in successive reviews of the completed session. By employing these quotes, the instructor can frame an elusive goal of finding previously hidden meanings in the patient's material. As the work of Pennebaker and Smyth (2016) makes clear, that writing is an essential route to enhanced self-understanding in a wide range of ways. The theme of the book not only addressed research into the positive effects on health and trauma, but many of the ideas were fundamentally demonstrating the value of written access to one's thoughts, whatever the context of the potential writer. As universally observed, many previously hidden ideas come to an individual involved in some general form of a writing exercise.

SUCCESSIVE OBSERVATIONS: THREE LOOKS

The importance of rereading as a foundation of real reading, of good reading, was described eloquently by Nabokov (1980). The particular theme of repetition in reviews is also echoed in a much-repeated "Fish Story" (Tierney, 1998, pp. 27–30) that describes a student who was told by an instructor to "carefully study a preserved fish from a jar. I will ask you later what you have learned." After several brief tries at conforming to the instructor's directions in which he either could not find the teacher or met up with the following response: "You have not looked very carefully. Why? You have not even seen one of the most conspicuous features of the animal . . . look again, look again." After reflecting further, he finally came into the laboratory and said: "Do you perhaps mean that the fish has symmetrical sides with paired organs?" The professor agreed and was pleased. Again, the student asked what he should do next, and the professor said "Look at the fish" and then left the room. The student did so with "renewed vigor and discovered one thing after another. 'Do you see it yet?' the professor asked." "No," replied the student. "I am certain I do not, but I see how little I saw before." This process played out and the student was asked to go home and look again. At that point the professor displayed a family of such fish, and the student understood the relationships between the fish and the family of fish. "Facts are stupid things until brought into connection with some general law."

I tell this story to demonstrate that this methodology is another source of process that is highly relevant to learning in a wide range of learning domains. This story can be articulated in a basic assignment for instructors to regularize "re-search" routine in a transcript history and review process. This expectation and its value can be easily inserted into the instructors' expectation for more extensive reception to and understanding of reactions in student presentations.

In the aforementioned contexts, I offer another general phase model that values the successive reviews of session material. I term the process a

"Three Looks" approach, which can be focused on the aforementioned and well-understood rationale that is basic to many different disciplines and even personal habits. In addressing the session material with the intent of three observations, I have found that performing all three of these successive looks is not easily achieved.

My essential purpose, however, is to identify a goal in the self-supervision processes of the student and experienced therapist. I recognize that sometimes such an expectation is unrealistic given the nature of practice demand. However, this well-understood process creates a vision and goal that can be achieved even if one applies such a model to one challenging patient a week. A subsidiary goal is the generalization of this repeated exercise of these looks, and the recognition that such return looks might also be selectively used sometimes in challenging cases. It is noted here that no one would disagree with this common practice for many. My purpose for saying the obvious is to refresh those activities that sometimes drift in the course of time (Hirsch, 2008).

As noted in the earlier example, the rationale behind these successive looks is one that acknowledges that significant meanings can accrue from revisiting the same material. What is often found in these revisits is material that has not been observed or has been dismissed from the therapist's central awareness. There is always an unconscious collection of items that are also disturbing to the therapist, which are also unconsciously ignored in the initial looks at the patient's commentary. Perhaps an apt metaphor can portray this mental process as planting a hook into the preconscious mind, and then the observational pulling up.

However, the significance of the first look is quite important. It is often more reactive than reflective in nature. However, therapists and other writers (Gladwell, 2005) also know that first impressions can also register important communications from patients. This is part of Reik's (1956) rationale for careful attention to the embedded knowledge hidden in certain first impressions or first communications in the session.

> And so we should pay attention to the first, hardly noticeable impressions that we receive of a person, however much they may soon be drowned by other, more insistent impressions. . . . First impressions may not be right, but they often contain true apprehensions in a distorted form. . . . The student is often taught to observe sharply and accurately what is presented to his conscious perception, but conscious perception is much too restricted and narrow. The student often analyzes the material without considering that it is so much richer . . . than what can be caught in the net of conscious observation. The small fish that escapes through the mesh is often the most precious. (p. 302)

In typical training settings, the second look is part of a preparation for supervision, as well as part of a discussion with the supervisor about the therapist's reactions to facets of the session material. This second look frequently captures the therapist's initial recognition of what was missed or marginalized in the first look. A beginning reconceptualization of what is important begins to emerge.

When the therapist is able to get to a third look, there is likely more available attention given to those patient comments or mood that appears to have more significance than initially thought. These observations might occur because in the multiple looks certain significant patterns emerge. This discovery of unconscious and preconscious patterns or themes then can be seen in the discovery phase of the recall, along with the observation of patterns and themes in the patient's presentation. The unpredictable and winding road to this discovery can only emerge from the preformulated domain after the revelation seen in the prior looks. Not infrequently, therapists are able to recall something about their prior participation in the relationship that provides a context for the session, whether it is a comment, a frame change, or an enactment. In short, these subsequent looks begin to access obscured data from the patient and therapist, formerly blocked in some fashion from therapist awareness (Stern, 1989).

So far, I have emphasized the value of capturing shadowy impressions, memories, and feelings through the note-taking process that includes both recall and reaction in the review process and the emergence of enhanced self-observations. At this point, the role of spoken observations will be reviewed. It constitutes another way of surfacing critical material that can be lost in the use of limited expressive domains.

The role of spoken self-exercises such as "imagined conversations" as a way of surfacing underlying countertransference experience. Arnd-Caddigan (2013) developed a study that asked practicing therapists to verbalize imagined conversations (IC) with their clients. These spoken conversations appeared to be successful in surfacing countertransference reactions formerly outside of the awareness of therapists.

> The participants in this study reveal that having ICs with clients between sessions is helpful in identifying and modulating negative feeling about the client or the treatment process. Some participants felt that the IC helped them to surface negative feelings that they had not previously identified. The most frequent response was that the IC helped the therapist prepare for a future conversation that they anticipated would be difficult. ICs appear to serve the function of helping the therapist modulate anxiety and center on the clients's needs rather than acting out a negative countertransference. (p. 8)

There were additional speculations as to the neurological implications related to the positive outcomes for the therapists in terms of greater self-awareness and higher sensitivity to the arousal of such reactions in future sessions with the client. The major point here is that this technique would appear to offer additional stimulation of therapist affective reactions and associations to the patient–therapist.

Casement (1991) has developed the concept of the "internal supervisor." He presents this concept as having certain elements. These items are useful in terms of spelling out a type of clinical target for therapists extending their reflective abilities. As part of employing this concept related to developing self-observing skills, Casement has identified earlier concepts such as inner "space" that has been used several times in this chapter to depict the therapists' conscious and unconscious collection of their own flows of self-observations.

> During the course of being supervised, therapists need to acquire their own capacity for spontaneous reflection within the session. They can thus learn to watch themselves as well as the patient, now using this island of intellectual contemplation as the mental space within which the internal supervisor can begin to operate. (p. 32)

TRIAL IDENTIFICATION

Going further Casement offers a direction for such reflections: "As part of the internal supervision that I am suggesting, I often find it helpful to use trial identification." This concept is derived from Fliess (1942) and is another way to articulate an immediate goal of reflective activity. One major purpose of this particular concept is directed toward the creation of empathy toward the patient.

> Now, when I use trial identification I do so in a number of different ways. I may, for example, think or feel myself into whatever experience is being described by a patient. I may also put myself into the shoes of the other person being referred to. From each of these viewpoints it is possible to pick up elements of the patient's object relating that might otherwise be missed. (p. 33)
>
> I first learned to monitor the therapeutic interaction in this way by trial identifying with the patient when following the clinical presentations of people whom I supervised. With practice it become possible to use these two viewpoints simultaneously, the patient's and one's own. (p. 33)

Casement goes on to mention how he discovered the internal supervisor when he identified a patient's reaction to a prior comment from the therapist. This focus emerged from his close observation of the session. This can be an important use of the type of micro-analytic attention that observes the impacts of therapy interventions on the experience of the patient. Considerable information and meanings from such observations can help with important implications of the relational field within the therapeutic interaction.

In the following statement, the linkage between accessing internal supervisor and post-session review is apparent in a designation of an "open" period that allows for therapist reflection. Theodore Jacobs has noted this immediate shift from in-session reflections to post-session observations:

> It was only after Mrs. A. was gone that I, like the adolescent who when alone can experience certain emotions that do not surface in a parent's presence, became aware that my responses during the hour were only one side of a complex countertransference reaction. (p. 296)

In this context, access to the external context or space in which the therapist can identify his or her reactions can be found again. Note the suggestion that the therapist allow for a "post-session" period in which underlying thoughts and feelings and observations of the patient can float to the surface without the constraints of listening and responding immediately to the patient. Casement explains the value of this model when he notes, "We can more readily learn to recognize the various clinical options when we are not subjected to the pressures that exist in an actual therapy session" (p. 37).

POST-SESSION IV: RECALL AND REFLECTION

This heightened post-session structure relates to a selected time in which therapist recall and reflection can be activated. Note again the parallels: That technique can be developed by taking time after the session when the therapist is "liberated" to more freely observe ideas that capture themes and patterns in the clinical material. Then when again in the presence of a patient, the associational products of internal supervision are more readily available "when they are most needed" (Casement, p. 38).

Unfocused listening, and remembering and their eventual integration into the therapeutic setting. One difficulty here resides in the therapist's capacity to remember all these factors in a nonrecorded context. The demands on a therapist to be able to reconstruct this sequence would take considerable support and guidance in terms of the role of the instructor or supervisor. At best, one can only aim for the achievement of this flexibility in shifting from self to other to self, and achieving a broad-based recovery of a significant exchange with the patient. In this context, the enhancement of self-observing skills would benefit from certain self- and supervisor-applied processes and support for reserved time structures in order to provide the space for recovering a fragment of a critical exchange. The eventual expansion of the therapists' inner space and awareness of his countertransference, along with a simultaneous recovery of forgotten moments in the session, can be seen as essential processes that can lead to a more receptive and understanding therapeutic stance toward the patient.

Again, the instructional support achieved by the teacher related to this domain of self-observation is to encourage student collection of a range of such observations in writing and speaking. By doing so, the therapist can then build a psychic repertoire of observations. In addition, this process is considered "muscle building," an exercise designed to engage and strengthen recall processes. The group helps to expand awareness of alternatives to the student's initially limited number of reactions to the clinical stimulus. If so, the aforementioned written and spoken activities can reinforce both therapeutic and teaching self-observations.

Chapter 9

Teaching and Learning from Microanalysis of Exemplar Transcripts

Detailed Approaches to the Clinical Data

> *The first distortion of truth in the "myth of the analytic situation" is that analysis is an interaction between a sick person and a healthy one. The truth is that it is an interaction between two personalities in both of which the ego is under pressure from the id, the superego, and the external world; each personality has its internal and external dependencies, anxieties and pathological defenses; each is also a child with its internal parents; and each of these whole personalities—that of the analysand and that of the analyst responds to every event of the analytic situation.* (Racker, 1968, p. 132)

This chapter is a detailed summary of the therapy exchanges with a detailed examination of the process of therapist discovery observed in the case. I then comment on the details of the aforementioned exchanges in terms of successive cycles of reactions to, and observations of, "triggers" and "reactions" in the moments of a charged clinical interaction. The purpose of this detailed review is to highlight and illuminate the ways through which Stern and Tansey/Burke were able to proceed to significant insights and attitudinal shifts in these therapists' relationships with their patients. A micro-analytic approach is used in which patient–therapist exchanges are examined in which identification of such levels of reactivity is part of the matrices of transcript review. The goal is to identify what might have accounted for the rather dramatic self-observations of the writers of the two clinical vignette articles to be reviewed. An important element of the teaching outcome and rationale of employing a micro-analytic approach is described in the following:

> When we focus at the local level made up of present moments, a different clinical sensibility arises. One becomes more aware of small events, especially

> nonverbal and implicit events. These also occur in the form of speech acts. The observer/listener must be attentive to the explicit verbal content and the implicit experience simultaneously. (D. N. Stern, 2004, p. 223)

In order to speculate further, I will consider what might have gone through the mind of the writer of this chapter, in providing a type of clinical and instructional response to the therapist's self-reflections. In short, the instructor's focus is to identify the potential learning moments in employing the use of a micro-analytic approach in the analysis of the patient–therapist exchange. This approach is drawn from the mother–infant micro-observations derived from the work of D. N. Stern (2004) and Beebe and Lachmann (2002).

A SEMINAR TEACHING APPLICATION

In the instructions for the student's presentation to the seminar group, the presenter initially determines the transcript focus and a definition of the problem she wishes to examine. This very process aids in the activation of an initial self-observing engagement with the instructor and the seminar. Students must attempt to surface an underlying observation of a sense of discomfort, confusion, frustration, anger, and so on. This begins to open the door to further exploration as the process develops.

The instructor then guides the presenter and seminar students in refining the initial problem definition of the presenting student, using transcript material to further identify the problem. Details of the sequence of oral and written transcript follow the presenter's introductory statement of her problem. As the discussion proceeds, the instructor, the student, and the group all pursue the subsequent patient comments and observations, sometimes connecting with their own experiences. The instructor also does so, keeping in mind making clear these connections to the student's stories. In fact, it is the student who sometimes discovers another critical memory detail when her peers contribute associations and speculations of their own. In that sense, the self-observations of the presenting student have found an enlarged arena within which to explore additional possibilities of understanding.

This finding that came out of a group process model helps the student presenter to have the experience of a line of associative and observational contributions of her colleagues to her own thoughts. It is this process that also becomes partly internalized in terms of the experience of an expansion of her internal repertoire of meanings around her presenting problem.

The instructor follow-up for this process then is a student write-up after the seminar and a meeting with the instructor, and a subsequent written follow-up to that meeting. The goal of these extended procedures is to continue an experience of exploration of a range of new understandings and their potential for further extension of those contributions going forward.

Gladwell (2005) has addressed a similar issue of explicit and implicit registrations of particular communications in *Blink*. He discusses a range of instances in which underlying reactions are explored in a wide range of situations. In this chapter, the student struggles with this very issue of instantaneous observations and their significance. While Gladwell's work is a mixture of journalistic and research elements, his observations and his quotes about these same processes can help to further reinforce the understanding and value of very brief and immediate observations. While anecdotal in nature, they are presented as another way to articulate the common theme and value of this micro-analytic approach to review of psychotherapeutic exchanges.

In Gladwell's "thin slicing" concept, one can find the micro-analytic perspective as a potential and valuable source of information as to what might underlay an initial patient presentation, verbal or behavioral in nature. In this sense, the subsequent session observations can help to surface what those initial observations might have been forgotten or blocked by the therapist. He employs the term "thin slicing" as a way of trying to track those initial, fleeting, and detailed impressions that might encode critical information. He suggests that sometimes these might well present latent perceptions that are actually quite accurate and revealing.

THREE LOOKS AT THE TRANSCRIPT

The discussion of the Three Looks model needs to take place in the seminar process as well as in individual transcript self-observations. The instructor guides the use of class time for therapist-spoken self-observations relevant to presentation of a challenging and difficult therapy episode. The focus at this point is on both the presenter and her peers exercising their views of self around a particular vignette exchange. Most important is the initial grounding of the therapist self-reflections, complemented by those of her colleagues and instructor, into a beginning process of understanding and sensitizing the seminar group. Emergent student associations to other observations related to patient history, therapeutic history, underlying and conflict, and whatever other factors occur to students and instructor are then considered. Later in the discussion, group associations to the therapy transcript frequently begin to locate patterns and themes between the aforementioned ideas and beginning formulations.

There are also highly focused analytically oriented faculty options for strong attention to the central role of open student emotional reactions to a series of commentaries on the patient's presentation. The instructor of that section then provides a conceptualization of the range of disclosed reactions and guides the class toward using such observations in the service of understanding the inner and interpersonal world of the patient. This particular approach has been quite successful in its structure and active student participation. In this process, the intense focus on the clinical value of such student reactions or possible ranges of countertransference again is folded into students valuing of their self-observations (M. MacMillin, PhD, personal communication, November 2014).

In what follows, I provide details of expert therapist–patient exchanges through the analysis of transcribed case material, along with the therapists' conscious associations at key moments or nodal points in the therapeutic impasse. The goal in this chapter is thus to observe and attempt to provide a broad outline for a general development or trajectory of emergent therapist self-awareness and insight. This awareness was developed by a preliminary tracking of both self-observation and observations of patients around interaction exchanges that appear in the transcripts and commentaries discussed in the exemplar materials.

Tracking these processes shows an evolution of therapist associations and memories associated with the session that evolved into the subsequent emergence of meaningful therapeutic insights and understanding.

These ideas can be the insights from which therapy stalemates can be addressed and understood by studying the processes by that experienced therapists utilize their countertransference awareness in a therapeutic manner. This approach can then provide the development of instructional guidelines for a range of possible tracking and micro-analytic ways of addressing countertransference access and subsequent processes.

This micro-analytic tracking approach is then designed to provide a teaching model for how new observations and insights can be activated in student-therapists revisiting the clinical material. Such a micro-analytic review might also provide guidance as to how an instructor might point out and model how student-therapists might independently apply this model to their own patients. In short, this instructor's approach also reflects the challenge of identifying and utilizing countertransference moments and therapist self-observations for therapeutic and teaching purposes.

GENERAL SUMMARY OF EXPERT THERAPISTS' TRANSCRIPT: AN INTRODUCTION

What follows are two examples reflecting the challenge of identifying and utilizing countertransference moments for therapeutic and teaching purposes. In the first example, Stern (1989) illustrates a process by which he was able to track and identify a type of chronic patient difficulty in exploring the patient's internal experience. This process was accompanied by his later awareness of his own chronic and particular countertransference attitude around her difficulty, unavailable to him before he embarked on this self-observing process. In the second example (Tansey & Burke, 1989), the therapist reported the experience of a patient's intense verbal attack on the therapist and an intense countertransference reaction to this attack, followed by an insight that also changed his understanding of his countertransference experience, and then a parallel change toward his attacking patient.

In examining this process, the writers were both able to demonstrate a way of eventually empathizing with the patient's motives in challenging treatment of the therapist. In both examples, I identify a general and fluid sequence as the therapists became increasingly aware of their countertransference reactions. This process of gaining these new perspectives might then provide guidance for the instructor in understanding ways in which therapists might learn how to activate and pursue such self-awareness in their own self-observations of the details in a series of exchanges. It appears that this type of accessing of inner experience draws upon the associational processes that are part of the psychoanalytic psychotherapy experience for both therapist and patient.

An underlying assumption here is that awareness of such processes is not sufficiently accessed and worked through in the usual course of therapy impasses. For that reason the extra step is going beyond the immediate therapeutic value of the therapists' approach to the transcript into a consideration of how that might then translate into a teaching experience for the instructor and a learning experience for the student and postgraduate therapist. This chapter's goals are ultimately to present the clinician-instructor-therapists in those roles.

The clinician part of the clinician/instructor role is most apparent when I present my process observations in this chapter. In this context, I will also provide two major and interwoven tasks: a clinician's and instructor's observations of critical interactional moments in the sessions when the therapists' self-reflections can provide teaching opportunities. This can occur in the instructor observations of those moments as "teaching opportunities," and when the meanings of these micro-events to the therapists can be generalized to wider lessons in self-observing in the experiences of the neophyte and experienced therapist. In presenting the reported session, I will track critical exchanges in search of finding ways through which Stern (1989) and Tansey and Burke (1989) eventually became aware of reactions being communicated in their relationships with their patients. It will be clear that getting to an insight is not simple, direct, nor predictable, but it does provide some clues as to how a therapist might get to that point.

As an instructor, I shall extract the self-observational components as examples for students to consider as they respond to the observations of the instructor.[1] The eventual expansion of the therapists' awareness of their countertransference and a simultaneous recovery of forgotten moments in the session can be seen as essential outcomes that can lead to a more receptive and understanding therapeutic stance toward the patient and, in the context of sessions reported, result in an attitude shift toward their patients.

It is clear, according to Stern (1989), that he is attempting to find the observations that lift the "unformulated" into the formulated and consciously observed. In this context, the use of a micro-analytic approach is also designed to provide a teaching model for how new observations and insights can be activated and integrated in revisiting clinical material by attending to these central moments in the session. Such a micro-analytic review might also provide a structure as to how an instructor might point out the specific new observations and insights that are stirred in the revisiting of clinical material by attending to these central moments in the session. The use of this approach will be described in a later segment of this chapter.

Instructional Reflections

In an instructional stance, the sometimes presession thoughts about the patient might be viewed as potential information as to a possible countertransference position, observable before the session starts. In this case, this possible predisposition might be embedded in the phrase "discussed many times." Such a statement for the instructor and his class might suggest that the repetition alludes to a lack of prior resolution of these problems for this patient and therapist. If this is true, this observation may constitute an awareness of a subtle therapeutic impasse between therapist and patient who perhaps could not share a common understanding on how to discuss her problems.

As an instruction point, this might just highlight helping students appreciate the presence of a possible impasse before the session begins. "Discussed many times" might suggest potential for conflict in both patient and therapist. This observation can find a receptive stance on the part of students applying that presession awareness to their own therapeutic relationships.

Illustration 1: Stern Exemplar—Relationship Problems

In this section, Stern (1989, pp. 28–30), an analyst (I use analyst for Stern and therapist for Tansey and Burke extracts), describes the analysis of a single woman executive in her late twenties, who began treatment to address her difficulties in establishing and maintaining a relationship with a man. Stern described this patient as having a primary "fix it" approach to her difficulties. She was eager to immediately work on solving her problems and uneasy with a more open and exploratory approach to her challenges. The nature of her approach to her problems had been discussed "many times" prior to the session described later. As noted, this patient was described as someone who preferred immediate action responses to conflict-related problems over a more reflective process that required self-observation and reflection. The patient's achievement of a reflective capacity would be an expected goal for the psychoanalyst.

Specifically, Stern's female patient began the session with resentment toward a male friend who did not share her preference for a planned night out. After the patient had expressed her preference, she observed the man's tone of voice became "more distant" (p. 29).

The Patient's Comment

Patient 1: At that point in the exchange, the patient said, in a tone that appeared "resentful" in her report of it, "Do you think you could be nicer to me" (p. 29)?

Analyst Intervention

Analyst 1: "The analyst interrupted the patient at this point, and asked her how she understood what seemed to have taken place in that moment with her male friend" (p. 29).

Possible countertransference and teaching implications. From a clinician's perspective the manifest story is about the patient expressing a date "preference" of an activity which in her mind seemed to create a pulling back by her friend. With prior knowledge of the suggested differences in approaching the session between patient and therapist, this theme with her friend may also capture an underlying theme already suggested by the therapist, which was her preference to "fix" versus explore conflicts. The comment "Do you think you could be nicer to me?" (p. 29) may also have expressed her sense of injury around the possibility of her therapist's apparent therapeutic preference disrupting hers. This was another central moment illustrating the impact of her vulnerability in this interaction with her friend in which she feels slighted.

In the instructional context, concepts such as "derivative communication" in her complaint to her friend might be considered as one model by the therapist and then by the students in a beginning speculation of an encoded communication to the therapist. If the therapist would have registered a sense of her somewhat victimized question to her friend, he might also consider a projective impact of such a comment. This again can illustrate the utility of identifying critical moments for the students, who can begin to reference parallel reactions to their patients. In addition, the instructor's listening and conceptualizing models, which might emphasize a transference focus by the use of derivative representations and projective communications ("could you be a little nicer?"), would provide an instructional moment for students.

The story then includes an additional central exchange—the interruption. The nature of Stern's interruption of the patient's commentary might have expressed a possible impatience with the patient in terms of Stern's not providing her with a full chance to respond to his immediate question "What do you think might have happened?" (p. 29). At this point, his sense of urgency that prompted the interruption might also have constituted a partial reaction to the long-standing impasse between him and the patient, a concern that this potential exploratory moment and opportunity would get lost (as it did later) if she continued to pursue her initial path. With a more reflective patient, this intervention would likely yield a reflective response. The nature of this patient's response will be reviewed next.

Another central moment: the interruption. In more general terms, the instructor might present questions as to the nature and meaning of an interruption with a particular patient. This can be another teaching focus as the instructor reviews this exchange in terms of what it can teach the student-therapist. The teacher's question for the students might be "what transpired in her communication that activated an interruption and immediate question?" The question that an instructor might have asked students about these moments would have touched on a sense of urgency that led to the therapist's interruption. This seminar or class inquiry might then have helped to launch students on a discussion about the meaning of interruptions within the therapeutic dialog.

In point of fact, students in a seminar group immediately associated with their own mixed feelings about the value of such an intervention, their own experience with it, the concerns over being polite or confrontative when such an interruption might be called for, all along with a range of countertransference feelings versus encouraging reflective functions in the patient around her exchange with her friend. Thus, the therapist in an extended post-session retrospective might have included the patient's response as to whether she was accessible to a reflective response at that point.

Lessons from that moment for students help them to acknowledge that interruptions have a range of possible meanings to their patients; timing, tone, and therapist motivation are critical elements. Thus, the therapists, in an extended post-session retrospective, might have observed the patient's response as to whether she was accessible to a reflective response at that point. Lessons from that moment can help them to acknowledge that interruptions have a range of possible meanings to their specific patients. The seminar discussion can activate future visibility of such interruptions and subsequent alertness to the emergence of such inclinations in the therapist. This is an exemplar item that can activate greater visibility of such moments and subsequent reflections for the student and graduate therapists.

Response Exchange: Tracking Patient Response to the Therapist

Patient 2: "She had not thought about it, she said, since in her report to me she had merely been on the way to the point she wanted to make, and had not meant to give any special emphasis to this part of the interaction. However, now that she thought about it, she could see that it had been at this point that the phone conversation had become uncomfortable, which it had remained until the end" (p. 29).

An evaluation of the interruption and the impact of the analyst's question appeared to be partly validated. She did appear to respond with a more direct set of immediate reactions to the question and revealed that she was not in a reflective mood when the question was asked. She revealed another key observation of recognizing the momentary discomfort as it emerged on the phone. In terms of the analyst's impact on the patient, these reactions suggest a partly successful intervention and a partly disruptive response from the patient.

The instructor could use this level of post-session attention to assessing the mixed qualities of the therapist's impact on the patient as a teaching session. Such a validating focus can demonstrate the utility of bringing more awareness to student-therapists as to the nature of a possibly mixed intervention and the evaluation of the validating and disruptive impact on the student.

This observation of outcomes to therapist interventions provides a major part of the self-supervision process in that the patient becomes the judge of the effectiveness of the therapist's work. It should be noted that the criteria for a validating response cover several areas: extension and deepening of the theme, associations to meaningful and relevant personal history, emergence of feelings that are strongly connected to the intervention, increase in adaptive and insightful response, and positive images of others in the patient's life, including the therapist. The meaning of manifest validation and agreement with the therapist is not necessarily confirmatory, given patient conscious agreement with the therapist does not necessarily address unconscious criteria. The criteria for indirect validation speaks more to an internal expression of confirmation than such direct validating statements.

The Analyst's Response to the Patient

Analyst 2: "I asked her whether she thought the resentful tone of the remark as she had told it to me represented the feeling she had conveyed at the time" (p. 29).

Patient 3: "She said ruefully that she thought it probably did, though she had not been aware of it at the time and did not understand it now. And then she said, in a sad and resigned kind of way, 'Look, I know I should think about what it means, but "'I just can't imagine what else I could have said to him.' She drifted into silence" (p. 29).

Reflections on the Interaction

One can see in this detailed review that the analyst's interpretive efforts were both requesting a reflective capacity and simultaneously confronting a key vulnerability for the patient. However, the patient seemed to struggle with acknowledging she had not thought of it, and was guilty and ashamed in the tone of her response to the analyst. In detailing her immediate response, it would appear that she possibly felt initial shame as she "ruefully" reported her reactions and added that she was not then aware and not understanding now. She then became "sad and resigned."

Her comments suggested a feeling of failure and a sense of disappointment in herself as she acknowledged that she should have "thought about it" but had no alternatives at the time. Her comment appears to be an acknowledgment of feeling stuck and having reached, for the moment, a type of "impasse," that preceded her "drift" into silence. She could not successfully address the therapist's questions, had fallen short of doing so in her mind, and appeared to sink into a sense of shame and failure. It appears that the very search for a fix-it answer for her therapist had failed at that moment.

In an instructional context, the example provides the value of attending to the microelements of such a specific exchange. An apparently appropriate question has evoked a guilty and sad reaction in the patient. This observation suggests that there is a communicative dimension to the intervention and patient response. The intervention was challenging the patient to reflect further on her reaction to her friend. It was likely another prompt to reflect versus fix.

For students, the instructor's focus on validation criteria also opens a door for students to assess the utility of an immediate validating process to assess the effectiveness of an intervention. Students frequently come to graduate school with an idea of correct and incorrect interventions, and sometimes have a perfectionistic goal in mind when assessing their interventions. For these reasons, the instructor emphasis on the process of reviewing a transcript provides a realistic and data-based set of observations. It also allows for an opportunity for an exploration of the students' reactions to a failed or mixed outcome of their interventions, thus grounding the students in both the intervention analysis and the personal impact of recognizing the patients' response to their comments to their patients. Instructors or supervisors are able to use these concepts as they guide the student toward a more empirical approach to the interaction.

The Analyst's First Look at the Exchange

Note the more direct accessing of the analyst's conscious countertransference affect as he initially observed and communicated in the following comment on his peripheral "sinking feeling" (p. 29) at this example of his patient's "fix-it attitude"(p. 29).

Analyst: "My initial response to this only peripherally noted by me, was a sinking feeling and frustration at what seemed to be another instance of her fix-it attitude. One more opportunity to explore something about this central problem seemed to be on the way down the drain."

The analyst here registers his first actual self-observation (in the written article) of his own disappointment and frustration, which are clearly part of an emotional response to her. One can see here in his comment the filtering in of his early formulation of her approach to her problems ("another instance of her fix-it attitude") noted in his introduction to the session. This comment might reveal a potential countertransference element embedded in the prior formulation, which articulated well the countertransference frustration around the conflicted goals of the patient and analyst (p. 29).

In this extended initial look, the analyst clearly identifies his investment in "exploration" and his acute disappointment, frustration, and even momentary despair at the loss of this opportunity. The instructor can use this self-observation of the analyst as a model for openness and curiosity in the student-therapists' internal reactions to the patient. In this extended initial look, the therapist clearly identifies his therapeutic investment in exploration and his acute disappointment, frustration, and even momentary despair at the loss of this opportunity. At this point, the analyst acknowledges his prior conceptualization as it was connected to his immediate questions and efforts to explore her "central problem." One can observe the analyst now beginning to identify his level of awareness in his immediate reactions in both their impact ("peripherally noticed") and his affective response: ("sinking feeling") (frustration) ("opportunity down the drain") as he describes a sequence of self-observations around a prior, depressively charged comment of the patient's. This "first look" might be seen to contain the more immediate affectively driven reactions that also might subsequently be seen in another review as part of the cycle of the impasse both he and his patient are experiencing.

Once again, the particulars of the analyst's disclosures can be a key part of both a modeling of internal reflections and self-acceptance of what might appear to be "inappropriate" by naïve or constricted students who are new to the process of acknowledging the reality of the internal world. There are multiple ways for the instructor to discuss student reactions to the disclosures of inner processes that conflict with students' idealized image of how a therapist needs to be. In addition, the encouragement of students to discuss their own reactions to reading about what might, on the surface, not be the always loving, understanding therapist can be helpful in engaging them in a significant process that draws them into a potentially meaningful self-exploration.

The Role of Silence and a Second Look

At this moment, the analyst noticed the emergence of a mutual silence, with the patient allowing him time for a second look at the impact of her prior comments: "For this initial moment I said nothing, though. As moments passed I was aware of something else, of her apology to me for fixing it rather than thinking about it, . . . and I began to see that I must many times have been subtly critical of this defense of hers" (p. 29).

Significantly, his new awareness followed the patient's silence, and his own parallel silence. It is not clear why the analyst became silent, but for purposes of learning about accessing the inner reactions of the therapist, it appears that the mutual silence from both patient and analyst at this crucial moment preceded this discovery of the analyst's. It appears there was some hidden, internal activity that was taking place in the analyst's mind. Most particularly, there was also the hidden process of revisiting and remembering those exchanges in the wake of having an open silence between him and his patient. In this silence, the analyst was suddenly able to access the tone and content of the patient's remarks, after his initial disappointment and sense of defeat following her earlier comments. The recovery of her affective tone was a critical micro-moment in his inner process. It could be considered a third look during which time he discovered a tone he had not been able to find earlier.

For purposes of tracking and accessing internal processes, and extracting a "lesson" from this process, it is helpful to consider that the mutual silence may have allowed access to, and acknowledgment of, these earlier eclipsed observations. The momentary joint withdrawal at this time may have provided both parties a chance to remember, recover, regulate, and move toward reparation. These observations appeared to draw on the recent recall of the affective tone of the prior patient comments, whereas the conscious perception of her apologetic tone was possibly disrupted by the preceding emotionally charged dialog.

It is also interesting to note that at that point the analyst was then able to remember another highly significant, specific, and embedded aspect of the exchange between the two of them. "I was aware of her apology to me for fixing it rather than thinking about it" (p. 29). He had missed this apology in his first look. It was the opportunity, afforded by the silence, to go beyond the first look that allowed renewed access to underlying affective and memory experience initially embedded in the first look.

The teaching implications here are not only to identify the silent and evocative moments and their fresh observations. This example illustrates an option afforded in consultative or supervisory interventions as well. Stern saw more clearly her fuller emotional reaction to him that then allowed him to proceed to a subsequent insight. This particular shift constitutes one of the factors noted in the effective management of countertransference (Gelso & Hayes, 2007, pp. 93–97). This second look then introduced a beginning reconceptualization and also a new perception of the patient. "She must have anticipated this critical attitude just now, so that she felt discouraged and hopeless" (p. 29).

Note here this new conceptualization dramatically released the therapist from an embedded position in his initial frustration. The therapist then linked the patient's hopeless tone to her perception of him in prior interactions. The major learning emerging from this insight was that Stern now understood her remarks and considered that her remarks were in part connected to a perception of him as critical and perhaps disappointed in her. Once the analyst heard the difference in her tone, he also became aware of his own attitudes that might have contributed to part of her sense of resignation. A subtle but dramatic shift had occurred in this moment. Such shifts can be blocked by a therapist's underlying focus on achieving a particular therapeutic goal. Along with this focus was an unconscious dismissal of a particular defensive pattern in the patient's communications. Both factors were then beyond the awareness of the therapist at the moment. Stern considers this moment a "breaking the grip" of an impasse, in which a fresh view of the relationship included a reconceptualization of the role of both parties in ways that help shift the therapist's attitudes toward the patient.

The instructor could use this shift as an indication of change for the neophyte student. This image of success can serve as a type of goal statement in observing the validation of mutual exchange processes.

Discovery Phase

Sequential tracking of therapist–patient exchanges and therapist observations can appear, at times, to set the internal stage for discovery. This particular sequence led from an examination of a presession case conceptualization, with elements of possible countertransference attitudes and evidence of a preexisting impasse, to an intensification of affective exchanges between patient and therapist. The examination of underlying reactions in both patient and therapist had led to an understanding of the ensuing silence as an expression of an impasse and the beginning of an insight. The mutual withdrawal actually then seemed to have had the effect of providing the therapist with the inner space needed to regroup. It was then, within this open space, that he was now able to identify his countertransference reactions and to have a new, more complete memory of the tone of his patient's final comments. Jacobs (2013) and Casement (1991) have made similar observations.

The results of this review allowed him to then reconceptualize his patient's behavior and alerted him to his prior contribution to the patient's experience. In short, the preliminary examination of the therapist's self-observations might have led to a more complete memory of his patient's preceding word and tone and stimulated a new attitude toward her: He recognized that it was his prior attitude that in part had accounted for his patient's apologetic tone. This recognition now allowed him to see his patient as a more whole and separate person (p. 30).

In broader terms, this particular observing sequence can provide one type of teaching model for a transcript analysis. This analysis of the immediate processes and post-session associations can help the instructor to guide students to a heightened alertness to a process that can be applied to other impasses. This type of approach might be one way of facilitating insight often found in significant micro-moments between therapist and patient.

Illustration 2: Tansey and Burke Exemplar—The Angry Patient

What might be learned from the sequence observed in Stern observations that could now be applied to the Tansey and Burke (1989) example? The following section will discuss possible connections through another application of a micro-analytic examination. In this context, the following segment of a "pre-discovery" process will now be observed in a case presented by Tansey and Burke (1989, pp. 164–171). From the summary, it seems evident that the dramatic past interactional cycles with this particular patient stood out for the therapist, as well as the need to understand and manage the cycles of attack and alliance in the therapeutic process.

Patient 1: The patient reported a call with his father in which the father was harshly critical of the recent TV appearance. His father's critique and lack of acknowledgment of the patient's TV achievement enraged and clearly hurt the patient. The patient was deeply angered by his father's lack of knowledge of his work and offering only trivial and critical observations of his appearance. "No wonder I don't feel I deserve that life should go well for me" (p. 165).

The therapist then asked him, "How did you respond to your father?" (p. 165).

While there is no subsequent and manifest self-reflection on why the therapist chose to ask that question at that time, it seems possible he thought it was useful to attempt to shift the patient's angry reactions into a more reflective domain in response to the patient's rage at his father. It also could have been an effort to create some emotional distance from the powerful and attacking tone of the patient's story and presentation. In that sense, the tracking of possible therapist countertransference might be observed not only in the intervention but also in the patient's angry reaction to it.

First Look: The Patient's Reaction to the Therapist's Question

This question was immediately met with protest from the patient, who said this type of response to his father would only have drawn a further attack from him. The patient then began criticizing the therapist and saying that the therapy itself was of no use and actually a way for the therapist to satisfy his greed.

After listening to these attacks on the therapy, the therapist experienced an intensifying of his anger toward the patient and an emerging retaliatory set of internal counteraccusations.

There followed a sense of deepening despair in both therapist and patient as the patient was describing how awful his life was and his deep sense of helplessness. After a period of time during which there was silence between the two, the patient then described how awful his life was and his deep sense of hopelessness. However, "as the therapist paid closer and closer attention to his own experience of the patients' attack," he noticed in himself a sense of despair as to the effectiveness in his work with his patient and a sense of hopelessness (p. 159). Maybe the patient was right about him.

At that point the therapist noticed a wish for the session to be over. Once he noted this feeling about wanting the "beating" from the patient to end, he began to recognize the parallels between his reactions to the patient and the patient's reactions to the father in wanting to get off the phone.

The therapist then made a connection between his patient's and his own sense of hopelessness and told the patient that he recognized his earlier question may have communicated to the patient that he did not fully understand how deeply the patient was feeling in response to his father. He then suggested that perhaps the patient's attacks on him were efforts to have the therapist have a similar experience to his own. The therapist's silent focus was then on seeing the patient's reactions from the patient's perspectives, and this allowed him a newfound empathy for the patient's attacks on him in this session.

The therapist finally told the patient that he felt that the patient's attack was a response to his question, and he then realized (toward the end of the session) that it activated the patient's aggressive response. He said that he thought the patient felt he was not really "with him" when he asked the question. He then explained to the patient that by attacking the therapist in the session he thought the patient needed to place the therapist in the emotional abusive situation he had just experienced with his father. He added that it seemed a way that the patient could communicate his feelings as to his experience with his father (p. 170).

To reemphasize the significance of the patient's response, another review of the patient's response might be helpful. The patient responded to this by saying that "I felt like you thought I should have been able to confront my father . . . some kind of wimp for not blasting him back. I know that I tend to turn around and do the same thing to other people, but you don't sound mad" (p. 170).

Teaching Moment

In considering this exchange as a teaching opportunity, the instructor might then point out the presence of Casement's recommendation as to "putting oneself in the patient's shoes," which had just happened in the process description.

In addition, an instructor might focus on this exchange as a useful learning topic for student-therapists around their awareness of the challenge of managing and understanding a highly agitated and accusatory patient. This exemplar can invite a conversation that brings this type of challenge to include students in becoming more aware of these types of situations along with their inner reactions to such challenges. This focus would be a type of "disembedding" of the type of experiences that would now be a teaching and learning target available for further student self-reflection now available for a focus.

Once again, the purpose of the proposed instructor interventions was to heighten student self-awareness vicariously through these teaching discussions. They would represent one more "practice" opportunity for student-therapists, outside the actual therapeutic interaction.

The Onset of Successive Looks at the Exchange

The First Look

As noted here, the therapist initially was in the first look segment of the sequence, and his internal responses were primarily affect-driven in terms of both his anxiety and subsequent aggressive fantasied reactions as to what was happening at the moment. The value of the first look concentrating retrospectively on the intensity of the patient–therapist exchange is the revelation, articulation, and beginning acceptance of the raw experience of the therapist as he describes his reactions to these attacks. For student-therapists, this segment can demonstrate a vision of a broader range of self-observations and a therapist's inner acceptance of the disturbing feelings that can come with it. A group discussion about these challenges can help these types of conflicted self-disclosures become more acceptable to the students as they might struggle with accepting the intensely negative responses that come in response to the sharp accusations of certain types of patients.

Second Look

As noted earlier, as the therapist began to reflect on his prior reactions, which Tansey and Burke describe as signal affect (Tansey & Burke, 1989, pp. 81–84), the therapist then tried to concentrate on his own thoughts as the patient's criticism continued. The therapist's aforementioned raw reactions were obviously painful to experience. His increased feeling of hopelessness and inadequacy intensified concerning his ability ever to help this patient. This particular feeling for the moment initially left the therapist feeling the patient was right and triggered the therapist's sense of hopelessness (p. 166). This in turn led to the wish for the session to be over.

As the reader can see, the therapist had made a conscious effort to begin to self-observe and access his feelings in the wake of the patient's attacks. This shift from reaction to observation now included a greater awareness and registration of the patient's feelings, thoughts, and memories starting to become available to the therapist. The teaching lesson here is a demonstration to student-therapists of the value of increased self-awareness that can come from witnessing the therapist's conscious effort to self-observe at a most challenging time. It also presents the deep value in the sequenced tracking and noting of such conflicted therapist self-images in reaching a different level of understanding.

This articulation of a "second look" illustrated the further emergence of an awareness of progression of affects and images that were flowing through the therapist's mind in his immediate response. These moments demonstrated the intensified onset of an observational stance that was experientially based.

In this process, the therapist was able to find a retaliatory impulse, which seemed to have been lacking in the patient's response to his father. He also discovered a depressive reaction in himself, which also might have been connected to the patient's discouraged reaction to his father.

Second Look: Extended to Onset of Discovery

As noted earlier, it was at that point the therapist decided to continue to study the exchange more carefully, attending to his reactions and discovering new insights about the patient in the process of this self-examination. This observation also may have included the therapist's possible identification at that moment with his patient's just "sitting and taking it" from the father. What is interesting here is that in his intense self-observations around the patient's attack, an association to his patient's prior comment emerged spontaneously.

This emerging discovery suggests that at some level the therapist had strongly registered the patient's comments and perhaps identified then with the feeling related to "getting off the phone" in such a way that the phrase was easily recovered when he had parallel thoughts toward this patient. Such vivid recall thus became available when a parallel and similar experience was registered in the therapist's memory. These types of experiences cannot be willfully recovered but are recovered following the conscious recognition of a particular inner reaction, which can then trigger these specific types of significant recollections. This indirect outcome supports the sometimes-invisible value of acknowledging a conscious pursuit of internal reactions. The critical discovery can depend on the therapist's fleeting registration of inner reactions that can, at a later point, be tapped for a richer formulation and sense of engagement with the patient.

At that point and following the awareness of this common affective connection, the therapist's attitude toward his patient changed dramatically. A qualitatively different reaction from the therapist emerged. "The therapist felt a rush of understanding as he recognized this connection" (p. 166). It was then the therapist's affect changed dramatically as he now understood what his reactions to his patient meant. The therapist became excited about this new understanding of his patient suddenly coming together.

In this context, the instructor can point out these sometimes-surprising discoveries can help boost the therapist's professional self-esteem and sense of competence. This deserves to be observed as it can become a motivator for both the student and experienced therapists to address these issues. The therapist's pride in discovering this connection was calming to the therapist. It then helped to increase his subsequent steady, nonreactive, and empathic response to the patient's projective identification.

The earlier conscious focus of the therapist's attention to his reactions to his patient was part of a containment process that led to the subsequent connection to the critical experience that increased the therapist's self-awareness. This awareness now included an association between an aspect of the therapist recognizing an empathic moment with his patient. He was now having a "concordant" identification (Racker, 1957) in terms of his inner experience matching that of his patient's. In these instances, the instructor can then attend to and emphasize the therapist's efforts to pay close attention in the midst of powerful projective forces. Clearly, another conceptual connection to the concordant identification is a strong example for students to observe in practice. At some level, the instructor also can collect student identifications with the therapist, along with their own open identifications with the therapist in this example.

Therapist Intervention

To return to the therapist's intervention in noting the patient wanted the therapist to know how it felt in being the subject of an abusive attack from his father, it was after those self-observing processes that the therapist felt more certain of his understanding of his patient. His countertransference was far more positive as he then felt he could understand him. All of this resulted in a more empathic understanding of the patient. He now had identified both his contribution to the patient's immediate rage toward him and his way of understanding it.

Patient Response

The patient's response in which he recognized this aggressive reaction toward others, and his recognition that the therapist appeared not to be angry with him, could be seen as a validation of the therapist's successful processing of the earlier patient attacks. In a sense he had successfully worked through a projective identification just received from the patient. In this account, it appears that the therapist had to traverse the sequence of retaliatory rage, hurt, despair, and feelings of incompetence and experience a sense of helplessness, submission, and despair before he could see the connection. As a result of his focus on observing these emotional reactions, his emerging awareness allowed him to locate the trigger for his reaction more fully. While this particular search or discovery process was not yet explicated, it would appear that as the therapist was able to access a concordant identification, a formulation emerged. It is hard to know here what observation might have preceded the other. However, it does seem plausible that the discovery of a concordant identification realigned the therapist's interaction model with that of the patient-victim, which then placed him in the world of his patient. He was now restored to a sense of feeling competent, and more truly understanding of his patient, and had in this moment become a new corrective figure in the patient's world.

The teaching goal of discussing the exemplar therapist's self-observations would be to model and engage student and postgraduate therapists' parallel efforts to enhance such processes in their own professional work. Most immediately, that goal would provide a pathway to accepting and working through the difficult identifications in relation to their own patients. Observing and discussing the positive results in this vignette can also be a valuable teaching tool in the class microanalysis of these episodes with both the student and the seminar group.

SUMMARY AND REFLECTIONS: EXEMPLAR OBSERVATIONS

In summarizing and integrating the potential learning students can gain with the preceding instructor observations, I highlighted the value of successive "looks" at the therapeutic impasse as it emerges within and after a session. The goal here is to find what it is in the therapist's in-session and post-session self-observations in both accounts that can help therapists to find ways to discover and work through defensive positions to locate new perspectives around moments of impasse. In short, the effort here is to consider ways in which identifying and then accessing therapist conscious experience of critical moments can help generate new understanding as presented by and with the instructor.

Part of this process can be organized in terms of a concept of "significant points," mentioned earlier, which captured critical exchanges. These are potential points of in-session attention that contain the possible presence of significant mutual impacts and communications between patient and therapist. Finding those overlapping observation points in both the Stern and Tansey and Burke vignettes was important to finding common themes in these two highly creative and dramatic therapeutic discoveries. Much of the data and speculations gathered here is based on a micro-analytic model, which emphasizes the specificity of the transcript data studied post-session. This focus allowed for the identification of these key moments in a therapeutic exchange.

It is important to note again that this model was limited to transcript analysis, which means that these findings must also be read in light of incomplete data and the absence of nonverbal observations. However, as we can see, valuable observations can still be made even given the limitations of transcript data. These segment analyses provided critical sources for successive observations, reflections, and conceptualizations in those cases as they moved from impasse to resolution. Correspondingly, while content driven, they can also open up other nonverbal areas for observation as they might occur to the therapists. This also points to the need for recall in nonrecorded sessions. The following section identifies these moments, looks, and points of interest.

Presession Reflections and the Impact of Prior Attitudes and Conceptualizations on the Therapist's Subsequent Reactions to the Patient

This particular component has been described as part of the "mental set" in the Tansey and Burke model. As described, presession formulations and clinical observations of both Stern and Tansey and Burke patients provided a conceptual and attitudinal foundation for the therapists' subsequent reactions in the reported sessions. In some instances, access to the foundation is helpful and facilitative. In others, the foundation may be considered as a concrete directive or dictum, and may well limit awareness and be used in a defensive fashion. In the Stern case, using his comments as possible presession formulations, the conceptualization identified the patient's "central defensive problem" that interfered with her fuller engagement in the therapeutic process. He added that there were prior, unsuccessful therapist attempts to address this patient problem. His remarks implied that efforts to engage this particular formulation in the past were not helpful. In this instance, it is possible the employment of this particular conceptualization at those times may have been too limiting or disconnected from the patient's immediate therapeutic needs. He also might have added that he shared a central defensive problem around this patient.

This observation can alert the therapist to be mindful of its meaning and potential impact on how clinical material will be understood at a given time. In the Tansey and Burke case, the ongoing presession conceptualization of the interactive patterns identified themes of patient anger and depression with oscillating exchanges of insight and attack toward the therapist. While this formulation provided a foundation for observing the sporadic stalemates, it did not fully immunize the therapist against such a momentary impasse. However, the advantage of being mindful of presession conceptual templates and potential biases might allow for increased awareness and mindful anticipation when the therapist experiences such an impasse again. It might also represent an early listening and interpretive bias in the therapist.

Another presession cue as to the presence of countertransference inclinations was presented by an example of Heinrich Racker (1957, p. 188):

> For instance if a feeling of annoyance before entering the consulting room is a countertransference response to the patient's aggressive or domineering

> behavior, the annoyance may enable the analyst to understand beforehand the patient's anxiety which, at the most superficial later, is fear of the analyst anger provoked by the patient's behavior.

It is clear that the ongoing observing powers of his mood before the session begins help establish a significant lesson: that countertransference is an ongoing problem until recognized and understood.

In-Session and Post-Session Analysis: Integrating Exemplar Findings

These initial in-session and post-session observations focused on immediate therapist reactions to their patients' comments. In applying a major part of the Tansey and Burke language, these moments can also constitute the onset of "interactional pressure" on the therapist. These reactions can be seen to be embedded in the initial interventions and were outside of the therapist's immediate awareness. However, at times they were articulated in therapist self-observations.

A review of those initial therapist reactions suggested that their more immediate responses reflected in part the emergence of selective presession conceptualizations and an experience of interactional pressure and frustration in both patient and therapist. For example, both therapists immediately raised questions to the patient after the initial patient statements. The nature of these questions, on close analysis, suggested that while appropriate and exploratory on one level, such immediate interventions may also have expressed therapist impatience, ambition, and/or underlying irritation with their patient's initial evocative comments. The onset of an immediate impasse may have begun in these early moments in the respective sessions as the therapists reacted to the patient's stories and tone. Both Gladwell (2005) and Reik (1956) note how immediate reactions might carry seeds of accurate perceptions as well as countertransference expressions. In terms of teaching, this focus, though, allows for student reflection and a beginning post-session focus on those early moments. They might be quickly forgotten in the narratives to follow.

Conceptualizing the Initial Patient–Therapist Exchange: The Therapist's Experience

In studying the patients' impact on the therapists' reactions, I have found possible countertransferential meanings communicated through the therapists' interventions and in their direct comments to their patients. As noted earlier, the patients' initially charged reactions to the therapists' first interventions in both vignettes and subsequent therapists' questions demonstrated an application of what both therapists described in their presession moments.

For example, the Stern patient was expressing frustration with her friend's withdrawing reaction to her date idea, a type of "withdrawal and rupture" (Safran & Muran, 2000) marker for her. Connected to this story, there is a possible implication of past therapist "withdrawal" markers in his prior responses to her. There was an emergence of the same reaction in her therapist's parallel withdrawal and rupture in his response to her resigned response to her friend's dismissal.

This quality might well have been expressed in the therapists' immediate questions back to their patients. Tansey and Burke's patient's angry depiction of his father's dismissive reaction to his TV performance might have been played out in the therapist's immediate "how did you respond?" question following his patient's very powerful and angry presentation, just as Stern's question elicited a patient withdrawal from the therapist's focus. Both questions may have had implicit critical implications and motivations expressed in their timing and their questions.

Those implications might have been fed by countertransference reactions to central issues in the patient's way of participating in treatment. Of course, they may have a constructive purpose in addressing particular patient defenses to the challenging intentions of the therapists. Both are plausible, but in terms of an instructional focus on significant moments in therapy, they can yield both thought and increased sensitivity to these therapeutic issues.

In addition, the teaching focus on the meanings of initial patient presentations might extend, as noted earlier, to the therapists' initial reactions to the patients' communications. In both of these micro-moments, an impasse was revealed in the underlying communicative meanings embedded in the patients' evocative comments and in the therapists' initial interventions. The value of observing these post-session observations in terms of a second look is that by accessing initially hidden meanings, they can subsequently alert therapists to the sometimes-unobserved communications embedded in their earlier and immediate reactions to their patients. This observation then allows for a greater awareness of the presence of such factors in further interventions, hopefully modifying the denial expressed in the early phases of these vignettes.

The Therapists' Processing Experience: Concepts Drawn from the Relevant Literature on Phases of Interactions

Tansey and Burke's subphases of reception, internal processing, and communication are helpful in conceptualizing the value of return looks at the therapists' experience. As the therapists continued their observations beyond their initial pressured reactions to the patient and their questions, they took second looks at the internal responses that activated these initial responses. They were then able to refine and further articulate their inner experiences. The examination of the latent implications of Stern's initial awareness of frustration and sense of defeat as "one more exploratory effort down the drain" as he registered his patient's story and struggle with his question reinforced therapist's momentary distress. In the Tansey and Burke vignette, the therapist's initial question of his patient ("how did you respond to your father?"), followed by an intense verbal attack by the patient, resulted in his co-occurring and oscillating reactions of both self-observations of rage and despair around the patient.

In both of these situations, the process of accessing internal experience in both therapists appears to have evolved from a focus on the more immediate and defensively driven questions to their underlying observations of internal thoughts and feelings in this second look (seen both in subsequent therapist associations).

In essence, the therapist's second looks suggested that a significant part of the therapists' set of inner reactions to their patients' initial comments (as communicated in their initial questions) might have expressed the therapists' initially hidden reactions to the projective identifications embedded in their patients' initial remarks. In this part of the process, one can note that a major component as observed by Tansey and Burke is the high potential for the disruption of this process by virtue of its carrying within it seeds of disavowed and painful recognitions of both therapist and patient. Rather than take such hidden self-observations any further, the second look of these therapists may not necessarily be followed by a third look, which may be defensively and protectively blocked, flat, disconnected, or unproductive.

A Shift in Process: Third Looks

A significant shift in the process for patient and therapist in both vignettes was the initial emergence of a mutual silence and withdrawal after the initial impact of their experiences registered in both participants. As observed, this period of silence appeared to allow the therapists an opportunity to notice a productive "third look" come to mind. This third look allowed for a clearer surfacing of a new view of the patient and at times a new view of the therapist's self. The therapists' experience then shifted from their earlier immersion in powerful countertransference responses to more reflective, observational mode, now focused on the patient's experience of the therapist.

In the Tansey and Burke model, this shift is registered in the next subphase of patient–therapist working models. A therapist key goal in this part of the process was to become more alert to the patient's thoughts and feelings toward the therapist during the critical exchanges. This alteration is the most challenging moment since the moves from therapist self-observation to focused observations about the patient ("patient-therapist interaction model") (p. 88) can then set up a subsequent move into a model that integrates both sides of the exchange. This shift can require conscious effort and increased awareness (as seen in the Tansey and Burke clinical material and "working model" subphase), and can easily slip away. But the fact that Stern found this new moment in which he was able to locate the patient's experience of him without such a conscious shift in his focus suggests that there was also a creative element in the prior collection of observations that was then coalesced in his unconscious functioning. This element appears to have used the silence to gather prior initially peripheral memories of earlier impressions of the patient in order to now imagine the patient's inner reactions to the therapist at those moments.

The third looks in each case witnessed a beginning shift in the experience of both therapists as each saw their patients in dramatically new lights. Specifically this observation appeared to occur during the silence in which Stern remembered the nuanced apologetic tone of his patient, missed in his earlier looks. At a similar point following a silence in the therapist–patient exchange, the therapist in Tansey and Burke recalled the prior comment of the patient wanting to get off the phone call from his attacking father as he heard himself echoing the same sentiment regarding wanting to end the session in response to his patient's diatribe.

What then followed was the therapist's emerging focus on the patient's experiences in the context of the therapist's earlier comment. He now was able to connect to the patient's experience of him in the context of that comment. In both instances, the therapists traversed their initially strong affective reactions and possible defensively driven responses (their questions to their patients), through an elaboration of further responses and associations. This led to the beginning of new observations of the patient's subsequent reactions to a somewhat different and more positive view of the patient.

One goal of reviewing these shifts in the process is to surface and explore what prior actions and conditions might have facilitated this type of subsequent shift to happen. It may be what matters to effective recall is the accumulation of significant earlier patient and therapist observations and associations that helps to provide the repertoire or pool for future connections. It is not a linear process since it depends on the sometimes-unpredictable and spontaneous memories and associations emerging from that pool that is more important. It is also a moment of attention to a collection of past and current critical moments that become a pool for recognizing patterns in clinical domains. It does seem in retrospect that many patient comments carried within them a clue as to what was transpiring between patient and therapist. Each subsequent "look" captured part of an evolving internal therapist observational process. This evolving process first captured a powerful initial image of the patient and then started to shift the therapist image of the patient, now including new perspectives on the therapist's prior image of the patient.

In short, the significant learning that the instructor provides to the student is the more immediate understanding of this "co-construction." This phenomena has benefited from the ongoing self-observational processes of both therapists. This view was aided by close attention to the patient's comments and the therapist's self-observations as they informed, impacted, and were elaborated. This was followed by the therapist's self-observations. In short, the co-construction benefited both from the ongoing self-observational processes of the therapists and from their close attention to their patients' comments.

It can then be that part of the readiness for this third look stage occurred as the therapists were able to observe a range of their earlier countertransference responses, captured in the first look phase. In doing so, they were able to listen differently to the patient. For example, Stern quite suddenly recalled his patient's apologetic tone, which he had missed in his earlier looks at the patient. This followed his openly acknowledged (to himself) frustrated feelings about his patient. In a sense, he needed to articulate his underlying resentment and disappointment before he could actually listen again to the patient, now for her accompanying affect. The fact that this followed his own recognition of the depth of his own affective response to her would appear to be significant, along with an internal commitment to understanding his patient in less subjectively driven terms.

Renik (2006) has commented at the end of an article on his own working through a subtle but powerful countertransference reaction:

> The way things developed, I had the opportunity to recognize retrospectively that important factors of which I had been quite unaware had also been in operation. Because (my patient) confronted me with my lack of attention, I realized that as I was listening to his . . . story, my sadness at my mother's illness and death, my urges to rescue her, my rivalry with other rescuers and a host of longstanding wishes, conflict, and anxieties had ben stirred up. . . . My session with my patient revealed to me with unusual vividness the limitations of my self-awareness . . . the analyst can never know, at any given moment to what degree or entirely in what manner his or her listening is being shaped by highly personal thoughts and feelings of which he or she is unaware. I had not been conscious of any of these concerns. Any useful conception of analytic technique has to take this condition into account. (p. 88)

I would add here that more attention to using retrospective activity, as Renik notes, is one way to provide time and space for the independent practitioner to address the various underlying factors that are influencing therapist understanding and reactions. Such time and space also have multiple benefits for the therapist and patient, especially when quality supervision and consultation and one's own therapy are not available.

In that context, Stern's recognition along with Tansey and Burke's suggested that the initial internal venting followed by subsequent self-questioning and exploration may have modified the initial underlying guilt and frustration that were initially blocked. It was not just the venting then but the subsequent reflections on the third look that appeared to release the critical coalescing observations that altered the therapists' initial attitudes toward their patients.

The instructor's lesson might be the importance of self-questioning at certain moments and pauses. Again, it is evident that discussions, written journals and recall, "imagined conversations" (out loud), group presentations, and the reading of exemplars and finding parallel countertransference experiences with their patients can awaken certain hidden reactions in student-therapists. This purview is that of the instructors and even supervisors as they might introduce questions into a nonreflective flow than helps to reset the therapist into a self-observing mode. This was what happened to me in the early exchange with Dr. Bettelheim.

One learning piece here is that a move from process/reactive responding can sometimes be broached, with mixed results, and set a somewhat compromised process in motion. That process contains elements of both a disrupted reaction to the interruption of the patient's comments and implications for the patient, along with a type of resistant collaboration and positive response to the interest and curiosity of the analyst. In terms of an instructor's explanations of the meanings of this intervention, students may then be open to considering the temptations of an interruption in both therapeutic and countertherapeutic perspectives.

Therapist Awareness of Countertransference: Interventions at Critical Points

The importance of being aware of one's internal countertransference reactions has been supported in the research cited early that demonstrated that such awareness is an important part of the therapist's empathic understanding of the patient, as well as the therapist's being responsive to the feelings the patient is expressing (Latts & Gelso, 1995; Peabody & Gelso, 1982; Robbins & Jolkovski, 1987).

In the subsequent observations of patients' immediate reactions to the therapists' initial questions, it appeared that in both instances the therapists' interventions had subtle elements of a challenging and affectively dismissive response to their patients' opening affectively charged statements. As noted earlier, while both therapist questions were partly motivated by the goal of exploratory work, the affective context in which both appeared could speak to the therapists' underlying reception and perception of the patients' evocative comments. The observation that in both instances the patients appeared emotionally unprepared and reluctant to address those questions at the moment suggested that the therapists might have shared an urgency and sense of hurt and anger as to their own particular therapeutic needs.

Again, an instructor can demonstrate that such reactions are not unusual, nor are they an unresolvable rupture. Despite the exploratory surface to the therapists' questions, their questions at those times suggest that those patients seemed to be reacting more to the therapists' timing, tone, and emotional disconnect from the patients' immediate feelings than to the therapists' conscious intent to encourage an exploration of their prior reactions.

The Value of Second and Third Looks in Psychotherapy: The Therapist's Self-Observations

The nature of the second and third looks as with any task (e.g., drafts, speeches, presentations) provides additional and alternate observations for the therapist to consider. Initial looks are altered by cues embedded in the subsequent set of patient communications. These cues then are supplanted by the emergence of new internal cues and information from the patient's ongoing comments and reactions. One can see the significance of this flow, described as "moving along" by D. N. Stern (2004). In the moment-by-moment associations and reactivation of earlier session memories, an expanded underlying network of a range of images and thoughts is created from which the therapist may draw. Such observations also can guide a reevaluation of the already-perceived events and thoughts in light of new information.

The observer may then be exposed to what was missed in a prior set of observations. In that exposure to new and insightful perceptions, the therapist may then feel a growing sense of pride, increased interest, and self-esteem in this new discovery. These factors then can be communicated to the patient in an implicitly different tone and manner, more accepting and even appreciative of the patient's co-construction participation in the exchange.

It is not only the finding of the missing observations but it is also the availability of connections that were not yet available in the first look. These connections are now enhanced from the associational network that was developed in the subsequent flow that followed the initial look. This first layer then provides a base for further fleeting connections stirred in the process. The connections can then include prior concepts, relevant experiences, and memories of related events or ideas. As the next look emerges, the initial layer of associations now activates new observations that were not available earlier. It then appears that with each successive look, the therapist finds something a bit different from even what might initially appear to be repetitive reviews. In fact, a particular critical eye toward what initially felt like a helpful intervention may begin to shift as the successive looks unfold.

It is common knowledge that such expanded vision comes with any endeavor that has subsequent "checks" and reviews a second time. In that context there is nothing new in this presentation about the value of successive observations. It is promoted here because in certain clinical settings noted earlier which do not routinely provide the multiple perspectives of supervisors and teachers, this self-review process is frequently dismissed. The major issue in this discussion is that this self-review may not be customary in the normal expectations of new and even experienced therapists, given the constraints of time, pressure, and possible resistance in actual clinical practice.

The inclusion of this feature throughout this document is employed primarily as a reminder of its value as one type of a self-supervisory alternative to being stranded and then avoidant when faced with the challenge of difficult patients without a structured consultative presence. It should not replace such a presence but provide a stronger backdrop and information cluster when such a presence becomes available. However, in less dramatic clinical circumstances, it offers an ongoing involvement with the task of understanding the relationship with the patient. With that involvement, there is a higher probability for new insight and discovery.

Matches between Microanalyses of Therapist Exchanges and Expert Traits and Qualities

There appears to be a connection between the capacities for self-observation that emerged in the successive microanalyses and the "expert" qualities identified in the research. The major focus in this chapter is to identify those qualities as they appeared "in action" rather than as abstract and discrete therapist qualities. Such exemplars reviewed in this chapter basically showed these factors in the clinical material. In each of the exemplars, anxiety management, self-insight, empathy, and conceptualizing skills were all evident in each of the accounts of psychotherapy (Gelso & Hayes, 2007).

Countertransference Management: Internal Factors

Apart from the topics identified in the therapist's stream of thoughts during and after the interaction with the patient, an overlapping series of self-observed topics identified in a student self-review can be found in areas embedded under the rubrics of "countertransference management" (Gelso & Hayes, 2007, pp. 93–111). In this context, effective countertransference management can be seen in therapists' awareness of their affective reactions. If such sequential looks are applied effectively, it might be assumed that more successful countertransference management would be a possible outcome. The five factors included in effective countertransference management are "self insight, conceptualizing skills, empathy, self-integration, and anxiety management skills" (Gelso & Hayes, 2007, p. 95). These items can also provide guidance in the areas selected for student self-observations that are reviewed by the student learners. These can be modeled in the Stern and Tansey and Burke activities. It is helpful to note that certain variables from Gelso and Hayes's (2007) countertransference management topics actually fall under the outcomes of these very processes of self-observation.

Self-insight is an outcome that represents one product of those self-observations that are embedded in the "first" and subsequent looks at the clinical exchanges and the sequelae of reactions. It is generated by the intensified therapist attention to facets of their exchanges that comes from a focused self-observing experience. The emergence of this increased self-attentiveness in both individual and class experience can have an impact on the subsequent observations of the therapist. This can be seen in the evolution of therapist insight in both Stern and Tansey and Burke.

As one student noted in a post-session discussion, her repeated reviews of the seminar transcripts seemed to bring her to a greater awareness of those clinical factors that might have been obscured by the passage of time and multiple distractions. In a sense, these renewed "visits" helped to create greater self-awareness in the therapist.

Conceptualizing skills are a second factor related to countertransference management. The emergence and potential application of relevant concepts were embedded in the successive looks review process. Stern drew on recognition of his impact on the patient as a missing piece. Students were asked to find connections between such phenomena and selective internal and interactional concepts as part of the assignment. These connections were also identified as the therapists spontaneously recognized such concepts emergent in their associations with the particular data. Instructor focus on student inclusion of the patient's perceptions in class assignments and discussions was also designed to facilitate student connections between their clinical observations and particular concepts. For example, in these learning contexts, careful and specific delineation of transcript exchanges and identifying of underlying therapist intentions and affects evoked further self-observations and conceptual connections.

These activities can help bring to life object relational perspectives such as projective identification and role responsiveness. Such concepts can then be another part of the representations of the students' picture of the self and patient, and facilitate a more reflective and less reactive therapist stance toward the patient. As an example, Gelso and Hayes (2007, p. 98) stated: "When the therapist can conceptualize the patient's behavior more objectively . . . as (for example) an attempt to recreate familiar relationship dynamics, the therapist is less likely to react in a counter-therapeutic manner." The use of this observation in drawing on relevant concepts such as projective identification can be a critical factor that can help disrupt certain ruminative and nonproductive associations in the student-therapist, and allow for the emergence of more reflective processes.

Empathy is a third factor that can be part of the immediate associational network (feeling "with" the patient). Most important, it also can be a desired outcome of the self-observing process described in the model, and illustrated in both the Stern and Tansey and Burke exemplars. In short, with the availability of personal reactions (including identifications with the patient and aspects of oneself) comes access to points of potential empathizing with the patient's experience. "The therapist who is able to stay attuned to the patient's communications, feelings, experiences, and needs is less likely to put her or his own needs ahead of the patient's" (Gelso & Hayes, 2007, p. 99).

Self-integration, a fourth factor, is one significant outcome of the self-review process and is essential for therapists' ultimate capacity to effectively access, understand, and conceptualize their own reactions to their patients. Note here Gelso and Hayes's (2007, p. 99) definition of this phenomena in the context of countertransference management: "Self integration refers to a therapist's having a relatively stable identity, being able to differentiate from others, and generally possessing sound psychological health." The therapist's increased self-observing capacities would contribute to this integrative process, and its positive psychological implications as well as an enhanced sense of competency. We could observe this experience in the Tansey and Burke description of the very positive self-image of the therapist that came with his new understanding of his patient.

Anxiety management, as a fifth factor, refers directly to the therapist's capacity to be aware of and contain a level of anxiety that is neither overwhelming nor unavailable. This capacity as observed in Tansey and Burke's observational acuity allows for the potential to access and identify the triggers for such reactions. These features are also critical factors in countertransference management, which facilitates both the observation and understanding of these reactions. In doing so, this capacity frees the therapist for a more complete focus on the patient's experience, and a conceptual model of the sequences and process.

Summary: Teaching Self-Observation and Countertransference Awareness in Multiple Clinical and Curricular Arenas

As noted earlier, teaching assignments can help structure and reinforce a sequence and process for evoking student awareness of potential countertransference experiences. This activity can be promoted by guiding student observations of the flow of therapy exchanges and the underlying thoughts occurring in the student-therapist. In doing so, the student and instructor can locate possible countertransference meanings in therapists' internal sequence of reactions to patient's earlier comments or behaviors. The information as to possible countertransference reactions might then be seen in explicit and emerging self-observations, and in specific student-therapist interventions (e.g., tone, timing, clarity, interpretations, questions, confrontations, silences, emotional meanings, interactional impacts, communications, projective qualities, and overall delivery).

Finding ways to translate concepts of countertransference awareness into the actual contexts and flow of an interpersonal exchange can then be critical to helping the students develop enhanced self-observing skills, memory retrieval capacities, and conceptualization skills. In this way, using the model of teaching multiple and progressive looks at the same clinical transcript material can concentrate attention on therapist's hidden motives, feelings, and intentions as they emerge in a series of observations of inner thoughts and feelings. Such a model can then also be expressed in written and class discussion assignments, which also focus on the student's subjectivities expressed in both personal and clinical exchanges.

In subsequent discussions of student responses to these assignments, students in the courses and seminars have reported that the micro-analytic focus on transcripts in both the written assignments and class discussions guided their more complete attention to and understanding of the dynamics of countertransference. The capacity to more directly see the impact of underlying countertransference feelings on the interactions was enhanced by this level of clinical review. Course learning exercises discussed earlier, then, appear to facilitate this process by detailed focusing on the therapist's actual thoughts and responses to patients, and subsequent student-therapist self-observations, and reflections on their own student intentions regarding their interventions.

Examples of the value of these activities can be found in the accessing of student self-awareness, parallel to those processes demonstrated in Stern's underlying thoughts described as existing on the "periphery" of his awareness in one particular set of his observations. For example, his acknowledgment of his disappointment in his patient's limited response to his question was a stimulus to further self-exploration and discovery. As noted, part of Stern's countertransference response to his patient's comments about her initial problem with her boyfriend was likely communicated in the timing and tone of his initial question. Very shortly after the session began and the patient's initial story, "I interrupted the patient here and asked what she thought might have happened in that interchange."

While a subtle communication, the suddenness of the intervention in the very early part of the session might have contained an example of a type of similar countertransference communication that was also evident in the Tansey and Burke therapist's question, "How did you respond to your father?" This question, communicated early in his session with his male patient, was another instance of an articulation of a countertransference manifestation in the session. In these instances, both the therapists' interruption and the rather sudden and immediate challenging questions in both examples might have had a type of countertransference communication of impatience and dissatisfaction embedded in the comment to the patient.

Additional examples of countertransference judgments seeping into therapist comments were also observed in the therapist's interruption of his patient as a possible expression of an acute disappointment in the patient's failure to reflect more fully on her attitudes toward the exchange with the boyfriend. Implicit judgments of self and the patient are also seen in Stern's disappointment in his description of the session insights "going down the drain" following his patient's failure to follow up on potential insights emerging in her account.

As is obvious, these observations are only a partial list. The purpose here is to identify further zones of interest, responsiveness, and identifications for the self-observing student. The effort here is to provide broad guidelines and examples for student-therapists' learning to negotiate the challenges of self-observation and awareness through a therapeutic exchange.

Where to Look?

As noted earlier, written and discussion self-observing assignments can promote identification of countertransference in student-therapists. These assignments are designed to focus student attention on discrete observations of critical interactional exchanges, impacts, and patterns. Part of the structure of the written assignments is to present a succession of targeted looks or observations of potentially significant interactional exchanges. The goal here is to assess the effectiveness of such an assignment for the development and enhancement of self-observing skills.

In writing responses to questions about particular experiences, students are expected to be able to describe, self-observe, and articulate their own thinking about such experiences. Specifically, the question is: What are the dimensions of the therapeutic exchange on which student-therapists may internally concentrate in order to first access the presence of countertransference? This is a type of template that might be useful for student-therapists. These territories can then be arenas for locating and heightening self-awareness of countertransference in their work with their patients.

In short, the question is "where to look?" in enhancing self-awareness in the therapy relationship. These skills in finding critical moments would help point the student-therapist toward enhanced self-awareness of countertransference as well as the activating of further associative and reflective activities. This, in turn, would address the larger question of countertransference management.

It is important to note here that the reflective activities or moments have a role in terms of not only the emergence of insight but the discovery of specific but formerly blocked or marginalized memories of the treatment relationship. As noted earlier, it is the student-therapists' observing of formerly unacceptable reactions to the patient and the surfacing of the conflicts activated by these experiences that help move the therapist beyond the acknowledgment phase. Acceptance of these conflictual feelings toward the patient requires the identification of the therapists' guilt and its impact on a fuller understanding of the patient. This topic will also be addressed later in the chapter.

These findings were also evident in the clinical insights described by Stern in one of the exemplars, quoted in the first chapter of this presentation. The reason I selectively repeated prior examples at this point is to reemphasize selected concepts more explicitly in this process.

The process of developing a beginning model for accessing countertransference and its impact on work with the patient was then observed in the successive looks at key points before and during the exemplar sessions. Careful observation of the transcripts and interventions detected a pattern of critical areas in which countertransference components could be identified. Those areas were presession attitudes toward the patient and conceptual models; anxiety management observed in the explicit therapist reactions to challenging patient comments; self-insight as a final outcome of the successive observational processes and patient responses; and conceptualizing skills, as located in the early formulations and countertransference understandings of both therapists. In short, the instructor's use and analysis of specific therapeutic examples may, in certain contexts, be found to facilitate the identification of a number of traits that contribute to the delivery of improved management of therapy impasses in psychotherapy.

Ultimately, the next step is to provide a flexible protocol for therapists that encourages the type of successive reflective activity present in both the exemplars and the research literature. We have seen that the importance of significant points or triggers can be one jumping-off point that can start an accessing process in a microanalysis of a transcript. At that point, one goal might then be to apply selected principles of the free associational method to the sequence of observations. These free associations, clustered into looks, may start to build a set of ideas and observations that enhance the therapist's self-awareness in the specific work with a therapy impasse. At some points, selected observations are found to connect to others. This discovery requires time to allow for a pattern recognition to take place, which begins to establish a basis for a therapist intervention.

The primary idea here is that what might not be a self-expectation in the daily work of experienced and busy therapists might be part of the work in cases of impasse. The second and third looks can then collect subsequent observations of what was missed and even misunderstood, as such observations expand and draw on a broader range of inner experiences of the therapist. This process widens the canvas for the therapist by creating more points of potential connection and a greater receptivity to the patient's participation. While major "insights" may not immediately follow, what does follow are a broader openness and a loosening of the "grip" that Stern described in the case he presented. This element was described in Stern's earlier remarks as to the value of receptivity to the patient's comments, as they may provide the critical point for a shift in the therapist's attitudes. At that point, the new awareness activates new anticipations. Therapists can then have new access to the recall of the interactional effects of earlier comments, which now informs subsequent interventions.

Finally, the findings of the exemplars study suggest in very general terms that allowing the flow between initial and reactive responses to an expanding vision of the patient's impacts to a shift in an identificatory experience is how a student or postgraduate therapist can track a flexible and receptive process. One major turning point then is the need for curiosity about the therapist's reactions and associations. Such self-curiosity and patience can allow the patient's perceptions of the therapist to become visible to the therapist. With this fuller and more complete visibility of both participants in the interaction comes the requisite empathy and ultimately a shift in attitude expressed in a change in the therapist's inner stance to the patient.

Because of this increased capacity to reflect and anticipate reactions within the interaction based on new information from the prior review, therapists have a choice as to evaluating, anticipating, and managing the new options that emerge in the second and third looks. These choices allow therapists to move from impasse into "opportunity and discovery."

NOTE

1. It is also important to state here that the notes presented by the therapists were likely developed post-session and therefore are not as complete or accurate as they would be if from audio or video recordings. However, since memory is the major

tool for most therapists in practice, this makes the focus on the significance of recall critically important. The emotional challenge of remembering the painful details of sometimes-conflicted inner experience often includes the disruption of therapist memory. This is why locating ways in which the therapist is able to recall specifics of critical moments in a session is often through associational freedom in reviewing a session. These moments, once recovered, can be attended by insight.

Chapter 10

Concluding Remarks

Throughout this book we endeavored to provide a broad overview of challenges awaiting the psychoanalytic practitioner who works in a university setting. Psychoanalytic clinicians bring particular ways of thinking about administering and teaching in a university culture and in relation to mainstream academic psychology. These challenges broadly transverse teaching students a model of self-reflectivity that promotes a psychoanalytic method of understanding relationship dynamics, dealing with the clinician-trainer tension that must identify and contain conflict associated with different roles, pressure toward increasing conformity and standardized ways of thinking and accountability that can be at odds with a psychoanalytic subjectivity, and interfacing with various systemic tensions in educational settings and programs. We also note the ongoing challenges and internal associated with traditional ways of understanding the training climate and share a great empathy for colleagues who approach their roles as clinicians and educators from different theoretical bases, understanding that they, too, are probably in conflict in these same areas but conceptualize differently. One might suspect that the pendulum swings in the other direction for those at the other end of the theory continuum, that is, too much, not too little, subjectivity. Forming alliances with colleagues of different orientations poses a challenge to everyone, but common ground is closer than what the surface shows. That said, the psychoanalytic clinician in the academic setting remains an outlier of sorts, especially as demands for quantification are the norm and must be satisfied. With these points in mind, what we endeavor here is a reminder of the complexity of teaching and training students within the larger university culture and the importance, as Freud suggested, of striving toward conscious recognition of conflict as, paradoxically, a means of reducing conflict and making contribution to the lives of others.

References

Allcorn, S. (2007). The psychological nature of oppression in an American workplace. *Organisational and Social Dynamics*, *7*(1), 39–60.

Allcorn, S. (2008). Diagnosing organizational narcissism. *Organisational and Social Dynamics*, *8*, 169–193.

Amado, G. (2013). Psychic imprisonment and its release within organisations and working relationships. In L. Vansina (Ed.), *Humanness in organisations: A psychodynamic contribution* (pp. 7–28). London, UK: Karnac.

American Psychiatric Association. (2013). *Diagnostic and statistical manual of mental disorders* (5th ed.). Washington, DC: American Psychiatric Press.

American Psychological Association. (2013). *Guidelines and principles for accreditation of programs in professional psychology*. Washington, DC: Author.

American Psychological Association. (2015). *Standards of accreditation for health service psychology*. Washington, DC: Author.

Anderson, D. K., & White, J. D. (2002). Psychoanalytic organizational theory: Comparative perspectives. *Free Associations*, *9*, 500–525.

Armstrong, D. (2004). Emotions in organizations: Disturbance or intelligence? In C. Huffington, D. Armstrong, W. Halton, & J. Pooley (Eds.), *Working below the surface: The emotional life of contemporary organizations* (pp. 11–27). London, UK: Karnac.

Arnd-Caddigan, M. (2013). Imagined conversations and negative countertransference. *Journal of Psychotherapy Integration*, *23*(2), 146–157. doi:10.1037/a0031415.

Auchincloss, E., & Kravis, N. M. (2000). Teaching Freud to under-graduates: A case report. *International Journal of Psychoanalysis, 81, 753–770.*

Balint, M. (1985). *Primary love and psycho-analytic technique*. London, UK: Karnac Books.

Beebe, B., & Lachmann, F. (2002). Organizing principles of interaction from infant research and the lifespan prediction of attachment: Application to adult treatment. *Journal of Infant, Child and Adolescent Psychotherapy*, *2*, 61–89.

Bellak, L., & Faithorn, P. (1981). *Crises and special problems in psychoanalysis and psychoanalytic psychotherapy*. New York, NY: Aronson.

Berg, D. N. (1998). Resurrecting the muse: Followership in organizations. In E. B. Klein, F. Gabelnick, & P. Herr (Eds.), *The psychodynamics of leadership* (pp. 27–52). Madison, CT: Psychosocial Press.

Bion, W. (1959). Attacks on linking. *International Journal of Psychoanalysis, 40*, 308–315.

Bion, W. R. (1961). *Experiences in groups*. London, UK: Tavistock.

Bion, W. (1967). Notes on memory and desire. In R. Langs (Ed.), *Classics in psychoanalytic technique* (pp. 243–244). New York, NY: Jason Aronson.

Blass, R. B. (2001). The teaching of the Oedipus Complex: On making Freud meaningful to university students by unveiling his essential ideas on the human condition. *International Journal of Psychoanalysis, 82*, 1105–1121.

Bollas, C. (1987). *The shadow of the object: Psychoanalysis of the unthought known*. London, UK: Free Association Books.

Bollas, C (1995). *Cracking up*: *The Work of Unconscious Experience. London, England*: Routledge Press.

Bollas, C. (1999). *The mystery of things*. London, UK: Routledge Books.

Bollas, C. (2003). Confidentiality and professionalism in psychoanalysis. *British Journal of Psychotherapy, 20*(2), 157–176.

Bollas, C. (2006–2007). *Chicago seminars*. Chicago, IL.

Bollas, C. (2011). *The Christopher Bollas reader*. London, UK: Routledge Books.

Bollas, C., & Sundelson, M. (1995). *The new informants*. Northvale, NJ: Aronson.

Bram, A. D., & Yalof, J. (2015). Quantifying complexity: Personality assessment and its relationship with psychoanalysis. *Psychoanalytic Inquiry, 35*(sup1), 74–97. doi: 10.1080/07351690.2015.987595, published online: January 6, 2015.

Brenner, C. (1976). *Psychoanalytic technique and psychic conflict*. New York, NY: International Universities Press.

Brightman, Baird K (1982). Narcissistic issues in the training experience of the psychotherapist. *The International Journal of Psychoanalytic Psychotherapy*, 10, 293–317.

Britzman, D. P. (1998). *Lost subjects, contested objects: Toward a psychoanalytic inquiry of learning*. Albany, NY: State University of New York Press.

Britzman, D. P. (2006). *Novel education: Psychoanalytic studies of learning and not learning*. New York, NY: Peter Lang.

Britzman, D. P. (2009). *The very thought of education: Psychoanalysis and the impossible professions*. Albany, NY: State University of New York Press.

Bryceland, C., & Stam, H. J. (2005). Empirical validation and professional codes of ethics: Description or prescription? *Journal of Constructivist Psychology, 18*, 131–155.

Bush, M., & William, M. (2011). Should supportive measures and relational variables be considered a part of psychoanalytic technique? Some empirical considerations. *International Journal of Psycho-Analysis, 93*, 377–399.

Casement, P. (1991). *Learning from the patient*. New York, NY: Guilford.

Chung, M. C. (2003). Examining the nature of psychoanalytic knowledge. In M. C. Chung & C. Feltham (Eds.), *Psychoanalytic knowledge* (pp. 1–19). Hampshire, UK: Palgrave MacMillan.

Collie, A. (2005). The dynamics of large groups and their effects on organizational functional. *Organisational and Social Dynamics*, *5*, 1–14.

Cooper, A., & Dartington, T. (2004). The vanishing organization: Organizational containment in a networked world. In C. Huffington, D. Armstrong, W. Halton, & J. Pooley (Eds.), *Working below the surface: The emotional life of contemporary organizations* (pp. 127–150). London, UK: Karnac.

Creswell, J. W., Wheeler, D. W., Seagren, A. T., Egly, N. J., & Beyer, K. D. (1990). *The academic chairperson's handbook*. Lincoln, NE: University of Nebraska Press.

Czander, W., Jacobsberg, L., Mersky, R. R., & Nunberg, H. (2002). Analysis of a successful consultative effort from four psychoanalytic perspectives. *Journal of Managerial Psychology*, *17*(5), 366–380. doi:10.1108/02683940210432619.

Czander, W. M. (1993). *The psychodynamics of work and organizations: Theory and application*. New York, NY: Guilford Press.

Deresiewicz, W. (2015, September). The neo-liberal arts: How college sold its soul to the market. *Harper's*, 25–32.

Diamond, M. (2012). Repetition and the compulsion to repeat: Psychodynamic challenges in organizational learning and change. *Administration & Society*, *45*(5), 499–521. doi:10.1177/009539971245183.

Diamond, M., Allcorn, S., & Stein, H. (2004). The surface of organizational boundaries: A view from psychoanalytic object relations theory. *Human Relations*, *57*(1), 31–53. doi:10.1177/0018726704042713.

Eisenhower, D. D. (1961). Farewell address. *American rhetoric: Top one hundred speeches*. Retrieved from http://www.americanrhetoric.com/speeches/dwightdeisenhowerfarewelladdress.

Field, K. (1989). Teacher-student dialogue. In K. Field, B. J. Cohler, & G. Wood (Eds.), *Learning and education: Psychoanalytic perspectives* (pp. 851–926). Madison, CT: International Universities Press.

Fink, B. (2011). *Fundamentals of psychoanalytical technique: A Lacanian approach for practitioners*. New York, NY: W.W. Norton.

Fliess, R. (1942). The metapsychology of the analyst. *Psychoanalytic Quarterly*, *11*, 211–227.

Freud. S. (1981). Project for a scientific psychology. In J. Strachey (Ed. & Trans.), *The standard edition of the complete psychological works of Sigmund Freud* (Vol. 1, pp. 281–397). London, England: Hogarth Press (Original work published in 1895.)

Freud, S. (1981). The interpretation of dreams. In J. Strachey (Ed. & Trans.), *The standard edition of the complete psychological works of Sigmund Freud* (Vols. 4–5, pp. 1–627). (Original work published in 1900.)

Freud, S. (1981). The dynamics of the transference. In J. Strachey (Ed. & Trans.), *The standard edition of the complete psychological works of Sigmund Freud* (Vol. 12, pp. 97–108). (Original work published in 1912a.)

Freud, S. (1981). Recommendations for physicians practicing psychoanalysis. In J. Strachey (Ed. & Trans.), *The standard edition of the complete psychological works of Sigmund Freud* (Vol. 12, pp. 109–120). (Original work published in 1912b.)

Freud, S. (1981). Remembering, repeating, and working through (further recommendations on the technique of psycho-analysis). In J. Strachey (Ed. & Trans.), *The standard edition of the complete psychological works of Sigmund Freud* (Vol. 12, pp. 145–156). (Original work published in 1914a.)

Freud, S. (1981). Those wrecked by success. In J. Strachey (Ed. & Trans.), *The standard edition of the complete psychological works of Sigmund Freud* (Vol. 16, pp. 316–331). (Original work published in 1914b.)

Freud. S. (1981). Observations on transference-love. In J. Strachey (Ed. & Trans.), *The standard edition of the complete psychological works of Sigmund Freud* (Vol. 12, pp. 157–171). (Original work published in 1915.)

Freud. S. (1981). Introductory lectures. In J. Strachey (Ed. & Trans.), *The standard edition of the complete psychological works of Sigmund Freud* (Vol. 15, pp. 157–171). (Original work published in 1915–1916.)

Freud. S. (1981). On the teaching of psycho-analysis in universities. In J. Strachey (Ed. & Trans.), *The standard edition of the complete psychological works of Sigmund Freud* (Vol. 17, pp. 169–173). (Original work published in 1919.)

Freud, S. (1981). Group psychology and the analysis of the ego. In J. Strachey (Ed. & Trans.), *The standard edition of the complete psychological works of Sigmund Freud* (Vol. 18, pp. 67–143). (Original work published in 1921.)

Freud, S. (1981). The ego and the id. In J. Strachey (Ed. & Trans.), *The standard edition of the complete psychological works of Sigmund Freud* (Vol. 19, pp. 3–66). (Original work published in 1923.)

Freud, S. (1981). The question of lay analysis. In J. Strachey (Ed. & Trans.), *The standard edition of the complete psychological works of Sigmund Freud* (Vol. 20, pp. 177–258). (Original work published in 1926.)

Freud, S. (1981). Analysis terminable and interminable. In J. Strachey (Ed. & Trans.), *The standard edition of the complete psychological works of Sigmund Freud* (Vol. 23, pp. 209–253). (Original work published in 1937.)

Freud. S., & Breuer, J. (1981). Studies on hysteria. In J. Strachey (Ed. & Trans.), *The standard edition of the complete psychological works of Sigmund Freud* (Vol. 2, pp. 1–306). (Original work published in 1893–1895.)

Gantt, S. P., & Agazarian, Y. M. (2007). Phases of system development in organizational work groups: The system-centred approach for intervening in context. *Organisational and Social Dynamics*, *7*, 253–291.

Gelso, C. J., & Hayes, J. A. (1998). *The psychotherapy relationship: Theory, research, and practice*. New York, NY: Wiley.

Gelso, C. J., & Hayes, J. A. (2001). Countertransference management. *Psychotherapy*, *38*(4), 418–422.

Gelso, C. J., & Hayes, J. A. (2007). *Countertransference and the therapist's inner experience: Perils and possibilities*. Mahwah, NJ: Erlbaum.

Gladwell, Malcolm. (2005). *Blink. The power of thinking without thinking*. New York, NY: Little, Brown, and Company.

Goffman, E. (1961). *Asylums: Essays on the social situation of mental patients and other inmates*. New York, NY: Penguin Books.

Gottdiener, W. H. (2006). Individual psychodynamic psychotherapy of schizophrenia: Empirical evidence for the practicing clinician. *Psychoanalytic Psychology, 23*(3), 583–589.

Gottdiener, W. H., & Haslam, N. (2002). The benefits of individual psychotherapy for people diagnosed with schizophrenia: A meta-analytic review. *Ethical Human Sciences & Services, 4*(3), 163–187.

Gottdiener, W. H., & Haslam, N. (2003). A critique of the methods and conclusions in the Patient Outcome Research Team (PORT) report on psychological treatments for schizophrenia. *Journal of the American Academy of Psychoanalysis & Dynamic Psychiatry, 31*(1), 191–208.

Grotstein, J. S. (1981). *Splitting and projective identification*. New York, NY: Aronson.

Halton, W. (2004). By what authority? Psychoanalytical reflections on creativity and change in relation to organizational life. In C. Huffington, D. Armstrong, W. Halton, & J. Pooley (Eds.), *Working below the surface: The emotional life of contemporary organizations* (pp. 107–122). London, UK: Karnac.

Heatherington, L., Messer, S. B., Angus, L., Strauman, T. J., Friedlander, M. L., & Kolden, G. G. (2012). The narrowing of theoretical orientations in clinical psychology doctoral training. *Clinical Psychology: Science & Practice, 19*(4), 364–374.

Herrick, C., Kvale, J. K., & Goodykoontz, L. G. (1991). Resolving faculty conflict: Application of a psychotherapeutic model in an encounter group process. *The Journal of Specialists in Group Work, 16*(1), 32–39.

Hirsch, I. (2008). *Coasting in the countertransference. Conflicts of self interest between analyst and patient*. Hillsdale, NJ: The Analytic Press.

Hirschhorn, L. (1988). *The workplace within: Psychodynamics of organizational life*. Cambridge, MA: The MIT Press.

Hirschhorn, L. (1998). The psychology of vision. In E. B. Klein, F. Gabelnick, & P. Herr (Eds.), *The psychodynamics of leadership* (pp. 109–126). Madison, CT: Psychosocial Press.

Hopper, E. (2012). Introduction: The theory of incohesion: Aggregation/massification as the fourth basic assumption in the unconscious life of groups and group-like social systems. In E. Hopper (Ed.), *Trauma and organizations* (pp. xxi–li). London, UK: Karnac.

Horstein, G. (1992). The return of the repressed: Psychology's problematic relationship with psychoanalysis, 1909–1960. In W. E. Pickren & D. A. Dewsbury (Eds.), *Evolving perspectives on the history of psychology* (pp. 471–491). Washington, DC: American Psychological Association.

Hoyle, L. (2004). From sycophant to saboteur-responses to organizational change. In C. Huffington, D. Armstrong, W. Halton, & J. Pooley (Eds.), *Working below the surface: The emotional life of contemporary organizations* (pp. 87–106). London, UK: Karnac.

Huffington, C., James, K., & Armstrong, D. (2004). What is the emotional cost of distributed leadership? In C. Huffington, D. Armstrong, W. Halton, & J. Pooley (Eds.), *Working below the surface: The emotional life of contemporary organizations* (pp. 67–82). London, UK: Karnac.

Jacobs, T. J. (2013). *The possible profession. The analytic process of change*. New York, NY: Routledge Press.

Jarecki, E. (Director). (2006). *Why we fight*.

Kabat-Zinn, J. (2005). *Wherever you go there you are there. Mindfulness meditation in everyday life*. New York, NY: Hatchette.

Kainer, R. (1999). *The collapse of the self*. Hillsdale, NJ: The Analytic Press.

Karon, B., & VandeBos, G. (1984). *Psychotherapy of schizophrenia: The treatment of choice*. New York, NY: Aronson.

Kaslow, N. J., Grus, C. L., Campbell, L. F., Fouad, N. A., Hatcher, R. L., & Rodolfa, E. R. (2009). Competency assessment tool-kit for professional psychology. *Training & Education in Professional Psychology, 3*(4-Supplment), S27–S45.

Kaslow, N. J., & Rice, D. G. (1985). Developmental stresses of psychology internship training: What training staff can do to help. *Professional Psychology: Theory and Practice, 16*(2), 253–261.

Kaslow, N. J., Rubin, R. J., Bebeau, M. J., Leigh, I. W., Lichtenberg, J. W., Nelson, P. D., Portnoy, S. M., & Smith, I. L. (2007). Guiding principles and recommendations for the assessment of competence. *Professional Psychology: Research and Practice, 38*(5), 441–451.

Kavanaugh, P. (1999). An ethic of free association: Questioning a uniform and coercive code of ethics. *Psychoanalytic Review, 86*(4), 643–662.

Kavanaugh, P. (2012). *Stories from the bog: On madness, philosophy, and psychoanalysis*. New York, NY: Rodopi.

Kernberg, O. F. (1965). Notes on countertransference. *Journal of the American Psychoanalytic Association, 13*, 38–56.

Kernberg, O. F. (1975). *Borderline conditions and pathological narcissism*. New York, NY: Aronson.

Kernberg, O. F. (1980). *Internal world and external reality*. New York, NY: Aronson.

Kernberg, O. F. (1987). Projection and projective identification: Developmental and clinical aspects. *Journal of the American Psychoanalytic Association, 35*, 795–819.

Kernberg, O. F. (1996). Thirty methods to destroy the creativity of psychoanalytic candidates. *International Journal of Psycho-Analysis, 77*(5), 1031–1040.

Kernberg, O. F. (2011). Psychoanalysis and the university: A difficult relationship. *International Journal of Psychoanalysis, 92*, 609–622.

Kets de Vries, M. F. R. (1977). Crises leadership and the paranoid potential: An organizational perspective. *Bulletin of the Menninger Clinic, 41*(4), 349–365.

Kibel, H. H. (2012). A study in institutional change: The experience of trauma and the role of rumour in a case of paranoiagenesis. In E. Hopper (Ed.), *Trauma and organizations* (pp. 3–22). London, UK: Karnac.

Kierwa, K. A. (1989). Review of note taking. The encoding, storage, paradigm, and beyond. *Journal of Educational Psychology, 1*(2), 147–172.

Klein (1975). Some notes on schizoid mechanisms. In M. Klein (Ed.), *Envy and gratitude and other works, 1946–1963* (pp. 1–24). New York, NY: Delacotte Press.

Klein, E. B., Gabelnick, F., & Herr, P. (Eds.). (1998). *The psychodynamics of leadership*. Madison, CT: Psychosocial Press.

Klerman, G. L. (1990). The psychiatric patient's right to effective treatment: Implications of *Osheroff v Chestnut Lodge. American Journal of Psychiatry, 147*(4), 409–418.

Kohut, H. (1971). *The analysis of the self.* New York, NY: International Universities Press.

Kram, K. E., & Hampton, M. M. (1998). When women lead: The visibility-vulnerability spiral. In E. B. Klein, F. Gabelnick, & P. Herr (Eds.), *The psychodynamics of leadership* (pp. 193–210). Madison, CT: Psychosocial Press.

Krantz, J. (2013). Approaching twenty-first century, information-based organisations. In L. Vansina (Ed.), *Humanness in organisations: A psychodynamic contribution* (pp. 51–69). London, UK: Karnac.

Kurzweil, E. (2002). The return of the repressed: Psychology's problematic relations with psychoanalysis, 1909–1960. In W. E. Pickren & D. A. Dewsbury (Eds.), *Evolving perspectives on the history of psychology* (pp. 471–491). Washington, DC: American Psychological Association.

Lacan, J. (1977). *Écrits: A selection* (A. Sheridan, Trans.). London, UK: Tavistock.

Latts, M. G., & Gelso, C. J. (1995). Countertransference behavior and management with survivors of sexual assault. *Psychotherapy, 32*, 405–415.

Leichsenring, F., & Rabung, S. (2008). Effectiveness of long-term psychodynamic psychotherapy: A meta-analysis. *Journal of the American Medical Association, 300*(13), 1551–1565.

Leichsenring, F., Leweke, F., Klein, S., & Steinert, C. (2015). The empirical status of psychodynamic psychotherapy: An up-date: Bambi's alive & kicking. *Psychotherapy & Psychosomatics, 84*, 129–148.

Levy, K. N., & Anderson, T. (2013). Is clinical psychology doctoral training becoming less intellectually diverse? And if so, what can be done? *Clinical Psychology: Science and Practice, 20*(2), 211–220.

Long, S. (1998). Discourse and corporate leadership: Transformation by or of the feminine. In E. B. Klein, F. Gabelnick, & P. Herr (Eds.), *The psychodynamics of leadership* (pp. 219–246). Madison, CT: Psychosocial Press.

Long, S. (2006). Organizational defenses against anxiety: What has happened since the 1955 Jaques paper? *International Journal of Applied Psychoanalytic Studies, 3*, 279–295.

Luborsky, L. (2001). The meaning of empirically supported treatment research for psychoanalytic and other long-term therapies. *Psychoanalytic Dialogues, 11*(4), 583–604. doi:10.1080/10481881109348630.

Lüdemann, S. (2012). As the case may be/from case-to-case: On case studies in literature and psychoanalysis. *Exemplarity/Singularity.* International Conference, The Franke Institute for the Humanities, University of Chicago, Chicago, Illinois, March 8, 2012.

Luria, A. R. (1987). *The man with a shattered world*, Cambridge, MA: Harvard University Press.

Mahler, M., Pine, F., & Bergman, A. (1975). *The psychological birth of the human infant: Symbiosis and individuation.* New York, NY: Basic Books.

McDougall, J. (1980). *A plea for a measure of abnormality*. New York, NY: International Universities Press.

McWilliams, N. (2013). Psychoanalysis and research: Some reflections and opinions. *Psychoanalytic Review*, *100*, 919–945.

Melville, H. (1991). *Moby-Dick, or, The Whale*. New York: Vintage Books.

Messer, S. B. (2004). Evidence-based practice: Beyond empirically-supported treatments. *Professional Psychology Research & Practice*, *35*, 580–588.

Messer, S. B. (2006). Psychotherapy integration based on contrasting visions of reality. In G. Stricker & J. Gold (Eds.), *Case-book of psychotherapy integration* (pp. 281–291). Washington, DC: American Psychological Association.

Messer, S. B., & Winokur, M. (1984). Ways of knowing and visions of reality in psychoanalytic therapy and behavior therapy. In H. Arkowitz & S. B. Messers (Eds.), *Psychoanalytic therapy and behavior therapy: Is integration possible?* (pp. 63–100). New York, NY: Plenum Press.

Miller, I. J. (1996a). Time-limited brief therapy has gone too far: The result is invisible rationing. *Professional Psychology: Research and Practice*, *27*(6), 567–576.

Miller, I. J. (1996b). Some "short-term therapy values" are a formula for invisible rationing. *Professional Psychology: Research and Practice*, *27*(6), 577–582.

Miller, I. J. (1996c). Ethical and liability issues concerning invisible rationing. *Professional Psychology: Research and Practice*, *27*(6), 583–587.

Milrod, B. L., Busch, F. N., Cooper, A. M., & Shapiro, T. (1997). *Manual of panic-focused psychodynamic psychotherapy*. Washington, DC: American Psychiatric Press.

Mintz, D. (2013). Teaching psychoanalytic concepts, skills, & attitudes to medical students. *Journal of the American Psychoanalytic Association*, *61*(4), 751–770.

Muller, J. P. (1999). The ethics of speech in psychoanalysis. *Psychoanalytic Review*, *86*(4), 513–528.

Muller, P. A., & Oppenheimer, D. M. (2014). The pen is mightier than the laptop. Advantages of long hand over laptop. *Psychological Science*, *25*(6), 1. doi:10.1177/0956797614552458 11.

Nabokov, V. (1980). *Lectures on literature*. In F. Bowers (Ed.). New York, NY: Harcourt.

Obholzer, A., with Miller, S. (2004). Leadership, followership, and facilitating the creative workplace. In C. Huffington, D. Armstrong, W. Halton, & J. Pooley (Eds.), *Working below the surface: The emotional life of contemporary organizations* (pp. 33–48). London, UK: Karnac.

Ogden, T. H. (1981). Projective identification in psychiatric hospital treatment. *Bulletin of the Menninger Clinic*, *45*(4), 317–333.

Ogden, T. H. (1994). *Subjects of analysis*. Northvale, NJ: Aronson.

Ogden, T. H. (1999). *Reverie and interpretation: Sensing something human*. New York, NY: Jason Aronson, an imprint of Rowman & Littlefield.

Parish, M. (2007). Reflections on the administrator's role. *Organisational and Social Dynamics*, *7*(1), 61–72.

Parker, I., & Revelli, S. (Eds.). (2008). *Psychoanalytic practice and state regulation*. London, UK: Karnac.
Parker, P. S. (2015). *Race, gender, and leadership*. New York, NY: Psychology Press.
Peabody, S. A., & Gelso, C. J. (1982). Countertransference and empathy: The complex relationship between two divergent concepts in counseling. *Journal of Counseling Psychology*, *29*(3): 240–245. doi:10.1037/0022-0167.29.3.240.
Pennebaker, J. W., & Smyth, J. M. (2016). *Opening up by writing it down*. New York, NY: Guilford Press.
Peper, R. I., & Mayer, R. E. (1978). Note taking as a generative activity. *Journal of Educational Psychology*, *70*(4), 514–523.
Phillips, A. (2001). *Promises, promises: Essays on literature and psychoanalysis*. New York, NY: Basic Books.
Piotrowski, C. (2015). Clinical instruction on projective techniques in the USA: A review of academic training settings 1995–2015. *Journal of Projective Psychology & Mental Health*, *22*, 83–92.
Racker, H. (1957). The meanings and uses of countertransference. *Psychoanalytic Quarterly*, *26*, 303–357.
Racker, H. (1968). *Transference and countertransference*. London, UK: Karnac.
Reik, T. (1956). *The search within. The inner experiences of a psychoanalyst*. New York, NY: Grove Press Books and Evergreen Books.
Reisner, S. (1999). Freud and psychoanalysis: Into the 21st century. *The Journal of the American Psychoanalytic Association*, *47*(4), 1037–1060.
Renik, O. (2006). "The Limits of self awareness," in *Practical Psychoanalysis for Therapists and Patients*. New York: Other Press.
Rilke, R. M. (2000). *Letters to a young poet* (J. M. Burnham, Trans.). Novato, CA: New World Library.
Rimer, S. (2007, October 13). First woman takes reins at Harvard. *The New York Times*, p. A12.
Robbins, S. B., & Jolkovski, M. P. (1987). Managing countertransference feelings: An interactional model using awareness of feeling and theoretical framework. *Journal of Counseling Psychology*, *34*, 276–282.
Rogers, A., & Pilgrim, D. (2005). *A sociology of mental health and illness* (3rd ed.), New York. NY: Open University Press.
Roudinesco, E. (2001). *Why psychoanalysis?* New York, NY: Columbia University Press.
Roustang, F. (1976). *Dire mastery: Discipleship from Freud to Lacan*. Washington, DC: American Psychiatric Press.
Rubin, J. (1985). Meditation and psychoanalytic listening. *Psychoanalytic Review*, *72*(4), 599–614.
Safran, J. D., & Muran, J. C. (2000). *Negotiating the therapeutic alliance. A relational treatment guide*. New York, NY: Guilford Press.
Schafer, R. (1983). *The analytic attitude*. New York, NY: Basic Books.
Schulten, K. (2013, November 6). Is it an unaffordable luxury to major in the humanities in college? *The New York Times*, 163, p. A17.

Searles, H. (1965). *Collected papers on schizophrenia and related subjects*. New York, NY: International Universities Press.

Searles, H. (1986). *My work with borderline patients*. New York, NY: Jason Aronson.

Shaw, D. (2006). Narcissistic authoritarianism in psychoanalysis. In R. Raubolt (Ed.), *Power Games* (pp. 65–82). New York: Other Press.

Shedler, J. (2010). The efficacy of psychodynamic psychotherapy. *American Psychologist*, *65*(2), 98–109.

Shedler, J. (2015). Where is the evidence for "evidence-based" therapy? *Journal of Psychological Therapies in Primary Care*, *4*, 47–59.

Shur, R. (1994). *Countertransference enactments: How institutions and therapists actualize primitive internal worlds*. Northvale, NJ: Aronson.

Sonnenberg, S. M. (2011). Psychoanalysis and the United States research university: Current trends. *International Journal of Psychoanalysis*, *92*, 641–659.

Stapley. L. (1996). *The personality of the organisation*. London, UK: Free Association Press.

Stein, H. F. (2005). From organizational meaning through splitting to organizational meaning through integration: Healing the great divide. *Organisational and Social Dynamics*, *8*, 298–321.

Stern, D. (1989). The analyst's unformulated experience of the patient. *Contemporary Psychoanalysis*, *25*(1), 1–33.

Stern, D. N. (2004). *The present moment in psychotherapy and everyday life*. New York, NY: W.W. Norton.

Stone, A. A. (1990). Law, science, and psychiatric malpractice: A response to Klerman's indictment of psychoanalytic psychiatry. *American Journal of Psychiatry*, *147*(4), 419–427.

Strupp, H. (2001). Implications of the empirically supported treatment movement for psychoanalysis. *Psychoanalytic Dialogues*, *11*(4), 605–619.

Symington, N. (1983). The analyst's act of freedom as agent of therapeutic change. *International Review of Psycho-Analysis*, *10*(3), 283–291.

Szasz, T. (1998). "The healing word." *Journal of Humanistic Psychology*, *38*(2), 8–20.

Tansey, M. J., & Burke, W. F. (1989). *Understanding countertransference: From projective identification to empathy*. Hillsdale, NJ. Analytic Press.

Thomas, K. M. (Ed.). (2008). *Diversity resistance in organizations*. New York, NY: Erlbaum.

Tierney, B. (1998). Let's take another look at the fish: The writing process as discovery. *The Quarterly*, *20*(4), 27–30.

Treweiler, S. J., & Stricker, G. (1998). *The scientific practice of professional psychology*. New York, NY: Plenum Press.

Trombly, R. M., Comer, R. W., & Villamil, J. E. (2002). Case III: Managing conflict—the case of the faculty stuck in the middle. *Journal of Dental Education*, *66*(4), 533–540.

US Department of Education. (2006). *A test of leadership: Charting the future of US Higher education*. Report of the Commission Appointed by Secretary of Education Margaret Spellings. Retrieved from http://www.ed.gov.

Van Servellen, G.M. (1984). *Group and family therapy: A model for psychotherapeutic nursing St.* Louis, MO: C.V. Mosby Co.

Vansina, L. (2013). General introduction. In L. Vansina (Ed.), *Humanness in organisations: A psychodynamic contribution* (pp. xv–xxvii). London, UK: Karnac.

Viney, W., & King, D. B. (2003). *A history of psychology: Ideas and Context* (3rd ed.). Boston, MA: Allyn & Bacon.

Waldron, S., Scharf, R. D., Hurst, D., Firestein, S. K., & Burton, A. (2004). What happens in a psychoanalysis: A view through the lens of the Analytic Process Scales (APS). *International Journal of Psychoanalysis, 85*, 443–466.

Wallerstein, R. S. (2011). Psychoanalysis in the university: The natural home for education & research. *International Journal of Psychoanalysis, 92*, 623–629.

Waska, R. T. (1998). Intrapsychic outcome in projective identification. *Bulletin of the Menninger Clinic, 62*(3), 366–377.

Winnicott, DW (1952). Psychoses and child care. In *Through Paediatrics to psychoanalysis* (pp. 212–228). New York: Basic Books, 1975.

Winnicott, D. W. (1955). Metapsychological and clinical aspects of regression in the psycho-analytical set-up. *International Journal of Psycho-Analysis, 36*, 16–26.

Winnicott, D. W. (1958). *Collected papers: Through paediatrics to psychoanalysis.* New York, NY: Basic Books.

Winnicott. D. W. (1965). *The maturational process and the facilitating environment.* New York, NY: International Universities Press.

Winnicott, D. W. (1971). *Playing and reality*. New York, NY: Routledge.

Yalom, I.D. (1983) *Inpatient group psychotherapy*. New York, NY: Basic Books.

Yalom, I.D. (1985). *The theory and practice of group psychotherapy*. New York, NY: Basic Books.

Yalof, J. (1996). *Training and teaching the mental health professional: An in depth approach*. Northvale, NJ: Jason Aronson, Inc.

Yalof, J. (2015). Teaching psychoanalytic concepts in the university setting: Issues, challenges, and promises. *Psychoanalytic Inquiry, 35*, 124–134. doi:10.1080/07351690.2015.987598, published online: January 6, 2015.

Zimmerman, B. J. (2005). Becoming a self regulated learner: An overview. *Theory into Practice, 41*(2), 69.

Zimmerman, B. J., & Bandura, A. (1994). Impact of self-regulatory influences on writing course attainment. *American Educational Research Journal, 31*, 845.

Index

academic programs: conformity rewarded, by accreditation commission, 48; consultations directed at helping, 25–26; evidence-based education and, 59, 107; military-industrial complex influence on, 55–57; projective identification example, 20–21; psychoanalytical theories and psychotherapies in, 1, 3, 62, 64–65; quantification in, 62; Spellings Commission and, 57–58
academic setting, psychoanalysts importance in, 85–86
accreditation: APA, doctoral program survival and, 99–100; commission, program conformity rewarded by, 48; federal governmental body reporting requirements for, 48; health care professionals and standards for, 47; nursing program conflict example and, 28–29; quantifiable outcomes demand for, 46; regulations governing, 3; self-studies, 59; student competencies emphasis and, 89
achievement, Freud on anxiety response to, 29
adaptive aspects, of projective identification, 10
administration: organizational dynamics and program leadership in, 3, 12–14, 25–27, 35, 36, 74–75, 77–79, 81; organizations task relationship with structure of, 9; psychoanalysts in positions within, 79–80; quantifiable outcomes pressure for, 10
administrators: Creswell on positive characteristics of, 22; group ego function of, 81; Parish on assets for, 22; program management role of, 10; psychodynamic architecture addressed by, 80–82; skills of, 9
affect containment and sacrifice, of leader, 14
Agazarian, Y. M., 22
aggregation/massification assumption, of group, 12, 35–36
aggression: defensive denial of, 16; reparative creativity for conflicts of, 18
"Aggressivity in Psychoanalysis" (Lacan), 65–66
agreeable without reflection conflict defensive retreat, of Hoyle, 40
Allcorn, S.: on organizations pathological subgroupings, 18–19; on workplace oppression, 15
Amado, G., 1, 13

American Object-Relational School, 78, 88
American Psychological Association (APA), 63–64, 99–100
analysts. *See* psychoanalysts
analytic third concept, of Ogden, 19
annihilation fear, in departmental conflict example, 39
anti-psychoanalytical bias, 55, 59, 70–71, 73–77
antisocial characteristics, of leader, 16
anxiety: management, in countertransference management, 173; response to achievement, Freud on, 29
APA. *See* American Psychological Association
apprenticeship/mentorship model, of psychoanalysis training, 66–67
Arnd-Caddington, M., 139
assessment: of quantifiable outcomes practices, 60; Spellings Commission, on student learning comparisons, 57
Asylums (Goffman), 49
attachment research, 134
authoritarian leader, 18

Bandura, A., 113
Beebe, B., 144
behavioral health, 49, 54, 88
Bellak, Leopold, 104
Bettelheim, Bruno: on observing before formulating, 116; psychoanalysis seminar of, 111–12; on self-observation, 116
Bion, W.: on group assumptions, 12, 15, 35–36, *42*; on psychoanalysts, 96–97; on work group productivity, 12, 35
blank screen metaphor, of Freud, 77
Bollas, C.: normotic illness concept of, 4, 47; on psychoanalysis absolute confidentiality, 72; on psychoanalysts, 91; on therapeutic listening inner space, 119; on transference, 97–98; on unconscious freedom, 98
Burke, W. F.: expert therapist-patient exchanges vignette of, 147–48, 157–62, 165–67; phase-focused model of, 135–36; on signal affect, 159
Bush, M., 22

capacity to be alone, of Winnicott, 4, 73–77
Casement, P., 140–41, 158
central defensive problem, of patient, 163
chairperson dilemma, in nursing program example, 33–34, 36
charismatic leader, 18
clinical data detailed approaches, in exemplar transcripts microanalysis, 143–44
clinical psychology doctoral education: conflict within, 2; internship in, 78; psychoanalytic theory integration with, 1
cognitive-behavioral orientation, 89, 100
Collegiate Learning Assessment, Spellings Commission recommendation of, 58
communication: derivative communication concept of, 150; in nursing program conflict example, 27; patient, in therapists transcripts, 5; systemic method, projective identification as, 10, 19–21; of therapist and patient meta, 135
competency assessment models, 60
conceptualizing skills, in countertransference management, 172–73
concordant identification, Racker on, 161
confidentiality, 93; Bollas on psychoanalysis absolute, 72; mandated reporting laws and, 71–72

conflicted aspects, of projective identification, 10
conflicts: within clinical psychology doctoral education, 2; creative leadership, from psychoanalytical perspective, 10; Freud Oedipal, 28–29; Gantt and Agazarian on group movement to collaboration from, 22; Hoyle agreeable without reflection defensive retreat from, 40; internal, of psychoanalytically informed faculty members, 46–47; management, of leader, 14; in organization subgroupings, 12, 27, 35, 36, 81; reparative creativity for aggression and, 18; resolution, in group dynamics, 26, 27. *See also* departmental conflict; nursing program conflict and crises
consultations: data organization and consultation model of, 41, *42*; directed at helping academic programs, 25–26
countertransference: in departmental conflict example, 40–41, *42*; descriptive phase-focused models on, 134–36; experience, in therapist transcripts, 5, 129–30; in expert therapist-patient exchanges, through transcripts, 171–72, 174–75; Gladwell on, 164; IC role in, 139; in nursing program conflict example, 36–37, *42*; Racker on response, 163–64; reactions, resolution model for withdrawal ruptures and, 135; Reik on, 164; Renik on, 168; research observations on, 131; self-observation and, 4–5, 130–31; Stern transcript vignette and, 149–50
countertransference management: anxiety management in, 173; conceptualizing skills in, 172–73; empathy in, 173; self-insight in, 172; self-integration in, 173
creative leadership, 10
Creswell, J. W., 22
critical exchanges recovery, of self-observation skills, 126–28
Cs system, 46–47, 98
culture of competency, Kaslow on, 60

data collection, self-observation skills and, 115; clinical data detailed approaches to, 143–44; recording data absence in, 114
data organization and consultation model, 41, *42*
defensive denial, of aggression, 16
departmental conflict, Trombly example, 25, 35–37; annihilation fear in, 39; basic assumptions for, 40, *42*; case study summary for, 38–39; conflict symptomatic expression in, 40, *42*; core conflicts in, *42*; fight-flight group assumption in, 40; interventions to strengthen program and, *42*; leadership characteristics and, 40, *42*; Oedipal questioning of authority in, 40–41; paranoid-schizoid type of, 40; precipitating event in, 39, *42*; program identity in, *42*; psychoanalytic reformulation in, 39–41; sibling rivalry in, 41; transference, countertransference and projective identification in, 40–41, *42*
dependency assumption, of group, 12, 35
depressive position, of Klein, 37, 40, 54
depressive society, Roudinesco on, 45, 47, 56
Deresiewicz, William, 84–85
derivative communication concept, 150
descriptive phase-focused models, on countertransference, 134–36
Diagnostic and Statistical Manual of Mental Disorders (*DSM)*, 47
disenfranchisement, in otherness, 50

disengaged subgroup, in nursing program conflict example, 27
DSM. See Diagnostic and Statistical Manual of Mental Disorders

economical and business pressures, in training, 67
ego functioning, in administration organizational dynamics, 78, 79, 81
ego psychology: *Cs* system overemphasis in, 46–47; normalizing trends in psychoanalytic, 54; psychoanalysis and, 46–47; societal norms adaptation emphasis in, 47; *Ucs* system de-emphasis in, 47
empathy, in countertransference management, 173
empirical study, 63–64, 99
encounter group: nursing program example intervention of, 26; process, in nursing program example, 36–37
enmeshed subgroup, in nursing program conflict example, 27
enterprise/identity boundaries, in organizations, 10
evidence-based education, 4, 59, 73, 82–83, 107
evidence-based treatment, 88, 99; Strupp on, 51–52; student competence demonstration for, 89
exceptionalism, in American psychoanalysis, 65
exemplar transcripts microanalysis: clinical data detailed approaches in, 143–44; expert therapists vignettes of, 147–62; group associations to, 144–46; observations in, 162–78; seminar teaching application of, 144–45; Three Looks model and, 145–46
expert therapist-patient exchanges, Stern transcript vignette on, 165, 167, 168; discovery phase in, 156; discussed many times phrase in, 148, 149; instructor teaching opportunities in, 147–48; interruption in, 150–51; patients comment in, 149; possible countertransference and teaching implications in, 149–50; psychoanalyst First Look at exchange in, 153–54; psychoanalyst intervention in, 149–51; psychoanalyst response to patient in, 152; reflections on interaction in, 152–53; on relationship problems, 149–56; response exchange: tracking patient response to therapist in, 151–52; role of silence and Second Look in, 154–55
expert therapist-patient exchanges, Tansey and Burke vignette on, 165–67; discovery onset and Second Look in, 160–61; discussed many times phrase in, 148; First Look in, 159; First Look: patient reaction to therapist question in, 157–58; instructor teaching opportunities in, 147–48; patient response in, 161–62; Second Look in, 159–60; teaching moment in, 158; therapist intervention in, 161
expert therapist-patient exchanges, through transcripts: countertransference management, 171–72; initial patient-therapist exchange conceptualization of, 164–65; in-session and post-session analysis for, 164; pre-session reflections and therapist subsequent reactions for, 163–64; Second and Third Looks value in, 170–71; teaching self-observation and countertransference awareness through, 174–75; therapist countertransference interventions awareness from, 169–70; therapist processing experience in, 165–66; Third Looks in, 166–69; written and discussion self-observing assignments in, 175–77

faculty members: nursing program conflict example scapegoat of, 27, 36; psychoanalysts as, 79–80; turnover impact, on nursing program, 20. *See also* psychoanalytically informed faculty members
Faust, Drew Gilpin, 58
federal government, accreditation reporting requirements to, 48
fight-flight assumption, of group, 12, 17, 35, 40
Fink, B., 54, 55
First Look, in Three Looks phase model, 138–39, 153–54, 157–59
"Fish Story" (Tierney), 137
Fliess, R., 140
Fonagy, Peter, 106
Foucault, 49, 55
free association, 90–91, 93, 98, 102
free speech, 90–91
Freud, S., 72, 87–88, 102; on anxiety response to achievement, 29; blank screen metaphor of, 77; Lacan on return to, 92–93; on leader, as transference object, 15; mainstream medicine departure by, 53, 93; on normalization trends, 53, 55; on Oedipal conflict, 28–29; philosophical perspective of, 63; psychiatry medical alignment of, 65; on psychoanalysis position, 48, 65, 66; on psychoanalytical diversity challenges, 69; on regression after success, 29, 30; Reisner on psychoanalysis of, 94; rule of abstinence of, 90; three-body psychology of, 96; on transference, 14, 91, 93
The Future of an Illusion (Freud), 72

Gantt, S. P., 22
Gilroy, 49–50
Giovacchini, Peter, 85
Gladwell, Malcolm: on countertransference, 164; thin slicing concept of, 145
Go-around intervention technique, of Yalom, 27
Goffman, E., 49, 53
Grotstein, J. S., 19
group collaboration: Gantt and Agazarian on moving from conflicts to, 22; leader and, 10
group dynamics, 10, 15; of administrators ego function, 81; Bion on work group productivity, 12, 35; of conflict resolution, 26, 27; dependency assumption, 12, 35; fight-flight assumption in, 12, 17, 35, 40; hierarchical protection in, 11; Hopper aggregation/massification assumption in, 12, 35–36; of large groups and leader, 16; leader regression management in, 14; of leaders authority challenges, 11; pairing assumption in, 12, 16, 35; of small groups and leader, 16
group process model, self-observation and, 144–46
Group Psychology and the Analysis of the Ego (Freud), 15

Halton, W., 18, 37
health-care professionals: accreditation and professional association standards for, 47; Freud departure from, 53, 93; psychoanalysis and, 47, 61, 63–64, 84, 101; psychoanalytically informed faculty members as, 52
Herrick, C., 25–37, *42*
hierarchy structure, group protection and, 11
holding environment, of Winnicott, 17, 74
Hopper, E., 12, 35–36
"How College Sold Its Soul" (Deresiewicz), 84–85

Hoyle, L.: agreeable without reflection conflict defensive retreat of, 40; on worker change responses, 13
Huffington, C., 21

imagined conversations (IC), countertransference role, 139
individual capacity to be alone, psychoanalyst and, 4, 73–77
inner space, in therapeutic listening, 119, 121
institutional controls, psychic imprisonment system of, 13
instructor: mindfulness perspective of, 118–19; note-taking experience assignments of, 124; role, in therapeutic listening student encouragement, 119, 121; teaching opportunities of, 147–48
instruments, of Spellings Commission, 58
intergroup communicator, in nursing program conflict example, 33, 36
internal conflict, for psychoanalytically informed faculty members, 46–47
internal supervisor, Casement concept of, 140–41
interpretation, normalization trends and, 54
interventions: in administration organizational dynamics, 25–26; Go-around technique, of Yalom, 27; model, for consultation data organization and, 41, *42*; nursing program conflict and crises use of, 27, 36–37, *42*; nursing program encounter group example of, 26; overlapping phases of, 5; psychoanalytic clinicians effective, 22; from Stern transcript vignette psychoanalyst, 149–51; from Tansey and Burke vignette therapist, 161; therapist countertransference awareness in, 169–70
intervention skills, Bush and William on psychoanalytic clinicians effective, 22

Jacobs, Theodore, 141
Jaques, 79–80

Kaslow, N. J.: on competency assessment principles, 60; on culture of competency, 60
Kernberg, O. F.: on effective program leadership, 21; on leader as transference object, 15–17, 34; on leadership regressive pressures, 17, 34; on leader systems approach, 10–11; on paranoiagenesis, 36; on psychoanalysis normalization, 52–53; on transference, 14
Kets de Vries, M. F. R., 18
Kibel, H. H., 14
Kieffer, Christine, 53
Klein, E. B., 37, 40, 54
Kurzweil, Edith, 85

Lacan, Jacques: on psychoanalysis, 65–66, 82; return to Freud by, 92–93
Lachmann, F., 144
leader: challenges to Oedipal authority of, 12; characteristics, in nursing program conflict example, 32–34, *42*; fight-flight assumption unification against, 12; group challenges to authority of, 11; group collaboration and, 10; group dependency assumption reliance, on omnipotent, 12, 35; Kernberg systems approach, on individual and mission relationship with, 10–11; large groups and, 16; pairing assumption defense against dependency on, 12; resistance to change and, 10; work setting personal issues reenactment, 10

leader, as transference object: affect containment and sacrifice of, 14; Allcorn on workplace oppression and, 15; conflict management by, 14; defensive denial of aggression by, 16; example, 17–18; Freud on, 15; group regression management by, 14; Halton on reparative creativity for, 18, 37; identification and idealization of, 16; Kernberg on, 15–17, 34; narcissistic or antisocial character features of, 14, 16, 18; paranoid-schizoid splitting by, 17–18, 40; power abuse and destabilization characteristics of, 18; sadomasochistic enactments avoidance by, 14; sexual tension enactment by, 10, 16; student impacted by, 15; types of, 18; Winnicott on secure holding environment of, 17, 74
leadership: departmental conflict example characteristics of, 40; Hoyle agreeable without reflection conflict defensive retreat and, 40; Huffington on, 21; Kernberg on regressive pressures, 17, 34; Locke on tasks of, 11; in nursing program conflict example subgroup, 27, 35, 36; organization task relationship with administration structure by, 9; psychoanalytic applications for, 10; qualities of, 10. *See also* program leadership
learning, Zimmerman on students, 113
Locke, 11
Luborsky, L., 100
Lüdemann, S., 50–51

Mahler, M., 78
managed care, 71, 72, 88, 99
management/structure boundaries, in organizations, 10
mandated reporting laws, 71–72
manualization, Strupp on research, 51–52
Mayer, R. E., 135
McDougall, Joyce, 49
"The Medical Model and Mental Hospitalisation: Some Notes on the Vicissitudes of the Tinkering Trades" (Goffman), 49
mental health professionals education, 87–88; cognitive-behavioral orientation in, 89; Freud impact on, 92–98; Lüdemann on mental health, 50–51; mono-culture for, 89–90; psychoanalytical ethos of praxis transmission in, 98–101; teaching psychoanalytical theories and courses in, 102–8
military-industrial complex, academic program influenced by, 55–57
mindfulness processes, teaching of, 4, 118–19
Mintz, D., 67
mono-culture, for mental health profession education, 89–90, 100
moving along, Stern on, 170
Muller, P. A., 96–97, 125
Muran, J. C., 134–35

narcissistic vulnerabilities, of leaders, 14, 16, 18
neutrality and relatedness, in psychoanalytical academic environment, 77–78
nonjudgmental self-attitudes model, 4
normalization trends, in professional psychology graduate training, 51–55, 94
normotic academic trends, 94; behavioral health and, 49; manufacturing of, 55–61; of Psychological Haves and Have-Nots, 49; quantifiable outcomes and, 48; training impacted by, 48–49
normotic illness concept, of Bollas, 4, 47

note-taking experience: benefits of, 128–30; challenges of, 114; handwritten compared to computer, 125; instructor assignments of, 124; Muller and Oppenheimer on, 125; Pennebaker and Smyth on self-understanding through, 137; Peper and Mayer on, 135; recording data absence in, 114; review before next session in, 127–28; self-observation skills and, 4, 124–26; vignette of, 128–29
numeric changes, in outcomes, 13, 26
nursing program conflict and crises, Herrick example of, 25; accreditation and, 28–29; Bion group assumptions on, 35–36, *42*; case study summary for, 26–27; chairperson dilemma in, 33–34, 36; communication difficulties in, 27; core conflicts in, *42*; disengaged subgroup in, 27; encounter group process in, 36–37; enmeshed subgroup in, 27, 35; faculty scapegoat in, 27, 36; faculty turnover impact on, 20; group dynamics in, 35–36; group facilitator for conflict resolution in, 27; Halton reparative creativity in, 37; Hopper aggregation/massification assumption in, 12, 35–36; intergroup communicator in, 33, 36; interventions used, 27, 36–37, *42*; Klein depressive position and, 37; leader characteristics in, 32–34, *42*; leadership subgroup in, 27, 35, 36; precipitating event in, 28–29, *42*; program identity in, *42*; program success impact on, 28–29; psychoanalytic reformulation in, 27–37; symptomatic expressions of conflict in, 30–32, *42*; transference, countertransference and projective identification in, 36–37, *42*; Van Servellens psychotherapeutic nursing model for, 26; Yalom conflict resolution group therapy concepts in, 26; Yalom Go-around intervention technique for, 27

observations, successive, 133–34, 137–40
obsessive leader, 18
Oedipal authority, challenges to leader, 12, 40–41
Oedipal conflict, 28–29
Ogden, T. H., 19
Oppenheimer, D. M., 125
oppressive organizations risks, 13
organizational dynamics, of administration, 3; ego functioning in, 78, 79, 81; interventions and, 25–26; psychoanalysts optimal functioning and, 77; qualitative processes for, 13–14; Shaw on, 74–75; subgroupings conflicts and, 12, 27, 35, 36, 81
organizations: Allcorn pathological subgroupings of, 18–19; enterprise/identity boundaries in, 10; Jaques on projective identification of, 79–80; management/structure boundaries of, 10, 78, 80; market forces and corporatization of, 88; personal relationships de-emphasized in, 11–12; psychodynamic architecture of, 80–82; risks of oppressive, 13; Stapley on, 74, 82; task relationship with administration structure in, 9; tasks/processes boundaries in, 10; technology impact on, 11
otherness, 92, 96; disenfranchisement in, 50; Foucault on madness and, 49; Gilroy on racism and, 49–50
outcomes, qualitative, 13–14
outcomes, quantifiable, 1, 62; accreditation demand for, 46; administration pressure to produce, 10; assessment practices for, 60; challenges producing, 3; forms of, 12; Luborsky on studies of, 100;

in normotic academic trends, 48; numeric changes impact on, 13, 26; program leadership accountability and production of, 13; psychic imprisonment system and, 13; Spellings Commission mandated, 58–59; variables for, 13

pairing assumption, of group, 12, 16, 35
paranoiagenesis, Kernberg on, 36
paranoid leader, 18
paranoid-schizoid splitting, 17–18, 40
Parish, M., 22
patients: central defensive problem of, 163; communication, in therapists transcripts, 5; impasses resolution for, 134–36; metacommunication of, 135. *See also* expert therapist-patient exchanges
pedagogy problematics, in professional psychology graduate training, 65–67; psychoanalysts and competencies and, 61; Spellings Commission measurement of, 58
Pennebaker, J. W.: on writing and self-understanding, 137; on writing and traumatic events, 125–26
Peper, R. I., 135
phase-focused models, 4; for therapeutic stalemates, 134–36; Three Looks approach of, 137–40, 145–46, 166–69
philosophical perspective, of Freud, 63
A Plea for a Measure of Abnormality (McDougall), 49
poethics, of psychoanalysis, 67
pressure to conform, training impacted by, 4
private practice, postgraduate self-supervision in, 4
professional associations, health-care professionals and standards for, 47
professional psychology graduate training: culture of competency in, 60; manufacturing normotics and, 55–61; normalization trends in, 51–55, 94; normotic elements of, 45–67; outside view of psychoanalysis and, 62–64; pedagogy problematics in, 65–67; psychoanalytical theories and psychotherapies in academy, 64–65; regulations for, 45–46; Roudinesco on depressive society and, 45; surveillance culture in, 49–51, 55, 85
program leadership: administration organizational dynamics and, 3, 12–14, 25–27, 35, 36, 74–75, 77–79, 81; final decisions in, 11; Kernberg on effective, 21; pressures and responsibilities of, 3; quantifiable outcomes and, 13; task relevance and, 21
program management, administrators role in, 10
projective identification: in academic program example, 20–21; adaptive and conflicted aspects of, 10; in departmental conflict example, 40–41, *42*; Jaques on organizations and, 79–80; in nursing program conflict example, 36–37, *42*; Ogden, Grotstein, Waska and Shur on, 19; as systemic communication method, 10, 19–21
psychiatry: departments, psychoanalysis integration in, 70; medical alignment, Freud and, 65
psychic imprisonment system, of institutional controls, 13
psychoanalysis: apprenticeship/mentorship model of, 66–67; Bettelheim seminar for, 111–12; Bollas on absolute confidentiality of, 72; *DSM* and, 47; ego psychology and, 46–47; elite and privileged status in, 46; exceptionalism and, 65; Fonagy on scientific validity of, 106; Freud philosophical perspective of, 63; Giovacchini on, 85; health-care

professionals and, 47, 61, 63–64, 84, 101; Kernberg on normalization of, 52–53; Kieffer on institutional suppression of, 53; Kurzweil on, 85; Lacan on, 65–66, 82; outside view of, 62–64; Phillips on poethics of, 67; psychiatry departments integration of, 70; quasi-religious devotion in, 99; research held in low regard by, 63; siege mentality of, 65; *Tarasoff* decision and, 47
psychoanalysts: academic setting importance of, 85–86; in administration and faculty positions, 79–80; Bion on, 96–97; Bollas on, 91; capacity to be alone by, 4, 73–77; on free association and speech, 90–91; optimal functioning, in administration organizational dynamics, 77; professional psychology graduate training, competencies and, 61; psychoanalytical diversity challenges of, 4, 73–77, 79–86; psychodynamic architecture and, 80–82; Reik on experience of, 112–13, 116; in Stern transcript vignette, 149–54; symptomatic relief provided by, 90
psychoanalytical academic environment, neutrality and relatedness in, 77–78
psychoanalytical diversity challenges: comments on, 82–85; confidentiality and, 71; Deresiewicz on, 84–85; Freud on, 69; lack of refinements training as, 70; managed care intrusion and, 71; on neutrality and relatedness, 77–79; psychoanalyst in academic setting importance, 85–86; on psychoanalysts capacity to be alone, 4, 73–77; psychoanalysts in administration and faculty positions and, 79–80; psychodynamic architecture and, 80–82; psychology department anti-psychoanalytical bias and, 70–71
psychoanalytical ethos, 4, 88; of praxis, transmission of, 98–101; research to support efficacy of, 90
psychoanalytically informed faculty members: challenges, 4, 179; as health-care professional, 52; internal conflict for, 46–47
psychoanalytical theories and psychotherapies, in academic program, 1, 3, 62, 64–65
psychoanalytic clinicians: effective intervention skills of, 22; training model for, 102–8
psychodynamic architecture, of psychoanalysts, 80–82
psychodynamic phase models, for self-observation: countertransference and, 134–36; patient impasses resolution in, 134–36
Psychological Haves and Have-Nots, 49
psychology departments: anti-psychoanalytical bias in, 70–71; psychoanalytical thought and theory in, 100

quantophrenic delirium, Amado on, 1, 13
quasi-religious devotion, in psychoanalysis, 99

racism, 49–50
Racker, Heinrich: on concordant identification, 161; on countertransference response, 163–64
radical behaviorism, 62
reflective time settings, for self-observation, 120–24
regression: after success, Freud on, 29, 30; group management of, 14; Kernberg on leadership pressures and, 17, 34; Winnicott on dependence from, 96

regulations: for governing accreditation, 3; for professional psychology graduate training, 45–46
Reik, Theodore, 136; on countertransference, 164; on first session embedded knowledge, 138–39; on psychoanalysts experience, 112–13, 116
Reisner, S., 94
Renik, O., 168
reparative creativity, Halton on, 18, 37
research, 83; attachment to, 134; on countertransference observations, 131; manualization, Strupp on, 51–52; psychoanalysis low regard of, 63; to support psychoanalytical ethos efficacy, 90
resistance to change, leader and, 10
resolution model for withdrawal ruptures, of Safran and Muran, 134–35
Rilke, Rainer Maria, 108
Roudinesco, E., 45, 47, 56
Roustang, F., 95
rule of abstinence, of Freud, 90

sadomasochistic enactments avoidance, of leader, 14
Safran, J. D., 134–35
schizoid leader, 18
Second Look, in Three Looks phase model, 154–55, 159–61, 166, 170–71
self-insight, in countertransference management, 172
self-integration, in countertransference management, 173
self-observations: assignments writing and discussion for, 175–77; Bettelheim on, 116; Casement trial identification and, 140–41; clinical learning significance of, 113; countertransference and, 4–5, 130–31; critical exchanges recovery in, 126–28; data collection for, 114–15, 143–44; group process model and, 144–46; note-taking as part of, 4, 124–26; note-taking benefits for, 128–30; psychodynamic phase models of, 134–36; recall and reflection from, 141–42; settings for reflective time of, 120–24; Stern unformulated experience for, 136–37, 148; successive, 133–34, 137–40; teaching goal and methodology on, 116–19, 121–24, 126, 130; teaching of, 4, 111–31, 133–42; therapist-patient relationship exchanges for, 121–24; of therapists transcripts, 4–5, 128–30
self-studies accreditation, 59
self-supervision, 4, 113
self-understanding, Pennebaker and Smyth on writing and, 137
seminar teaching application, 144–45
sexual tension enactment, 10, 16
Shaw, D., 74–75
Shur, R., 19
sibling rivalry, in departmental conflict example, 41
siege mentality, of psychoanalysis, 65
signal affect, Tansey and Burke on, 159
small groups, leader as transference object in, 16
Smyth, J. M.: on writing and self-understanding, 137; on writing and traumatic events, 125–26
societal norms, ego psychology emphasis on adaptation of, 47
Spellings, Margaret, 57
Spellings Commission: on assessments for student learning comparisons, 57; Faust on, 58; instruments of, 58; on learning objectives reports and outcomes, 58; on mandated quantifiable outcomes, 58–59
Stapley, L., 74, 82
Stern, Daniel, 144; expert therapist-patient exchanges transcript

vignette of, 147–56, 165, 167, 168; on moving along, 170; on tracking progression of patient-therapist exchanges, 122–23; on unformulated experience, 136–37, 148
Strupp, Hans, 51–52, 101
students: accreditation competencies emphasis for, 89; evidence-based treatment competence by, 89; instructor role, in inner space encouragement, 119, 121; leader transference impact on, 15; personal psychotherapy requirement for, 114–15; self-supervision development need for, 113; Spellings Commission on learning comparison assessment of, 57; -therapist self-experience target, 116–18; Zimmerman on learning by, 113
subgroupings, organization conflict, 12, 27, 35, 36, 81
success, Freud on regression after, 29, 30
surveillance culture, 51, 85; Foucault on madness as other, 49, 55; Gilroy on otherness and racism, 49–50; normalization through pathologization in, 50
symptomatic relief, psychoanalysts provision of, 90
systemic communication, projective identification as method of, 10, 19–21
systems approach, of Kernberg, 10–11
Szasz, Thomas, 105

Tansey, M. J.: expert therapist-patient exchanges vignette of, 147–48, 157–62, 165–67; phase-focused model of, 135–36; on signal affect, 159
Tarasoff decision, American psychoanalysis and, 47
tasks/processes boundaries, in organizations, 10
teaching: from exemplar transcripts microanalysis, 143–78; goals and targets for, 4; mindfulness processes in, 4; nonjudgmental self-attitudes model and, 4; note-taking settings and, 4, 114, 124–30, 137; of self-observation skills, 4, 111–31, 133–42
teaching goal and methodology, of self-observation: Bettelheim on observing before formulating, 116; goal activation for, 117; instructor encouragement of students inner space and, 119, 121; instructor mindfulness perspective in, 118–19; safe supervisory and instructional space in, 122–23, 126; seminar process for, 117; student-therapist self-experience target in, 116–18; therapist-patient relationship exchanges in, 121–24, 130; therapist resistance to intrasession focus in, 118
technology, organizations impacted by, 11
A Test of Leadership: Charting the Future of US Higher Education, Spellings Commission report, 57–58
therapeutic listening, inner space in, 119, 121
therapeutic stalemates, 133–35, 134
Therapeutic State, of Szasz, 105
therapists: -patient relationship exchanges, for self-observation, 121–24, 130; resistance to intrasession focus by, 118; student self-experience target and, 116–18; transcripts of, 4–5, 128–30. *See also* expert therapist-patient exchanges
thin slicing concept, of Gladwell, 145
"Thirty Methods to Destroy the Creativity of Psychoanalytic Candidate" (Kernberg), 52–53
three-body psychology, of Freud, 96
Three Looks phase model, 137, 140, 166–71; reactive first look in, 138; seminar process for, 145–46;

successive looks rationale in, 138; supervision preparation in, 138–39; unconscious and preconscious patterns in, 139
Tierney, B., 137
training: Lüdemann on mental health, 50–51; mandated reporting laws impact on, 71–72; mental health professionals education and, 87–108; Mintz on economical and business pressures in, 67; model, for psychoanalytic clinicians, 102–8; model, on unconscious and field of speech, 102–8; normotic professional psychology elements and, 45–67; psychoanalysis apprenticeship/mentorship model and, 66–67; psychoanalytical diversity challenges and, 4, 69–86; regulations governing accreditation and, 3; Winnicott capacity to be alone and, 4, 73–77. *See also* professional psychology graduate training
transcripts, of therapists: countertransferential experience from, 5, 129–30; self-observations of, 4–5, 128–30. *See also* expert therapist-patient exchanges
transference: Bollas on, 97–98; in departmental conflict example, 40–41, *42*; Freud on, 14, 91, 93; Kernberg on, 14; in nursing program conflict example, 36–37, *42*; Roustang on, 95. *See also* leader, as transference object
transitional space concept, of Winnicott, 77, 82, 104, 107
traumatic events, Pennebaker and Smyth on writing and, 125–26
treatment, manualization of, 52
trial identification, Casement on, 140–41
Trombly, R. M., 25, 37–41, *42*

Ucs system, 47, 98
unconscious processes: Bollas on freedom and, 98; psychoanalytically informed faculty member focus on, 46; Three Looks phase model and preconscious patterns as, 139; training model, on unconscious and field of speech, 102–8

Van Servellen, 26

Waska, R. T., 19
William, M., 22
Winnicott, D. W., 81, 91; on holding environment, 17, 74; on individual capacity to be alone, 4, 73–77; on regression to dependence, 96; transitional space concept of, 77, 82, 104, 107
work setting: Allcorn on oppression, 15; Bion on productivity of group in, 12, 35; Hoyle on workers change responses, 13; leader and personal issues reenactment in, 10
writing: discussion and, in self-observing assignments, 175–77; Pennebaker and Smyth on self-understanding and, 137; Pennebaker and Smyth on traumatic events and, 125–26. *See also* note-taking experience

Yalom: Go-around intervention technique of, 27; on group therapy concepts for conflict resolution, 26

Zimmerman, B. J., 113

About the Authors

David L. Downing, PsyD, ABPP, is a board-certified psychoanalyst and clinical psychologist and professor of clinical psychology at the University of Indianapolis, School of Psychological Sciences. He received his certificate in psychoanalysis from the Center for Psychoanalytic Study in Chicago in 1994. He is a Division 39 (Psychoanalysis) Representative to the Council of Representatives of the American Psychological Association (APA), as well as the past president of other sections of Division 39. His other publications include *Object Relations and Self-Psychology: A User-Friendly Primer*, with the late Barry J. Weber, PhD. Downing is interested in the psychoanalytical treatment of severe psychopathology; psychoanalytical perspectives on the arts and humanities; applied analyses of culture, professional trends, professional identity formation, and organizations. He has an abiding interest in emerging trends in accreditation, professional licensure, teaching/supervision of professionals-in-training, and health-care policy. He maintains a private practice in psychoanalysis, psychoanalytical psychotherapy, consultation, and supervision in both Chicago, Illinois, and Indianapolis, Indiana.

Marc Lubin, PhD, is professor at the American School of Professional Psychology at Argosy University, Southern California, where he directed the clinical psychology program for many years. He received his doctorate in human development and clinical psychology from the University of Chicago in 1968. After postdoctoral fellowships at Michael Reese Hospital in Chicago and an advanced fellowship and staff position at the Austen Riggs Center in Stockbridge, Massachusetts, he returned to Chicago to become a teacher of emotionally disturbed children at the Orthogenic School at the University of Chicago, founded by Bruno Bettelheim. He later became the first faculty chair at the newly created Illinois School of Professional Psychology in 1977. Lubin's ongoing focus on teaching doctoral students is reflected in his multiple publications and presentations about teaching clinical psychology students over the past thirty years in the National Council of Schools and Programs in Professional Psychology (NCSPP) publications, as well as APA's Division 39 annual programs. He is currently writing a new book to further deepen our understanding of the psychotherapist's clinical experiences.

Jed Yalof, PsyD, is professor and chair of the Department of Graduate Psychology and Counseling at Immaculata University and coordinator of the PsyD program in clinical psychology. He is board-certified in clinical psychology, school neuropsychology, assessment psychology, and adult psychoanalysis. He is a graduate in psychoanalysis from the Psychoanalytic Center of Philadelphia, where he is now on the faculty. His other works include *Training & Teaching the Mental Health Professional*. He has presented and published extensively on diverse psychoanalytically related topics as psychoanalytic interviewing, personality assessment, learning disability, supervision, psychotherapy, and ethics. Yalof's interests and activities include psychotherapy, psychoanalysis, and personality evaluations; school neuropsychology evaluations; neuropsychological evaluations; and consultation. Yalof maintains a clinical practice in psychoanalysis, psychoanalytical psychotherapy, personality assessment, neuropsychological assessment, and consultation in Haverford, Pennsylvania.

www.ingramcontent.com/pod-product-compliance
Ingram Content Group UK Ltd.
Pitfield, Milton Keynes, MK11 3LW, UK
UKHW012039150926
475560UK00001B/88